FREE MONEY
FOR
FOREIGN
STUDY

FREE MONEY
FOR
FOREIGN
STUDY

A Guide to More
Than 1,000 Grants
and Scholarships
for Study Abroad

Laurie Blum

Facts On File
New York • Oxford

Free Money for Foreign Study: A Guide to More Than 1,000 Grants and Scholarships for Study Abroad

Copyright © 1991 by Laurie Blum

Facts On File, Inc.	Facts On File Limited
460 Park Avenue South	Collins Street
New York NY 10016	Oxford OX4 1XJ
USA	United Kingdom

Library of Congress Cataloging-in-Publication Data

Blum, Laurie.
    Free money for foreign study : a guide to more than 1,000 grants and scholarships for study abroad / Laurie Blum.
      p. cm.
    Includes bibliographical references.
    ISBN 0-8160-2450-2
    1. Scholarships—Directories.   2. Foreign study—Scholarships, fellowships, etc.—Directories.   I. Title.
LB2337.2.B575   1991
378.3'4'025—dc20   91-4386

ISBN: 0-8160-2450-2 (Hardcover)
ISBN: 0-8160-2710-2 (Paperback)

British CIP data available on request from Facts On File.

Jacket Design by Ellie Nigretto
Composition by the Maple-Vail Book Manufacturing Group
Manufactured by the Maple-Vail Book Manufacturing Group
Printed in the United States of America

10 9 8 7 6 5 4 3 2 1

This book is printed on acid-free paper.

Contents

SUBJECT LISTINGS

Introduction

Have you thought about spending a year studying abroad or perhaps doing your graduate work in a foreign country?

As I have shown in my other financial aid books, there is an enormous amount of free money available, much of it from the institutions themselves. Moreover, many of these sources fund students regardless of their financial need or academic excellence.

Do you just walk up, hold out your hand, and expect someone to put money in it? Of course not. On your part, you're going to have to fill out applications. You may meet with frustration or rejection somewhere down the road. The odds, however, are in your favor that you will qualify for some sort of financial aid to study abroad.

The hardest part has always been finding the sources of money, which is why I wrote this book. As with my undergraduate and graduate scholarship books, this book provides you, the reader, with the actual sources of monies available.

The listings are divided into two alphabetical sections—countries and subjects of study (see the table of contents). The information available defined the structure of the book, as well as the countries and subjects included. Check both sections to see which grants apply to you. Subject listings apply for the most part to your major or intended field of study. I have noted in each listing if the award is made to undergraduate, graduate or postgraduate students. Regardless of your field of study or the country in which you choose to pursue your education, you can qualify for at least some of the grants in this book.

I have included wherever possible the number of grants given to students, the size of the average award, and the range of monies given. Often dollar amounts are given in the currency of the given country. Conversions of foreign currencies are accurate as of March 1, 1991. Conversion rates fluctuate almost daily; you might want to check the exchange rate at the time of application. Do not be dissuaded from applying if the average award is only $100.00 (the same material you put together for one application can be used for most, if not all, of your other applications). You might get more, you might get less. But remember, this is free money!

How to Apply

Applying for grants and scholarships is a lot like applying for school; it takes work, thought, and organization. But at this stage in your life, you know what you have to do. You've done it before.

First comes the sorting out process. Go through this book and note all the listings that could be possibilities for you. Pay close attention to the restrictions. Write the possible foundations to get a copy of their guidelines (in cases where a contact's name is not listed, begin your letter: To Whom It May Concern).

Grant applications, like college applications, take time to fill out. Often you will be required to write one or more essays. Be neat! Proposals should always be typed, double-spaced, and be *sure* to make a copy of the proposal before putting it in the mail. I've learned the hard way that there is nothing worse than having the foundation unable to find your proposal and having to reconstruct it because you didn't keep a copy. Many applications will require any previous college transcripts. You may be asked to include personal references (be sure to notify the people you are planning to use as references; there is nothing worse than having a foundation contact your reference, who has no idea what it is about). Remember, you have to sell yourself and convince the grantors to give the money to you and not to someone else.

One Final Note

By the time this book is published, some of the information contained here will have changed. No reference book can be as up-to-date as the readers (or the author) would like. Names, addresses, dollar amounts, telephone numbers and other data are always in flux. Therefore, it's always a good idea to double-check these items.

Good luck!

FREE MONEY
FOR
FOREIGN
STUDY

Country Listings

ARGENTINA

Inter American Press Association
Scholarships for Study in Latin America and the West Indies
2911 NW 39th St.
Miami, FL 33142
305-634-2465
RESTRICTIONS: For young journalists and graduate students (ages 21–35). Must be U.S./Canadian citizen. Fluency in the designated country's language is required.
AMOUNT GIVEN: $10,000. 1 academic year of study/research in a Latin American or West Indian country.
DEADLINE: August 1.

AUSTRALIA

Australian Federation of University Women
Georgina Sweet Fellowship
P.O. Box 123
Nedlands 6009 Western Australia
RESTRICTIONS: Doctoral and postdoctoral fellowships open to women who are members of the International Federation of University Women. To assist women who do not habitually reside in Australia to carry out some advanced study or research in Australia.
AMOUNT GIVEN: Aus. $8,000 biannually awarded for a 4–12 month duration.
DEADLINE: July 31.

Australian National University
Master's Degree Scholarships
Registrar
G.P.O. Box 4
Canberra, ACT 2601 Australia
49-5111

1

RESTRICTIONS: Open to students holding a first degree with a minimum level of second-class honors (upper division) or equivalent for study in arts, Asian studies, economics, law and science.
AMOUNT GIVEN: Aus. $7,375 per year + possible dependents allowance. 1 year duration, possibly renewable.
DEADLINE: October 31.

Australian National University
Ph.D. Scholarships
G.P.O. Box 4; Graduate Students Section
Canberra, ACT 2601 Australia
49-5111
RESTRICTIONS: Limited to graduate students for full-time study for doctorate of philosophy. High academic record with capacity for research required.
AMOUNT GIVEN: Aus. $7,375 per year + possible airfare and dependents allowance. Scholarship for 3 years, possibly extendable to 4.
DEADLINE: September 30.

Australian Telecommunications and Electronics Research Board
Post Doctoral Fellowship
P.O. Box 76
Epping NSW 2121 Australia
02-868-0459
RESTRICTIONS: For graduate students. Postdoctoral research fellowships open to young scientists and engineers of all nationalities. Preference for students under 30 years old.
AMOUNT GIVEN: Aus. $55,000. 2 years of research at an approved Australian institute.
DEADLINE: July 30.

Australian-American Educational Foundation
Fulbright Awards
P.O. Box 1559
Canberra, ACT 2601
Australia
RESTRICTIONS: U.S. citizens. All fields. For lecturing and research; some awards for postgraduate degrees at approved institutions in Australia. All grantees are expected to return to their home countries when program is completed. Each year one-half of the awards may be reserved for nominated fields of study announced in advance.
AMOUNT GIVEN: Travel expenses or full scholarships for 3–12 month durations. Possibly renewable.
DEADLINE: Graduate students—November 1. Others—June 1.
CONTACT: Graduate students:
                Institute of International Education
                890 United Nations Plaza
                New York, NY 10017

Others:
Council for International Exchange of Scholars
11 Dupont Circle
Washington, DC 20036

British Federation of University Women
Johnstone & Florence Stoney Studentship
Crosby Hall; Cheyne Walk
London SW 3 5BA England
01-352-5354
RESTRICTIONS: Open to members of the British and Irish Federations of University Women for postgraduate research in Australia, New Zealand or South Africa. Study in biological, geological, meteorological and radiological sciences.
AMOUNT GIVEN: Up to 3,000 British pounds.
DEADLINE: September 15.

Deakin University
Post-Graduate Research Scholarships
Secretary Graduate Studies and Research Committee
Victoria 3217 Australia
47-1183
RESTRICTIONS: Full-time postgraduate study and research at Deakin University in all fields. Must hold at least upper second class honors degree or its equivalent.
AMOUNT GIVEN: Aus. $7,000 per year.
DEADLINE: October 31.

Farrer Memorial Trust
Farrer Memorial Research Scholarship
Secretary
c/o NSW Dept. of Agriculture
P.O. Box K 220
Haymarket, NSW 2000
Australia
RESTRICTIONS: Open to graduate students for research into agricultural problems. Selected by trustees on the basis of exhibition of superior ability after graduation.
AMOUNT GIVEN: 1 year scholarships, available at irregular intervals. Possible extension.

Flinders University of South Australia
Research Scholarships
Stuart Road
Bedford Park, South Australia 5042
08-275-3911
RESTRICTIONS: Full-time study and research in all fields as a graduate student under supervision of a member of the staff appointed by the

board of the appropriate school. Scholarship renewable with satisfactory progress.
AMOUNT GIVEN: Aus. $6,150 per year.
DEADLINE: None.

Griffith University
Post-Graduate Research Scholarship
Kessels Road; Graduate Studies Office
Nathan, QLD 4111 Australia
07-275-7111
RESTRICTIONS: Master's or Ph.D. candidates in all fields accepted at the University. Renewable subject to satisfactory assessment at end of each year.
AMOUNT GIVEN: Aus. $7,184.
DEADLINE: October 31.

James Cook University of North Queensland
Post-Graduate Research Awards Scholarships
James Cook University
Townsville, QLD 4811 Australia
RESTRICTIONS: For overseas students to obtain research degrees in any department. Recipients chosen by heads of departments based on exceptional merit. Must have minimum of a class 2A honors degree. Fluent English required.
AMOUNT GIVEN: 3 scholarships of 3 years' duration.
DEADLINE: October 31.

La Trobe University
Registrar
Attn: Scholarships officer
Bundoora, Victoria 3083 Australia
RESTRICTIONS: Research scholarships for Master's and Ph.D. candidates. Available to students from any country holding the equivalent to a 4-year first-class honors degree from an Australian university. Proof of significant written work required. Must be efficient in English. Renewable if progress is satisfactory.
AMOUNT GIVEN: Aus. $7,000 + possible spousal and dependents allowance. Thesis allowance up to Aus. $800 and possible general service fee and travel allowance. 2 yrs. (master's); 4 yrs. (Ph.D.).
DEADLINE: July 31.

Macquarie University
Attn: Registrar
North Ryde, NSW 2113 Australia
RESTRICTIONS: All fields of study. Available to students of all nationalities. Minimum requirement of a bachelor's degree with second-class

honors from an Australian or overseas university or equivalent. Test in English language proficiency by Australian Embassy in country of origin. **AMOUNT GIVEN:** 1 year scholarship renewable for up to 2 years for masters or 3 years for Ph.D. **DEADLINE:** October 31.

Macquarie University
Attn: Registrar
North Ryde, NSW 2113 Australia
RESTRICTIONS: For students of all nationalities to obtain a Master of Arts in linguistics and its applications. Must have completed a first degree in linguistics or a related subject such as language, literature, psychology of speech pathology.
AMOUNT GIVEN: Tuition + student activities fee.
DEADLINE: November 1.

Macquarie University
Attn: Registrar
North Ryde, NSW 2113 Australia
RESTRICTIONS: For students of all nationalities to obtain an M.A. in population and development (in English). Must have a sound background in economics or demography and a knowledge of first year statistics and computing.
AMOUNT GIVEN: Tuition + student activities fee.
DEADLINE: November 1.

Monash University
Attn: Registrar
Clayton, Victoria 3168
Australia
RESTRICTIONS: All fields. All nationalities. Graduate Students from any recognized university. Reading and writing proficiency in English required.
AMOUNT GIVEN: Aus. $7,000–$9,490 + allowance per year. Renewable to 2 years (Masters) or 3 years (Ph.D.).
DEADLINE: October 31.

Murdoch University
Attn: Secretary
Murdoch, Western Australia 6150
RESTRICTIONS: All fields. All nationalities. Postgraduate students with English proficiency.
AMOUNT GIVEN: 10 awards. Aus. $7,000 per year + allowances for dependents, thesis, and fares.
DEADLINE: October 31.

Murdoch University
Attn: Secretary, Board of Research and Post-Graduate Studies
Murdoch, Western Australia 6150
RESTRICTIONS: Postgraduate students of all nationalities not already holding a Ph.D. For study leading to a master's degree in fields of applied psychology, education, or public policy.
AMOUNT GIVEN: 4 scholarships per year. Aus. $7,000 + dependents, incidentals, thesis, and fares allowances.
DEADLINE: September 30.

Murdoch University
Board of Research and Post-Graduate Studies
Murdoch University Research Studentship
Attn: Secretary
Murdoch, Western Australia 6150
RESTRICTIONS: All fields. All nationalities. Minimum of an honors degree level 2A or equivalent with proficiency in English.
AMOUNT GIVEN: Aus. $7,000 per year + allowances for dependents, thesis, and fares.
DEADLINE: October 31.

Queen's Fellowships Committee
Marine Science Grants
Department of Science and Technology
P.O. Box 65
Belconnen, ACT 2616
Australia
RESTRICTIONS: For fellowships in marine science. Applicants of all nationalities holding a Ph.D. or equivalent in research and work experience in marine science. Must be under 30.
AMOUNT GIVEN: 2 year fellowships.
APPLICATIONS: Send written inquiry to the National Research Fellowships Scheme at the above address.

University of Adelaide
Scholarships for Post-Graduate Research
Registrar
G.P.O. Box 498
Adelaide, South Australia 5001
RESTRICTIONS: All fields. All nationalities. For a master's or Ph.D. degree by research at the University of Adelaide. Must have equivalent of Australian first-class honors degree. Must be proficient in English.
AMOUNT GIVEN: Aus. $7,000 per year for up to 2 years (master's) or 3 years (Ph.D.).
DEADLINE: September 30.

University of Adelaide
G.O. Lawrence Scholarship
Registrar
G.P.O. Box 498
Adelaide, South Australia 5001
RESTRICTIONS: For students of all nationalities with a B.D.S. degree or equivalent qualifications for study in Dentistry at the University of Adelaide.
AMOUNT GIVEN: 1 year scholarship renewable to 2 years. Not offered yearly, but when vacancy occurs.

University of Adelaide
Clive E. Boyce Fellowship
Registrar
G.P.O. Box 498
Adelaide, South Australia 5001
RESTRICTIONS: Fellowships in architecture or urban and regional planning open to students of all nationalities with proper degree from a recognized university. Tenable at the University of Adelaide.
AMOUNT GIVEN: Minimum of Aus. $5,000. Awarded as available.

University of Melbourne
Post-Graduate Scholarships
Office for Research
Parkville, Victoria 3052 Australia
RESTRICTIONS: All fields. For graduate students at the University of Melbourne who are enrolled in a master's degree research program or a doctorate of philosophy degree program.
AMOUNT GIVEN: Aus. $11,500.
APPLICATION: Send written inquiry.
DEADLINE: October 31.

University of New England
Research Scholarships
Registrar
Armidale, NSW 2351 Australia
067-733333
RESTRICTIONS: All fields. All nationalities. Must hold a bachelor's degree at level at least 2nd class. Honors in first division at the University of New England or a qualification judged to be equivalent.
AMOUNT GIVEN: Living allowance of Aus. $7,500 for applicants with first-class honors. Aus. $7,000 for others.
DEADLINE: October 31.

University of Newscastle
Post-Graduate Research Scholarships
Secretary Graduate Studies

Newcastle, NSW 2308 Australia
049-680-401
RESTRICTIONS: For graduate students in all fields. To support research for higher degree studies (2 years master's; 3–4 years Ph.D.) at
the University of Newcastle. Competitive awards.
AMOUNT GIVEN: Aus. $7,000 + allowances for dependents. 8 awards
per year.
DEALINE: October 31.

University of Queensland
F.G. Meade Post-Graduate Scholarship
Academic Registrar; Scholarships Section
St. Lucia, QLD 4067 Australia
617-377-3512
RESTRICTIONS: For graduate students. Applicants must hold the
equivalent of an Australian first-class honors or master's degree. Awards
renewable if satisfactory progress is made in the 1st year.
AMOUNT GIVEN: Aus. $12,000 per year. Scholarships for full-time
graduate study in the biological sciences at the University of Queens-
land.
DEADLINE: October 31.

University of Sydney
Scholarships Office
Sydney, NSW 2006 Australia
02-692-2222
RESTRICTIONS: Graduate research scholarships tenable at the Univer-
sity's selection based on academic merit. Open to law students from
Australia or overseas. Accepted at the University of Sydney.
AMOUNT GIVEN: Aus. $10,500 plus travel allowances.
DEADLINE: November 30.

University of Sydney
Post-Graduate Research Awards
Scholarships Office
Sydney, NSW 2006 Australia
02-692-2222
RESTRICTIONS: For graduate study in all fields at the university based
on academic merit, with minimum qualification being second-class hon-
ors division 1 or equivalent.
AMOUNT GIVEN: Aus. $7,100. 20 awards a year.
DEADLINE: October 31.

University of Tasmania
Post-Graduate Course Awards
GPO Box 252 C
Hobart, Tasmania 7001 Australia

RESTRICTIONS: For graduate study at the University in the fields of educational studies, environmental studies, financial studies, fine arts, humanities, music, pscyhology, social science, special education and welfare law. Open to postgraduate students from Australia and overseas who hold a first- or second-class honors degree or equivalent qualifications from a recognized institution or other university.
AMOUNT GIVEN: Aus. $7,000. Renewable for 2 years maximum or length of degree (whichever is the lesser).
DEADLINE: October 31.

University of Tasmania
Post-Graduate Research Awards;
University Research Scholarships
GPO Box 252 C
Hobart, Tasmania 7001 Australia
002-2021-01
RESTRICTIONS: For graduate students in all fields. For non-Australian citizens or residents to study at the master's or Ph.D level. Master's awards tenable for 2 years. Ph.D. awards tenable for 5 years.
AMOUNT GIVEN: Aus. $7,000 plus travel/dependants allowances. 10 awards to foreign students per year.
DEADLINE: September 30.

University of Western Australia
James & Sith Annie Chester Scholarships
Mounts Bay Rd.
Crawley, Perth, Western Australia 6009
09-380-3838 or 09-380-3030
RESTRICTIONS: Open to Medical graduates from U.W.A. or other recognized universities. For study at the University of Western Australia.
AMOUNT GIVEN: Variable stipend plus travel allowances.
DEADLINE: July 31.

University of Western Australia
University Research Studentships
Nedlands, Western Australia 6009
Attn: Registrar
RESTRICTIONS: All fields. Australian and overseas applicants. Minimum requirement of an upper-division class 2 honors degree. Must be proficient in English. Preferences for candidates under 35 years old.
AMOUNT GIVEN: 35 to 40 awards. 2 years for master's, 3–4 years for Ph.D.
DEADLINE: October 31.

University of Western Australia
University Research Fellowships

Nedlands, Western Australia 6009
Attn: Staffing Office.
RESTRICTIONS: Fellowships in fields announced yearly. All nationalities with fluent English. Must be within 5 years of obtaining Ph.D. or equivalent and be proven researchers.
AMOUNT GIVEN: Approximately 4 awards per year. Renewable to 3 years.
DEADLINE: September.

University of Wollongong
Post-Graduate Research Awards
P.O. Box 1144
Wollongong, NSW 2500 Australia
Attn: University Secretary
RESTRICTIONS: All fields. All nationalities. Minimum of a bachelor's degree with first-class honors.
AMOUNT GIVEN: 4 awards per year. 3 years for Ph.D. 2 years for master's.
DEADLINE: October 31.

Victoria College
Prahen Faculty of Art and Design
142 High Street
Praran, Victoria 381 Australia
Attn: Lecturer in charge, Industrial Design
RESTRICTIONS: For undergraduate students of all nationalities for study leading to a diploma of art and design in industrial design or a B.A. in industrial design or graphic design with minors in exhibition, furniture and work environments. Interview, folio and possible entry tests required. Arrangements available for handicapped students.
AMOUNT GIVEN: 16 awards per year for 3 years for diploma of art and design and 4 years for B.A.
DEADLINE: November 30.
APPLICATIONS: Written inquiry for interview.

AUSTRIA

Federal Ministry of Science and Research
Minoritenplatz 5
1014 Wien 1 Austria
RESTRICTIONS: For unmarried undergraduate and graduate students in all fields. Awards for U.S. citizens to study in Austria. Preference to candidates under 35 years old.
AMOUNT GIVEN: 5,700 schillings per month. 3 awards per year for 1 year.

DEADLINE: April 1st for following academic year.
CONTACT: Institute of International Education
             809 United Nations Plaza
             New York, New York 10017
             or for students enrolled in a U.S. college
             the Fulbright Programme Adviser on campus.

Federal Ministry of Science and Research
Minoritenplatz 5
1014 Wien 1 Austria
RESTRICTIONS: Scholarships for music students of any nationality with very high musical ability.
AMOUNT GIVEN: 5,700–7,200 schillings per month for 1 year.
DEADLINE: March 1.
CONTACT: Austrian embassies abroad.

Institute of European Studies
875 N. Michigan Ave #1540
Chicago, Ill. 60611
RESTRICTIONS: Open to any student accepted into one of the institute's programs with proof of financial need.
AMOUNT GIVEN: Tuition, fees, one-way transportation, lodging, board, and books.
DEADLINE: December 10; February 25.

University of Music and Performing Arts
Lothrinerstrasse 18
Postfach 146
1037 Wien III Austria
RESTRICTIONS: Postgraduate students of all nationalities for studies in performance using all musical instruments; composition, and voice. Must have outstanding musical ability and good knowledge of German. Must be between 17 and 30 years of age.
AMOUNT GIVEN: 6,500 schillings per month for 1 year. Renewable.
DEADLINE: February.
CONTACT: Nearest Austrian embassy.

BAHAMAS

Inter American Press Association
Scholarships for Study in Latin America and the West Indies
2911 NW 39th St.
Miami, FL 33142
305-634-2465

RESTRICTIONS: For young journalists and graduate students (ages 21–35). Must be U.S./Canadian citizen. Fluency in the designated country's language is required.
AMOUNT GIVEN: $10,000. 1 academic year of study/research in a Latin American or West Indian country.
DEADLINE: August 1.

BARBADOS

Inter American Press Association
Scholarships for Study in Latin America and the West Indies
2911 NW 39th St.
Miami, FL 33142
305-634-2465
RESTRICTIONS: For young journalists and graduate students (ages 21–35). Must be U.S./Canadian citizen. Fluency in the designated country's language is required.
AMOUNT GIVEN: $10,000. 1 academic year of study/research in a Latin American or West Indian country.
DEADLINE: August 1.

McGill University
Faculty of Graduate Studies and Research
Associate Dean, Faculty of Graduate Studies and Research
Fellowship Office, Dawson Hall
853 Sherbrooke Street West
Montreal, Quebec H3A 2T6
RESTRICTIONS: Fellowships open to postdoctoral students of all nationalities for study of tropical problems at Bellaire Research Institute, Barbados. Applicants must collaborate with a McGill staff member.
AMOUNT GIVEN: Can. $20,000 year + essential travel expenses.
DEADLINE: March 16th.

Organization of American States
Department of Fellowships and Training
OAS PRA Fellowships for USA Residents
Trainee Selection Division
Washington, DC 20006
202-789-3902
RESTRICTIONS: Graduate fellowships for U.S. citizens/permanent residents who wish to study abroad in an OAS member country. Must have undergraduate degree and have proven ability to pursue studies at advanced level in chosen field. Should be fluent in language of country of intended study. All fields except medicine.

AMOUNT GIVEN: Tuition and fees. Travel expenses and stipend.
DEADLINE: April 30; August 31.

BELGIUM

Belgian American Educational Foundation
Graduate Fellowships
195 Church St.
New Haven, CT 06510
203-777-5765
RESTRICTIONS: All fields. For graduate study in Belgium. Should have speaking and reading knowledge of French or Dutch and have master's degree or be working towards Ph.D. Preferences to applicants under 30.
AMOUNT GIVEN: $10,000. 8–10 awards per year. Includes round-trip airfare to Belgium, lodging, living expenses, tuition, and fees.
DEADLINE: December 31.

North Atlantic Treaty Organization
NATO Science Fellowships for U.S.A. Citizens
B-1110; Science Affairs Division
Brussels, Belgium
2-241-00-40
RESTRICTIONS: Graduate and postdoctoral fellowships for almost all scientific areas including interdisciplinary areas. Open to U.S. citizens who wish to study/research in another NATO member country. Administered in each country by a national administration.
AMOUNT GIVEN: Amount varies with country.
DEADLINE: January 1–March 1.
APPLICATIONS: Write for address of your country's administration.

Von Karman Institute for Fluid Dynamics
Diploma Course Scholarship
72 Chaussee de Waterloo
1640 Rhode-St-Genese, Belgium
02-358-1901
RESTRICTIONS: For aeronautics, aerospace, turbomachinery, or industrial fluid dynamics. Must be citizen of NATO country. For postgraduate study at the Von Karman Institute.
AMOUNT GIVEN: 21,500 Belgian francs per month. 35 scholarships per year.
DEADLINE: May 31.
CONTACT: J.J. Gineux, Director.

BOLIVIA

Inter American Press Association
Scholarships for Study in Latin America and the West Indies
2911 NW 39th St.
Miami, FL 33142
305-634-2465
RESTRICTIONS: Open to young journalists and graduate students (ages 21–35). Must be U.S./Canadian citizen. Fluency in the designated country's language is required.
AMOUNT GIVEN: $10,000. 1 academic year of study/research in a Latin American or West Indian country.
DEADLINE: August 1.

BRAZIL

Inter American Press Association
Scholarships for Study in Latin America and the West Indies
2911 NW 39th St.
Miami, FL 33142
305-634-2465
RESTRICTIONS: For young journalists and graduate students (ages 21–35). Must be a U.S./Canadian citizen. Fluency in the country's language is required.
AMOUNT GIVEN: $10,000. 1 academic year of study/research in a Latin American or West Indian country.
DEADLINE: August 1.

CANADA

Acadia University
Graduate Fellowship in Biology
Welfville, NS BOP 1XO Canada
902-542-2201
RESTRICTIONS: Candidate must meet requirements for entrance to the M.Sc. course in biology at Acadia University. The fellow will work half-time as graduate assistant in the department and study half-time in graduate classes.
AMOUNT GIVEN: $5,000.
DEADLINE: None.
CONTACT: Dr. M. E. Peach

American Academy for Dermatology
ADA Student Fellowship Program
1567 Maple Ave.
Evanston, IL 60201
312-869-3950
RESTRICTIONS: Graduate fellowships for medical students in the field of dermatology. Work undertaken must be done at a university or college in the U.S. or Canada not for credit or degree. Must be U.S. or Canadian citizen.
AMOUNT GIVEN: Up to $1050.
DEADLINE: March 30.

American Assembly of Collegiate Schools of Business Doctoral Fellowship in Business Administration
605 Old Ballas Rd #220
St. Louis, MO 63141
314-872-8481
RESTRICTIONS: Fellowships for Ph.D. candidates in business administration or management who plan to pursue faculty careers at U.S. or Canadian business schools. Awards tenable at colleges and universities accredited by AACSB. Must be Canadian or U.S. citizen.
AMOUNT GIVEN: Tuition + $10,000 stipend.
DEADLINE: January 1.

American Institute of Architects Foundation
AIA/AIAF Scholarship Program
1735 New York Avenue NW
Washington, D.C. 20006
202-626-7349
RESTRICTIONS: For graduate students and undergraduate students in their final 2 years pursuing their master's degree for study at institutes in Canada and the U.S. in the field of architecture.
AMOUNT GIVEN: $500–$2,500.
DEADLINE: February 1.

American Lung Assocation
1740 Broadway
NY, NY 10019
212-245-8000
RESTRICTIONS: Open to U.S. citizens for study in U.S. or Canada or Canadian citizens to train in the U.S. Must be physicians entering at least second year of residency in lung-related specialties. Also open to M.D., Ph.D., or S.C.D. holders for further training as investigators in this field.
AMOUNT GIVEN: $25,000.
DEADLINE: October 1.

American Medical Association
Rock Cleyster Memorial Scholarship

Director of Undergraduate Medical Education
535 North Dearborn St.
Chicago, IL 60610
312-645-4691
RESTRICTIONS: Open to rising undergraduate seniors who are nominated by their medical school. Awards based on demonstration of interest and need and are tenable at accredited medical schools in the U.S.
or Canada. Must be U.S. citizen or legal resident.
AMOUNT GIVEN: Approximately 20 scholarships. $2,500.
DEADLINE: May 1.

American Society for Enology and Viticulture
P.O. Box 1855
Davis, CA 95617
916-753-3142
RESTRICTIONS: Candidate must be enrolled/accepted in an ac-
credited college in North America in curriculum stressing a science
basic to the wine and grape industry. Must be North American resident.
AMOUNT GIVEN: $1,000–$3,000.
DEADLINE: March 1.

American Vacuum Society
Russell & Sigurd Varian Fellow Award
335 E. 45th Street
New York, NY 10017
212-661-9404
RESTRICTIONS: Award to recognize and encourage excellence in
graduate studies in vacuum science. Recipients selected on academic
merit. Finalists must interview with trustees. Candidates must be full-
time graduate students in a regular institution in North America.

Arthritis Society
Studentships
250 Bloor St. E. #401
Toronto, Ontario M4W 3P2 Canada
416-967-1414
RESTRICTIONS: Highly competitive awards open to qualified candidates to promote research training in the general area relating to arthritis research. Research training may be part of an M.D./Ph.D. program. Preference to Canadian citizens/legal residents. 12-month awards
renewable with satisfactory progress.
AMOUNT GIVEN: Canadian $12,570.
DEADLINE: February 1.

AUCC
Awards Division
Emergency Planning Canada Research Fellowship

151 Slater St.; Enquiries Clerk
Ottawa, Ontario K1P 5N1 Canada
613-563-1236
RESTRICTIONS: For graduate research fellowships. Open to Canadian citizens or legal residents who have a first Canadian degree or equivalent. Particularly to encourage applicants in planning; geography; risk analysis; system science; sociology; business administration; health administration to develop ongoing interest in emergency planning. Preference to Ph.D. candidates, but master's candidates are considered.
AMOUNT GIVEN: Tuition fees + Canadian $10,810 stipend. Awards tenable for 4 years at a Canadian institution.
DEADLINE: February 1.

AUCC
Awards Division
Petro Canada Inc. Graduate Research Program
151 Slater St.; Enquiries Clerk
Ottawa, Ontario K1P 5N1 Canada
613-563-1236
RESTRICTIONS: For full-time graduate study at an accredited Canadian Institution. Granted primarily on the basis of academic standing and demonstrated potential for advanced study/research. Must be Canadian citizen or legal resident.
AMOUNT GIVEN: Canadian $10,000. Possibly renewable pending satisfactory progress.
DEADLINE: February 1.

AUCC
Awards Division
Sara-Lee Corp. Nathan Cummings Scholarship Program
151 Slater St.; Enquiries Clerk
Ottawa, Ontario K1P 5N1 Canada
613-563-1236
RESTRICTIONS: Competitive scholarships for High School students who are natural or adopted children of regular, full-time Sara-Lee employees. All fields. Winners picked by merit.
AMOUNT GIVEN: Canadian $1,500.
DEADLINE: June 1.

AUCC
Awards Division
Telecommunications Research Fellowship
151 Slater St.; Enquiries Clerk
Ottawa, Ontario K1P 5N1 Canada
613-563-1236

RESTRICTIONS: Open to master's or Ph.D. candidates for thesis research relating to engineering of broadbench communications systems. Must be Canadian citizen or legal resident.
AMOUNT GIVEN: Canadian $5,000
DEADLINE: February 1.

AUCC
Awards Division
Teleglobe Canada
151 Slater St.; Enquiries Clerk
Ottawa, Ontario K1P 5N1 Canada
613-563-1236
RESTRICTIONS: Open to graduates of a Canadian university. Must have achieved a high level of academic excellence and exhibited superior intellectual ability and judgment. Must be a Canadian citizen or legal resident.
AMOUNT GIVEN: Canadian $7,500.
DEADLINE: February 1.

Banff Centre School of Fine Arts
Scholarships
P.O. Box 1020
Banff, Alberta T0L 0C0 Canada
403-762-6180
RESTRICTIONS: Scholarships for study at the university for artists who have completed formal training and are pursuing studies at an advanced level. Young artists are given an opportunity to design postgraduate work programs.
AMOUNT GIVEN: 150 scholarships per year of approx. Canadian $6,000. Renewable for two years.
DEADLINE: March 15.

British Federation of University Women
(BFUW)
A. Vibert Douglas International Fellowship
Crosby Hall; Cheyne Walk
London SW3 5BA England
01-352-5354
RESTRICTIONS: All fields. Postgraduate fellowship for research in Canada. Applicants must have completed at least 1 year of graduate study and intend to study in a country other than their own. Open to members of the BFUW or association affiliated with the International Federation of University Women who are nominated by the BFUW.
AMOUNT GIVEN: 6,000 British pounds.
DEADLINE: September 15.

Canada Roads and Transportation Association
RTAC Scholarships

1765 Blvd. St. Laurent
Ottawa, Ontario K19 3V4 Canada
613-521-4052
RESTRICTIONS: To financially assist graduate students displaying high promise of future achievement in transportation. Award can be used in Canada or U.S.A. Must be Canadian citizen or legal resident.
AMOUNT GIVEN: Canadian $3,000. 3 awards per year. Possibly renewable.
DEADLINE: March 1.

Canadian Heart Foundation
Research Traineeships
1 Nicholas Street, Suite 1200
Ottawa, Ontario K1N 7B7 Canada
613-237-4361
RESTRICTIONS: Research fellowships for qualified research workers of all nationalities in Cardiovascular Research at approved Canadian institutions. Applicants must make their own arrangement with the university or institution and submit a statement of acceptance from the head of the department with their application.
AMOUNT GIVEN: Canadian $11,550– $46,500.
DEADLINE: December 1.
APPLICATIONS: Send written inquiry for prescribed forms.

Canadian Lung Association
Canadian Nurses Respiratory Society
Fellowships & Research Grants
72 Albert Suite 908
Ottawa, Ontario K1P 5E7 Canada
613-237-1208
RESTRICTIONS: For those studying at master's level or above. To increase the number of nurses with expertise in the clinical practice of respiratory nursing resulting in improved quality of patient care.
AMOUNT GIVEN: Varies.
DEADLINE: November 1.

Canadian Paraplegic Association
Joseph Hall/Don Vaux/John Macneal Schoalrships
780 S.W. Marine Dr.
Vancouver, BC V6P 5Y7 Canada
604-324-3611
RESTRICTIONS: All fields. Undergraduate students. For disabled persons to further their vocational or academic training. To be used specifically for tuition, tools, equipment, or books. Must be Canadian citizen or legal resident.
AMOUNT GIVEN: Varies.
DEADLINE: August 15.

Canadian Society of Exploration Geophysicists
206 7th Ave SW; Suite 501
Calgary, Alberta T2P 0W7 Canada
403-262-0015
RESTRICTIONS: Scholarships available to students in an academic program leading to an exploration geophysics career in teaching, industry, or research. For study at Canadian universities or technical schools.
AMOUNT GIVEN: Approx. 35 awards per years. Canadian $1250–$1500.
DEADLINE: June 30.
CONTACT: W. J. McCormack, Chairman.

Concordia University
Graduate Fellowships
Graduate Admissions
1455 de Maisonneuve Boulevard West
Montreal, Quebec H3G 1M8 Canada
514-848-3809
RESTRICTIONS: Graduate students. All fields. All nationalities. Based on academic record. For study at Concordia University.
AMOUNT GIVEN: 3–4 awards per year. Canadian $6,500 (master's) $7,500 (doctoral).
DEADLINE: February 1.

Concordia University
David J. Azzreli Graduate Fellowship
Graduate Admissions
1455 Boulevard de Maisonneuve
Montreal, Quebec H3G 1M8 Canada
514-848-3809
RESTRICTIONS: Graduate students. All fields. All nationalities. Based on academic record. For full-time study at Concordia University.
AMOUNT GIVEN: 1 award per year. Minimum of Canadian $10,000. Not renewable.
DEADLINE: February 1.

Concordia University
John W. O'Brian Graduate Fellowship
Graduate Admissions
1455 de Maisonneuve Boulevard West
Montreal, Quebec H3G 1M8 Canada
514-848-3809
RESTRICTIONS: Graduate students. All fields. All nationalities. Based on academic record.
AMOUNT GIVEN: 1 award per year. Minimum of Canadian $6,500 per year. Not renewable.
DEADLINE: February 1.

Concordia University
Stanley G. French Graduate Fellowship
1455 de Maisonneuve Boulevard West
Montreal, Quebec H3G 1M8 Canada
514-848-3809
RESTRICTIONS: Graduate students. All fields. All nationalities. Based on academic record.
AMOUNT GIVEN: 1 award per year. Minimum of Canadian $6,500 per year. Not renewable.
DEADLINE: February 1.
CONTACT: Director of the graduate program of application.

Concordia University
Alcan Doctoral Fellowship in Commerce and Administration
Attn: Graduate Admissions
1455 de Maisonneuve Boulevard West
Montreal, Quebec H3G 1M8 Canada
514-848-3809
RESTRICTIONS: For graduate students who are Canadian citizens or legal residents. For fully-time study in Ph.D. administration program at Concordia University in business administration.
AMOUNT GIVEN: Canadian $10,000.
DEADLINE: February 1.

Concordia University
Shell Canada Ltd. Doctoral Fellowship
1455 de Maisonneuve Boulevard West
Montreal, Quebec H3G 1M8 Canada
RESTRICTIONS: Doctoral fellowship in commerce and administration open to qualified students of all nationalities. Based on academic record.
AMOUNT GIVEN: Canadian $7,500 per year.
DEADLINE: February 1.
CONTACT: Director of the graduate program of application.

Council for International Exchange of Scholars
Fulbright Scholar Grant Programs
11 Dupont Circle NW #300
Washington, DC 20036
202-939-5401
RESTRICTIONS: All fields. Graduate students. Designed to increase mutual understanding between people of the U.S. and people of other countries. For U.S. citizens to conduct research and/or lecture abroad. Open to Ph.D.'s or equivalent.
AMOUNT GIVEN: Varies with country.
DEADLINE: June 15; September 13; January 1; February 1.

Dalhousie University
Izaak Walton Killam Post-doctoral Fellowships

Office of the Dean
Faculty of Graduate Studies
Halifax, Nova Scotia B3H 4H6 Canada
902-424-2416
RESTRICTIONS: Most fields. All nationalities. Must meet Canadian immigration requirements and be fluent in English. Applicants must have obtained a Ph.D. from a recognized university before receiving the award.
AMOUNT GIVEN: Canadian $21,000 per year + travel expenses.
DEADLINE: December 15.

Dermatology Foundation
Post-Doctoral Fellowship Award Program
1567 Maple Ave.
Evanston, IL 60201
312-869-3950
RESTRICTIONS: Competitive awards to support training in research skills and methods or research projects. Must be U.S. or Canadian citizen.
AMOUNT GIVEN: 18 awards. $15,000–$25,000 per year.
DEADLINE: September 15; February 1.
CONTACT: Sandra Rahn Goldman, Executive Director.

Dermatology Foundation
Post-Doctoral Grant Program
1567 Maple Ave.
Evanston, IL 60201
312-869-3950
RESTRICTIONS: Postdoctoral grants for M.D.s for "seed support" of research projects. Competitive awards. Must be Canadian or U.S. citizen.
AMOUNT GIVEN: $5,000–$10,000.
DEADLINE: September 15.
CONTACT: Sandra Rahn Goldman, Executive Director.

Electrochemical Society
Summer Research Fellowships
10 South Main St.
Pennington, NJ 08534
609-737-7882
RESTRICTIONS: Summer Fellowships open to graduate students at accredited colleges in universities in the U.S. and Canada for research of interest to the electrochemical society and research aimed at reducing energy consumption.
AMOUNT GIVEN: $2,000–$6,000.
DEADLINE: January 15.

Entomology Society of America
4603 Calvert Road

College Park, MD 20740
301-864-1334
RESTRICTIONS: Must be enrolled at a recognized college or university in the U.S., Canada, or Mexico and have accumulated at least 30 semester hours at the time award is presented. For study in fields of entomology, biology, or related science.
AMOUNT GIVEN: $500–$1,000.
DEADLINE: July 1.

Geological Society of America
Research Grants Program
P.O. Box 9140
330 Penrose Place
Boulder, CO 80301
303-447-2020
RESTRICTIONS: Open to master's and Ph.D candidates in the field of geology at colleges and universities in the U.S., Canada, Mexico, and Central America. To support thesis research. GSA membership not required.
AMOUNT GIVEN: Approx. 200 awards per year. $500–$1,700.
DEADLINE: February 15.

Institute of Electrical & Electronics Engineers
Charles Le Geyt Fortescue Fellowship
345 East 47th St.
NY, NY 10017
212-705-7882
RESTRICTIONS: For first year graduate students in field of electrical engineering at recognized engineering schools in the U.S. or Canada.
AMOUNT GIVEN: $24,000.
DEADLINE: January 31.

Institute of Food Technologies
Graduate Fellowships
221 North La Salle St. #300
Chicago, IL 60601
312-782-8424
RESTRICTIONS: Graduate Fellowships to encourage and support research in food science and technology at an accredited institution in the U.S. or Canada.
AMOUNT GIVEN: 23 awards of $1,000–$10,000 per year.
DEADLINE: February 1.

Institute of Food Technologies
Undergraduate Scholarships
221 North La Salle St. #300

Chicago, IL 60601
312-782-8424
RESTRICTIONS: Open to high school graduates planning to enroll/enrolled in an accredited institution in the U.S. or Canada in fields related to food science and technology. Based on academics (minimum 2.5 average) and personality.
AMOUNT GIVEN: $500–$2,000. 30 freshman/sophomore & 52 junior/senior awards per year.
DEADLINE: February 1 (junior/senior); February 15 (freshman); March 1 (sophomore).

Institute of International Education
International Fellowships for USA Residents
809 U.N. Plaza
New York, NY 10017
212-984-5328
RESTRICTIONS: Graduate fellowships for U.S. residents to study/research in a foreign country. All fields. Must be proficient in language of county of intended visit. At least half of B.A. must have been completed in the U.S.
AMOUNT GIVEN: Varies with country.
DEADLINE: May 1–October 31.

International Association of Bridge Structural and Ornamental Iron Workers
John H. Lyons Scholarship Program
Suite 400
1750 New York Ave NW
Washington, DC 20006
202-383-4800
RESTRICTIONS: For children of members or decreased members who were in good standing at time of death. Must rank in upper ½ of graduating class. For undergraduate study in U.S. or Canada.
AMOUNT GIVEN: Maximum of $1,500 per year.
DEADLINE: January 15.

International Order of the Kings Daughters and Sons
Student Ministry Scholarship Fund
Headquarters; P.O. Box 1017
34 Vincent Ave.
Chataqua, NY 14722
716-357-6200
RESTRICTIONS: Available to graduate students accepted or enrolled in an accredited U.S. or Canadian school or seminary or are preparing for a full-time religious career.
Must have minimum of "B" average. Must be U.S. or Canadian citizens.
AMOUNT GIVEN: 18–25 awards of $1,000 per year.

DEADLINE: April 30.
APPLICATIONS: Send a self-addressed, stamped, legal-sized envelope to the director; Mrs. Thad Welch Jr.; 1318 Walthour Rd.; Savannah, GA 31410

Jewish Welfare Board
JWB Scholarship Program
Grants Coordinator
15 E. 26th St
NY, NY 10010
212-532-4949
RESTRICTIONS: Open to U.S. and Canadian citizens of the Jewish faith. For master's degree programs only in fields of adult education, early childhood education, physical education and social work. Should have a strong desire to enter and work in the Jewish community center field.
AMOUNT GIVEN: $7,500. 18 awards per year.
DEADLINE: February 1.

Kappa Kappa Gamma
Graduate Fellowships
c/o Betty Cameron
P.O. Box 2079
Columbus, OH 43216
614-228-6515
RESTRICTIONS: For women who have completed a B.A. at a campus with a KKG chapter or attend a graduate school where a chapter is located in the U.S. or Canada. For applicants with high academic standing who need assistance for graduate study. Membership not required. All fields except rehabilitation services.
AMOUNT GIVEN: 24 awards per year. $1,000.
DEADLINE: February 15.

Kappa Kappa Gamma
Rehabilitation Scholarships
c/o Mrs. La Williams
4720 Pickett Rd.
Fairfax, VA 22032
RESTRICTIONS: Open to U.S. or Canadian citizens. For women who are undergraduate students in their last two years or graduate students having completed at least 2 years of study on a campus with a KKG chapter. Limited to study in rehabilitation or related fields (e.g., mental health rehabilitation and speech/hearing therapy). Membership not required.
AMOUNT GIVEN: $750 (undergraduate)–$1,000 (graduate).
DEADLINE: February 15.

Kidney Foundation of Canada
Nephrology/Urology Scholarship Fellowship and Grant Programs

4060 St.-Catherine St. W.; #555
Montreal, Quebec H3Z 2Z3 Canada
514-934-4806
RESTRICTIONS: To support study and research in fields of nephrology/urology. Open to graduate and postgraduate teachers, doctors, Ph.D.s and researchers. Many programs limited to Canadian citizens.
AMOUNT GIVEN: Amount varies with program.
DEADLINE: Varies.

Landscape Architecture Foundation
Harriet Barnhart Wimmer Scholarship
c/o Wimmer Yamada & Associates
516 Fifth Ave.
San Diego, CA 92101
619-232-4004
RESTRICTIONS: Awarded to a female undergraduate student in her final year of studies in Landscape Architecture at a University in the U.S. or Canada who had demonstrated excellence in her design ability and sensitivity to the environment and quality of life.
AMOUNT GIVEN: $500.
DEADLINE: April 15–May 15.

Medical Research Council
Studentships
20th Floor Jeanne Mance Bldg.
De'Lengantine St.
Tunney's Pasture Ottawa, Ontario K1A 0W9 Canada
RESTRICTIONS: Awards for Canadian citizens and non-citizens tenable in Canada. Applicants must have or be about to receive an honors B.S. degree (or its equal).
AMOUNT GIVEN: Canadian $11,400.
DEADLINE: December 1; April 1.

Mycological Society of America
Graduate Fellowships
c/o P.O. Box 5130; Forest Products Lab
Center for Forest Mycology Research
Madison, WI 53705
608-264-5634
RESTRICTIONS: Scholarships in the field of mycology available to Ph.D. candidates at accredited U.S. or Canadian universities. Can't be previous fellowship recipient.
AMOUNT GIVEN: $1,000.
DEADLINE: March 1.

National Federation of Press Women Inc.
Helen Malloch Scholarship

P.O. Box 99
1105 Main St.
Blue Springs, MO 64015
816-229-1666
RESTRICTIONS: For undergraduate juniors and seniors or graduate
students majoring in journalism at an accredited university in the U.S.
or Canada.
AMOUNT GIVEN: $1,000.
DEADLINE: April 15.

National Institute for Architectural Education
Van Alen Architect Memorial Fellowship
30 W. 22nd St.
New York, NY 10010
212-924-7000
RESTRICTIONS: Design competition for travel and study abroad open
to undergraduate or master's students enrolled in an accredited archi-
tectural or engineering program in the U.S. or Canada.
AMOUNT GIVEN: Up to $6,000.
DEADLINE: April 6.

National Research Council of Canada
Research Associateships
Research Associates Office
Ottawa, Ontario K1A 1H5 Canada
RESTRICTIONS: Open to recent Ph.D.s in natural sciences or recent
master's or Ph.D.s in engineering. Tenable at NRCC Laboratories
throughout Canada. 2–5 years duration. Preference to Canadian citizens
or legal residents.
AMOUNT GIVEN: Up to Canadian $31,423 stipend.
DEADLINE: November 30.

Natural Sciences and Engineering Research Council of Canada
Science and Engineering Scholarships
200 Kent Street
Ottawa, Ontario K1A 1H5 Canada
613-996-2009
RESTRICTIONS: For graduate students in the fields of agriculture, biology, chemistry, computer science, engineering, food science, forestry,
and geography, with superior scholastic or research ability for study
and research in Canada leading to Ph.D.
AMOUNT GIVEN: 60 awards per year of Canadian $17,500.
DEADLINE: December 8.

Natural Sciences and Engineering Research Council of Canada
Undergraduate Student Research Awards
200 Kent Street

Ottawa, Ontario K1A 1H5 Canada
613-996-2009
RESTRICTIONS: Open to Canadian citizens or legal residents for undergraduate research at universities or industrial labs in the fields of
agriculture, biology, computer science, engineering, food science, forestry, geography, and geology to encourage students to undertake graduate studies. Tenable during summer or may be used during academic
year.
AMOUNT GIVEN: Canadian $750 for a maximum of 4 months.
DEADLINE: Set by university.

Natural Sciences and Engineering Research Council of Canada
Visiting Fellowships in Canadian Government Laboratories
200 Kent Street
Ottawa, Ontario K1A 1H5 Canada
RESTRICTIONS: Fellowships for research in science and Engineering
available to applicants of all nationalities who meet all Canadian immigration requirements. Must possess a Ph.D. from an accepted university
or a master's degree with a minimum of two years of post-master's experience. Must have proven ability to successfully conduct independent
research. No more than five years may have passed since applicant received his or her doctorate.
AMOUNT GIVEN: Canadian $28,992 per year + travel allowances.
DEADLINE: December 15.

North Atlantic Treaty Organization
NATO Science Fellowships for U.S.A. Citizens
B-1110; Science Affairs Division
Brussels, Belgium
2-241-00-40
RESTRICTIONS: Graduate and postdoctoral fellowships for almost all
scientific areas including interdisciplinary areas. Open to U.S. citizens
who wish to study/research in another NATO member country. Admin-
istered in each country by a national administration. Write for address
of your country's administration.
AMOUNT GIVEN: Amount varies with country.
DEADLINE: January 1–March 1.

Nova Scotia College of Art and Design
5163 Duke St.
Halifax, Nova Scotia B3J 3J6 Canada
902-4222-7381
RESTRICTIONS: Individual grants awarded to advanced graduate students during the fall and spring semesters for study at the college in the
master of fine arts program.
AMOUNT GIVEN: Canadian $300–$500

Professional Plant Growers Scholarship Foundation
Carl Dietz Memorial Scholarships
P.O. Box 27517
Lansing, MI 48909
517-694-7700
RESTRICTIONS: Open to undergraduate and graduate students in horticulture with a specific interest in bedding plants. Tenable at accredited universities in the U.S. and Canada.
AMOUNT GIVEN: $1,000 (undergraduate)–$1,500 (graduate).
DEADLINE: May 1.

Professional Plant Growers Scholarship Foundation
Harold Bettinger Memorial Scholarship
P.O. Box 27517
Lansing, MI 48909
517-694-7700
RESTRICTIONS: Open to graduate and undergraduate horticulture majors with business and/or marketing emphasis or business and/or marketing majors with horticulture emphasis. Tenable at accredited 4-year universities or colleges in the U.S. or Canada.
AMOUNT GIVEN: $1,000.
DEADLINE: May 1.

Pulp and Paper Research Institute
McGill University
Harold Hibbert Fellowship
Attn: Chairman Education Committee
Montreal, Quebec
Canada
RESTRICTIONS: Fellowship in chemistry, chemical engineering, mechanical engineering in relation to the pulp and paper industry. Open to students of all nationalities who have a Ph.D. or equivalent in chemistry or physics from an approved university. Full-time study and research in department of chemistry at McGill and in the Pulp and Paper Research Institute of Canada is required.
AMOUNT GIVEN: Canadian $20,000.
DEADLINE: February 1.

Pulp and Paper Research Institute
McGill University
F.L. Mitchell Fellowship
Attn: Chairman Education Committee
Montreal, Quebec
Canada

RESTRICTIONS: Fellowship open to applicants from the U.S. or from the Commonwealth for research in chemistry, chemical engineering, mechanical engineering in relation to the pulp and paper industry.
AMOUNT GIVEN: Canadian $11,000.
DEADLINE: February 1.

Pulp and Paper Research Institute of Canada
Mount Allison University
Entrance Scholarships
Sackville, New Brunswick E0A 3C0 Canada
RESTRICTIONS: All fields. All nationalities. Must have high academic marks and financial needs. Selections made by the committee.
AMOUNT GIVEN: Canadian $1,000–$5,000 first year. $750–$2,500 subsequent years.
DEADLINE: March 15.

Pulp and Paper Research Institute of Canada
Fowler Fellowships; Papricorn Fellowships
570 St. John's Blvd.
Pointe Claire, Quebec H9R 3J9 Canada
514-630-4100
RESTRICTIONS: Open to graduate and postdoctorate students in chemical engineering, electrical engineering and mechanical engineering, to research topics relevant to the pulp and paper industry.
AMOUNT GIVEN: Up to Canadian $20,000.
DEADLINE: February 1.

Queen's University at Kingston
Clarence J. Hicks Fellowship
School of Graduate Studies and Research
Kingston, Ontario
Canada
RESTRICTIONS: Fellowship in industrial relations open to M.A. candidates and graduate students of all nationalities.
AMOUNT GIVEN: Varies.
DEADLINE: March 1.

Queen's University at Kingston
D. W. Stewart Graduate Fellowship
School of Graduate Studies and Research
Kingston, Ontario
Canada
RESTRICTIONS: Fellowships for master's and doctoral degrees in humanities open to applicants of all nationalities who hold degrees from recognized universities.
AMOUNT GIVEN: 1 year fellowship of Canadian $6,500. Not renewable.
DEADLINE: March 1.

Queen's University at Kingston
R. Samuel Mclaughlin Teaching Fellowships
School of Graduate Studies and Research
Kingston, Ontario
Canada
RESTRICTIONS: Fellowships in mechanical engineering for applicants of all nationalities. Recipients must fulfill teaching or demonstrating duties.
AMOUNT GIVEN: Canadian $5,000 per year.
DEADLINE: March 1.

Queen's University at Kingston
W. W. King Graduate Fellowships
School of Graduate Studies and Research
Kingston, Ontario
Canada
RESTRICTIONS: Fellowships in engineering for applicants of all nationalities who are candidates for the master's of science degree.
AMOUNT GIVEN: Canadian $4,500 per year. Not renewable.
DEADLINE: March 1.

Queen's University at Kingston
Gerald Row Foundation Scholarship
School of Graduate Studies and Research
Kingston, Ontario
Canada
RESTRICTIONS: English fellowship available to graduate students of all nationalities. Recipients must assist in teaching English composition.
AMOUNT GIVEN: Canadian $3,000 per year.
DEADLINE: March 1.

Richard D. Irwin Foundation
1818 Ridge Road
Homewood, IL 60430
708-798-6000
RESTRICTIONS: For Ph.D. candidates in the fields of business administration or economics who have completed all course work except dissertation. Awards tenable at U.S. and Canadian institutions. Preference given to those who plan to teach in the U.S. or Canada.
AMOUNT GIVEN: 20 awards per year of $2,000–$2,500.
DEADLINE: February 1.

Rotary Foundation of Rotary International
Graduate Study Abroad Scholarships
One Rotary Center

1560 Sherman Ave
Evanston, IL 60201
312-866-3000
RESTRICTIONS: Open to graduate students 18–30 years of age who received their bachelor's degree in the U.S. and wish to complete 1 academic year of study in a foreign country where rotary clubs exist. Rotary members and employees not eligible.
AMOUNT GIVEN: Full tuition, travel + living expenses.
DEADLINE: January 1–July 1.
APPLICATIONS: Do not write to above address. Applications must be obtained through local chapter of rotary club listed in phone directory.

Rotary Foundation of Rotary International
Undergraduate Study Abroad Scholarships
One Rotary Center
1560 Sherman Ave
Evanston, IL 60201
312-866-3000
RESTRICTIONS: Open to unmarried undergraduate students aged 18–24 who have completed 2 years of study in the U.S. and wish to complete their junior and senior year in a foreign country where rotary clubs are located.
AMOUNT GIVEN: Full tuition, travel + living expenses.
DEADLINE: January 1–July 1.
APPLICATIONS: Do not write to above address. Applications must be obtained through local chapter of rotary club listed in phone directory.

Royal Society of Canada
Attn: Awards Committee
NATO Fellowship Program
344 Wellington Street
Ottawa, Ontario K1A ON4 Canada
RESTRICTIONS: Fellowships for postgraduate students with established reputations from NATO states for study and research culminating in publication on various aspects of the common interests, traditions and perspectives of the countries of the North Atlantic Alliance. Recipients must conduct their research in one or more member country. Must have knowledge of language of host country.
AMOUNT GIVEN: 180,000 Belgian francs (or equivalent in country's currency).
DEADLINE: December 31.

Saint Mary's University
Entrance Scholarships; Achievement Scholarships
Financial Aid Office
Halifax, Nova Scotia B3H 3C3 Canada
902-420-5609

RESTRICTIONS: Open to undergraduate students in all fields accepted or enrolled at the University.
AMOUNT GIVEN: 180 awards per year. Canadian $200–$2,000.
DEADLINE: May 25.

Simon Fraser University
Graduate Fellowships
Dean of Graduate Studies Office
Burnaby, British Columbia V5A 1S6 Canada
RESTRICTIONS: All fields. All nationalities. Graduate students beginning studies.
AMOUNT GIVEN: Canadian $3,200 per semester (master's). $3,800 per semester (Ph.D.).

Simon Fraser University
Graduate Teaching Assistantships
Dean of Graduate Studies Office
Burnaby, British Columbia V5A 1S6 Canada
RESTRICTIONS: Teaching assistantships in all fields for graduate students of all nationalities to study in master's or doctoral programs.
AMOUNT GIVEN: Canadian $3,324 (master's). $3,816 (Ph.D.).

Simon Fraser University
President's Research Grant Stipends
Dean of Graduate Studies Office
Burnaby, British Columbia V5A 1S6 Canada
RESTRICTIONS: For Ph.D. students of all nationalities who have completed at least 2 residence semesters and all degree specifications aside from their thesis for the doctoral program.
AMOUNT GIVEN: Canadian $3,800.

Simon Fraser University
C. D. Nelson Memorial Graduate Scholarships
Burnaby, British Columbia V5A 1S6
RESTRICTIONS: Graduate students beginning studies. All fields. All nationalities.
AMOUNT GIVEN: Canadian $12,000 per year. 3 awards.
CONTACT: Department concerned.

Society of Manufacturing Engineering Education Foundation
Alfred V. Bodine/SME Award
One SME Drive; P.O. Box 930
Dearborn, MI 48121
313-271-1500
RESTRICTIONS: Granted for best paper on machine tool justification and its relationship to manufacturing productivity submitted by a graduate student. Must be U.S. or Canadian citizen.

AMOUNT GIVEN: 1 student award of $5,000 per year; $1,500 and a medallion awarded to the winning student's major professor.
DEADLINE: February 1.

Society for Technical Communication
Undergraduate and Graduate Scholarships
815 15th St. NW
Washington, DC 20005
202-737-0035
RESTRICTIONS: Open to full-time undergraduate student or graduate students who are enrolled in an accredited master's or doctoral degree program for a career in any area of technical communications. Tenable at recognized colleges and universities in the U.S. and Canada.
AMOUNT GIVEN: $1,500.
DEADLINE: February 15.

Swann Foundation
Fellowship for the Study of Caricature & Cartoon
655 Madison Ave.
New York, NY 10021
212-838-2424
RESTRICTIONS: Doctoral dissertation fellowship in caricature/cartoon open to students enrolled in a doctoral program in a university in the U.S. or Canada. Award must be used in the school year following its receipt.
AMOUNT GIVEN: $10,000.
DEADLINE: February 15.

Trent University
Graduate Teaching/Research Assistantships
P.O. Box 4800; Graduate Studies & Research Officer
Peterborough, Ontario K9J 7B8 Canada
705-748-1245
RESTRICTIONS: Open to master's candidates in the fields of anthropology, archaeology, biology, Canadian studies, and geography. For teaching/research assistantships at the university.
AMOUNT GIVEN: 28 awards of Canadian $2,140 per year for up to 2 years of study.

University of Alberta
Killam Scholarships
Director of Student Awards
Edmonton, Alberta T6G 2EI Canada
RESTRICTIONS: Doctoral students. All fields. All nationalities. English proficiency required.
AMOUNT GIVEN: 10 scholarships yearly.
DEADLINE: February 1.

University of Alberta
Graduate Research Assistantships
Edmonton, Alberta T6G 2EI Canada
RESTRICTIONS: Graduate students. All fields. All nationalities. English required.
AMOUNT GIVEN: 125 awards per year.
DEADLINE: March 1.
CONTACT: Chairman of department concerned.

University of Alberta
Graduate Teaching Assistantships
Edmonton, Alberta T6G 2EI Canada
RESTRICTIONS: Teaching assistantships open to graduate students. All fields. All nationalities. English required.
AMOUNT GIVEN: 800 awards per year.
DEADLINE: March 1.
CONTACT: Chairman of department concerned.

University of Birmingham
Student Travel Scholarships
The Registry
P.O. Box 363
Birmingham B15 2TT England
021-472-1301
RESTRICTIONS: Various Scholarships available to full-time registered students of the university for overseas study programs. All fields. Graduate students.
AMOUNT GIVEN: Up to 400 British pounds.

University of British Columbia
Faculty of Graduate Studies
235-2075 Wesbrook Mall
Vancouver, British Columbia V6T IZ3 Canada
RESTRICTIONS: Graduate fellowships and graduate teaching assistantships in all fields open to graduate students from all nationalities. Competitive awards. First class standing preferable.
AMOUNT GIVEN: Canadian $8,500–$13,000 per year.
DEADLINE: February 8.

University of Calgary
Department of Archaeology
2920 24th Avenue NW
Calgary, Alberta T2N 1N4 Canada
RESTRICTIONS: Research assistantships and teaching assistantships available to graduate students of all nationalities for study in archaeology.
AMOUNT GIVEN: 33 assistantships awarded yearly.
DEADLINE: February 1.

University of Calgary
Environmental Design Scholarships
Design Graduate Assistantships
2500 University Dr.
Rm. 275 Arts Bldg.
Calgary Alberta T2N 1N4 Canada
403-220-5690
RESTRICTIONS: Open to graduate students who are or will be enrolled in the Dept. of Environmental Design at the university. Based on
merit.
AMOUNT GIVEN: 10–12 scholarships of Canadian $1,000. 8-month
duration. 25 assistantships of Canadian $3,232 renewable session by ses-
sion.

University of Guelph
Guelph, Ontario N1G 2WI Canada
RESTRICTIONS: Teaching and service assistantships in all fields for
graduate students of recognized universities. All nationalities with pro-
ficiency in English.
AMOUNT GIVEN: Up to Canadian $10,740 per year.
CONTACT: Chairman of desired department.

University of Guelph
Graduate Visa Student Scholarships
Faculty of Graduate Students
Guelph, Ontario N1G 2WI Canada
519-824-4120 ext. 2441
RESTRICTIONS: Visa student scholarships in all fields open to out-
standing students with high GPA of all nationalities who are qualified
for graduate study. Must have nominations from academic department
and class 1 academic record.
AMOUNT GIVEN: Canadian $4,200–$6,300 per year.
DEADLINE: Open.

University of Guelph
Dean of Graduate Studies
Guelph, Ontario N1G 2WI Canada
RESTRICTIONS: Awards for postgraduate study in fields of agriculture,
arts, biological science, physical sciences, social sciences, veterinary sci-
ences. Open to students of all nationalities having graduated from a
recognized university.
AMOUNT GIVEN: Canadian $2,400–$3,000 per year.
CONTACT: Desired department.

University of Manitoba
J. W. Dafoe Graduate Fellowship

500 University Center
Winnipeg, Manitoba R3T 2N2 Canada
RESTRICTIONS: For graduate students of all nationalities planning to earn a higher degree in International Studies. Must have B.A. honors degree or equivalent and fluent English.
DEADLINE: February 15.

University of Manitoba
Graduate Fellowships
500 University Center
Winnipeg, Manitoba R3T 2N2 Canada
204-474-9836
RESTRICTIONS: For graduate study at the University of Manitoba in all fields. Mostly for Canadian citizens but some for international students. Must have a high GPA.
AMOUNT GIVEN: Canadian $8,000.
DEADLINE: March & July.

University of New Brunswick
School of Graduate Studies and Research
P.O. Box 4400
Fredericton, New Brunswick E3B 5A3 Canada
RESTRICTIONS: Graduate assistantships and teaching assistantship in the fields of computer science, education, engineering, forestry, humanities, mathematics, physical education and recreation, science and social sciences. Available to students of all nationalities who fulfill requirements for admission as higher degree candidates in the School of Graduate Studies and Research.
AMOUNT GIVEN: Up to Canadian $12,000 per year.
DEADLINE: March 1.
CONTACT: Director of appropriate department.

University of Ottawa
Merit Graduate Research Scholarships
School of Graduate Studies
115 Wilbrod
Ottawa, Ontario K1N 6N5 Canada
RESTRICTIONS: Scholarships for study at the University of Ottawa in fields of humanities and social sciences available to qualified applicants of all nationalities. Fluency in English or French required.
AMOUNT GIVEN: Canadian $4,600 (master's). $6,000 (Ph.D.).
DEADLINE: Fall session by July 1. Winter session by December 1. Summer session by April 1.

University of Ottawa
Excellence Supplementary Scholarships
School of Graduate Studies

115 Wilbrod
Ottawa, Ontario K1N 6N5 Canada
RESTRICTIONS: Scholarships for study at the University of Ottawa in fields of humanities and social sciences available to qualified applicants of all nationalities. Fluency in English or French required.
AMOUNT GIVEN: Maximum of Canadian $4,500.
DEADLINE: Fall session by July 1. Winter session by December 1. Summer session by April 1.

University of Ottawa
Merit Graduate Research Scholarships in Sciences and Engineering
Graduate Studies Scholarships
School of Graduate Studies
115 Wilbrod
Ottawa, Ontario K1N 6N5 Canada
RESTRICTIONS: Scholarships for study at the University of Ottawa in fields of sciences and engineering available to qualified applicants of all nationalities. Fluency in English or French required.
AMOUNT GIVEN: Canadian $1,000– $2,000.
DEADLINE: Fall session by July 1. Winter session by December 1. Summer session by April 1.

University of Ottawa
Research Excellence Scholarships in Sciences and Engineering
School of Graduate Studies
115 Wilbrod
Ottawa, Ontario K1N 6N5 Canada
RESTRICTIONS: Scholarships for study at the University of Ottawa in fields of sciences and engineering available to qualified applicants of all nationalities. Fluency in English or French required.
AMOUNT GIVEN: $3,500 per year. Renewable for one year at $2,500.
DEADLINE: Fall session by July 1. Winter session by December 1. Summer session by April 1.

University of Ottawa
Entrance Scholarships in Sciences and Engineering
Graduate Studies Scholarships
School of Graduate Studies
115 Wilbrod
Ottawa, Ontario K1N 6N5 Canada
RESTRICTIONS: Scholarships for study at the University of Ottawa in fields of sciences and engineering available to qualified applicants of all nationalities. Fluency in English or French required.
AMOUNT GIVEN: Canadian $1,500.
DEADLINE: Fall session by July 1. Winter session by December 1. Summer session by April 1.

University of Regina
Teaching Assistantships
Dean of Graduate Studies and Research
Regina, Saskatchewan S4S 0A2 Canada
RESTRICTIONS: Teaching assistantships in education, engineering, fine arts, humanities, science, and social sciences available to students from all nationalities.
AMOUNT GIVEN: 35 awards of up to Canadian $3,310 per semester (limit of 2 semesters).
DEADLINE: April 1.

University of Regina
Graduate Scholarships
Dean of Graduate Studies and Research
Regina, Saskatchewan S4S 0A2 Canada
RESTRICTIONS: Scholarships for graduate students accepted by the graduate faculty as fully qualified participants in the master's or Ph.D. programs in the fields of education, and social sciences available to students from all nationalities.
AMOUNT GIVEN: 11 awards of up to Canadian $3,100 per semester (limit of 3 semesters).
DEADLINE: April 1.

University of Saskatchewan
Awards Office
Saskatoon, SAS S7N 0W0 Canada
306-966-6722
RESTRICTIONS: All fields. Undergraduate awards open to full-time students who have successfully completed at least one winter term at the university.
AMOUNT GIVEN: 1,000 awards per year. Amount varies.
DEADLINE: July 1.

University of Saskatchewan
College of Graduate Studies and Research
Saskatoon, Saskatchewan
Canada
RESTRICTIONS: Graduates of all nationalities with B.A. (honors) or equivalent from recognized university. Scholarships available in fields of agriculture, education, engineering, health sciences, humanities, physical education, science, and social sciences.
AMOUNT GIVEN: up to Canadian $8,800 for eight months with possible addition of Canadian $4,400 for summer semester.
DEADLINE: February 1.

University of Toronto
School of Graduate Studies
Toronto, Ontario M5S 1A1 Canada

RESTRICTIONS: Fellowships open to graduate students of all nationalities in all fields who have an excellent academic record and fluent English.
AMOUNT GIVEN: 1-year fellowships.
DEADLINE: February 1.

University of Toronto
Trinity College
Attn: Registrar
Toronto, Ontario M5S 1H8 Canada
RESTRICTIONS: All fields. All nationalities. Graduate students. Must have degree from accepted university outside of Canada.
AMOUNT GIVEN: Free room and board.
DEADLINE: February 3.

University of Victoria
Faculty of Graduate Studies
Victoria, British Columbia V8W 2Y2 Canada
RESTRICTIONS: Graduate fellowships and teaching assistantships in many subjects available to graduate students of all nationalities.
AMOUNT GIVEN: Canadian $3,000 (assistantships)–$8,500 (fellowships).
DEADLINE: February 1.

University of Windsor
Undergraduate Scholarships
Dean of Undergraduate Studies
Windsor, Ontario N9B 3P4 Canada
519-253-4232
RESTRICTIONS: For U.S. students meeting all admissions requirements who wish to study at the university in all fields. In-course awards available to those who are already enrolled.
AMOUNT GIVEN: Approx. Canadian $500.
DEADLINE: May 31; December 31.

University of Windsor
Graduate Studies & Research Scholarships
Dean of Graduate Studies and Research
Windsor, Ontario N9B 3P4 Canada
519-253-4232
RESTRICTIONS: For any student accepted as a Master's or Doctoral candidate at the University of Windsor.
AMOUNT GIVEN: Tuition + Canadian $4,000–$5,000 stipend. 100 scholarships per year. Renewable.
DEADLINE: February 1; April 1.

CHILE

Inter American Press Association
Scholarships for Study in Latin America and the West Indies
2911 NW 39th St.
Miami, FL 33142
305-634-2465
RESTRICTIONS: For young journalists and graduate students (ages 21–35). Must be a U.S./Canadian citizen. Fluency in the country's language is required.
AMOUNT GIVEN: $10,000 for 1 academic year of study/research in a Latin American or West Indian country.
DEADLINE: August 1.

CHINA, PEOPLE'S REPUBLIC OF

AUCC
Awards Division
People's Republic of China Graduate Scholarships
151 Slater St; Enquiries Clerk
Ottawa, Ontario K1P 5N1 Canada
613-563-1236
RESTRICTIONS: Graduate scholarships and doctoral research scholarships in the field of Chinese studies open to Canadian citizens who have obtained a first degree from a recognized university. Awards tenable in China. Knowledge of Chinese language is preferred.
AMOUNT GIVEN: Tuition, accommodations, medical services.
DEADLINE: October 31.

National Academy of Sciences
Graduate Program—Grants for Study in the PRC
2101 Constitution Ave NW
Washington, DC 20418
202-334-2718
RESTRICTIONS: Grant support for graduate students enrolled in the social sciences or humanities to do coursework in an academic discipline at a Chinese university. Also support for dissertation and coursework. Must be U.S. citizen with proficiency in the Chinese language.
AMOUNT GIVEN: Amount varies.
DEADLINE: October 10.

National Academy of Sciences
Post-Doctoral Visiting Scholar Exchange Program

2101 Constitution Ave NW
Washington, DC 20418
202-334-2718
RESTRICTIONS: Postdoctoral grants to support research in the People's Republic of China by U.S. scholars and research in the U.S. by Chinese scholars. Open to U.S. or PRC citizens in fields of engineering, humanities, natural sciences and social sciences. For 1 to 3 months' research visits only; does not support study leading to academic degree.
AMOUNT GIVEN: Amount varies.
DEADLINE: October 10.

CHINA, REPUBLIC OF

Taiwan Ministry of Education
Scholarships for Foreign Students
5 South Chung-Shan Road
Taipei, Taiwan R.O.C.
321-6375
RESTRICTIONS: Undergraduate and graduate scholarships for foreign students wishing to study in Taiwan. Must study full time in Chinese studies.
AMOUNT GIVEN: $7,000 New Taiwan dollars.
DEADLINE: Between February 1 and April 30.

COLOMBIA

Colombia Ministry of Education
Educational Loans; Scholarships for Foreign Students
Apartade Aereo 5735
Bogota, Colombia
286 55 86
RESTRICTIONS: All fields. Financial aid and loans for study in Colombia by foreign students.
AMOUNT GIVEN: Amount varies.
DEADLINE: None.

Inter American Press Association
Scholarships for Study in Latin America and the West Indies
2911 NW 39th St.
Miami, FL 33142
305-634-2465
RESTRICTIONS: For young journalists and graduate students (ages 21–35) for 1 academic year of study/research in a Latin American or West

Indian country. Must be a U.S./Canadian citizen. Fluency in the country's language is required.
AMOUNT GIVEN: $10,000.
DEADLINE: August 1.

COSTA RICA

Inter American Press Association
Scholarships for Study in Latin America and the West Indies
2911 NW 39th St.
Miami, FL 33142
305-634-2465
RESTRICTIONS: For young journalists and graduate students (ages 21–35) for 1 academic year of study/research in a Latin American or West Indian country. Must be a U.S./Canadian citizen. Fluency in the country's language is required.
AMOUNT GIVEN: $10,000.
DEADLINE: August 1.

DENMARK

American-Scandinavian Foundation
Exchange Division
127 East 73rd St.
New York, NY 10021
212-879-9779
RESTRICTIONS: All fields. Graduate students. For study or research in Denmark, Norway, or Sweden. Open to U.S. citizens and legal residents who have completed their undergraduate education at the time the overseas program begins. Should have some ability in language of country of intended study.
AMOUNT GIVEN: $2,000–$10,000.
DEADLINE: November 1.

Danish Ministry of Education
Danish Government Scholarships for Foreign Nationals
Frederiksholms Kanal 25D
DK-1220 Copenhagen K Denmark
01-92-50-00
RESTRICTIONS: Scholarships for advanced students, graduates, and specialists to study or conduct research at an appropriate educational institution in Denmark. Fluency in Danish, German, or English required.

AMOUNT GIVEN: Free tuition + monthly allowance.
DEADLINE: April 1.

Fulbright Commission
Institute of International Education Study Abroad Program
809 United Nations Plaza
New York, NY, 10017
RESTRICTIONS: American graduate students. All fields.
AMOUNT GIVEN: Approximately 69,000 kroner + travel expenses.

Nordenfjord World University (NWU)
Grundvig Scholarships
Folk School Programs
Skyum Bjerge
7752 Snedsted THY Denmark
RESTRICTIONS: Courses offered by Folk High School Movement Adult
Education tenable at folk high schools in Denmark, Sweden, Norway,
and Finland. For applicants of all nationalities between the ages of 18
and 60 years who have experience in community organization and abilities working with people. Must be proficient in English.
AMOUNT GIVEN: Up to 9,000 kroner.
DEADLINE: April 1.

North Atlantic Treaty Organization
NATO Science Fellowships for U.S.A. Citizens
B-1110; Science Affairs Division
Brussels, Belgium
2-241-00-40
RESTRICTIONS: Graduate and postdoctoral fellowships for almost all
scientific areas, including interdisciplinary areas. Open to U.S. citizens
who wish to study or conduct research in another NATO member
country. Administered in each country by a national administration.
AMOUNT GIVEN: Amount varies with country.
DEADLINE: January 1–March 1.
APPLICATIONS: Write for address of your country's administration.

DOMINICA/DOMINICAN REPUBLIC

Inter American Press Association
Scholarships for Study in Latin America and the West Indies
2911 NW 39th St.
Miami, FL 33142
(305) 634-2465
RESTRICTIONS: For young journalists and graduate students (ages 21–
35) for 1 academic year of study/research in a Latin American or West

Indian country. Must be a U.S./Canadian citizen. Fluency in the country's language is required.
AMOUNT GIVEN: $10,000.
DEADLINE: August 1.

Organization of American States
Dept. of Fellowship Training
OAS PRA Fellowship for USA Residents
Trainee Selection Division
Washington, DC 20006
RESTRICTIONS: Graduate fellowships for U.S. citizens/permanent residents who wish to study abroad in an OAS member country. Must have undergraduate degree and have proven ability to pursue studies at advanced level in chosen field. Should be fluent in language of country of intended study. All fields except medicine.
AMOUNT GIVEN: Tuition and fees. Travel expenses and stipend.
DEADLINE: April 30; August 31.

ECUADOR

Inter American Press Association
Scholarships for Study in Latin America and the West Indies
2911 NW 39th St.
Miami, FL 33142
305-634-2465
RESTRICTIONS: For young journalists and graduate students (ages 21–35) for 1 academic year of study/research in a Latin American or West Indian country. Must be a U.S./Canadian citizen. Fluency in the country's language is required.
AMOUNT GIVEN: $10,000.
DEADLINE: August 1.

EL SALVADOR

Inter American Press Association
Scholarships for Study in Latin America and the West Indies
2911 NW 39th St.
Miami, FL 33142
305-634-2465
RESTRICTIONS: For young journalists and graduate students (ages 21–35) for 1 academic year of study/research in a Latin American or West Indian country. Must be a U.S./Canadian citizen. Fluency in the country's language is required.

AMOUNT GIVEN: $10,000.
DEADLINE: August 1.

FINLAND

American-Scandinavian Foundation
Exchange Division
127 East 73rd St.
New York, NY 10021
212-879-9779
RESTRICTIONS: All fields. Graduate students. For study or research in Denmark, Norway, or Sweden. Open to U.S. citizens and legal residents who have completed their undergraduate education at time the overseas program begins. Should have some ability in language of country of intended study.
AMOUNT GIVEN: $2,000–$10,000.
DEADLINE: November 1.

Ministry of Education
Exchange Scholarships
Scholarship Centre
Pohoisvant 4 A 4
00170 Helsinki 17 Finland
RESTRICTIONS: Exchange scholarships offered to graduate and postgraduate students from the U.S., Canada, and other countries for studies in all fields at Finnish universities.
AMOUNT GIVEN: 2,200 markka per month (4–9 months), free tuition, lodging, and approved study travel.
DEADLINE: March 1.
APPLICATION: Through authority of applicant's country.

Ministry of Education
Post-Doctoral Fellowships
Scholarship Centre
Pohoisvant 4 A 4
00170 Helsinki 17 Finland
RESTRICTIONS: Fellowships and research grants for postdoctoral students of all nationalities in all fields who plan further research at Finnish institutions of higher learning.
AMOUNT GIVEN: 2,700 markka per month (1–5 months) + boarding and study travel.
DEADLINE: March 1.

Ministry of Education
Finnish Language Scholarships

Scholarship Centre
Pohoisvant 4 A 4
00170 Helsinki 17 Finland
RESTRICTIONS: Scholarships open to undergraduate and postgraduate students of all nationalities for studies in the Finnish language and related subjects at Finnish universities.
AMOUNT GIVEN: 2,200 markka per month (4–9 months).
DEADLINE: March 1.

Sigrid Juselins Foundation
Medical Research Grants
Aleksanterinkatu 48 B
00100 Helsinki, Finland
90-634461
RESTRICTIONS: Grants for advanced postdoctoral research work in the field of medicine. For study in Finland.
AMOUNT GIVEN: 10,000–650,000 markka.
DEADLINE: November 15.

FRANCE

American College in Paris
French Nationality Scholarships
Attn: Director of Financial Aid
Office of Admission
31 Avenue Bosquet
75007 Paris, France
RESTRICTIONS: Scholarships for students of all nationalities in the fields of art history, comparative literature, computer science, European cultural studies, French studies, international affairs, international business administration, international economics who have demonstrated English proficiency and established need.
AMOUNT GIVEN: Full tuition.
DEADLINE: July 31 or December 15.

American College in Paris
Work/Study and Tuition Reductions
Attn: Director of Financial Aid
Office of Admission
31 Avenue Bosquet
75007 Paris, France
RESTRICTIONS: Scholarships for students of all nationalities in the fields of art history, comparative literature, computer science, European cultural studies, French studies, international affairs, international business

administration, international economics who have demonstrated English proficiency and established need. Must be 18 years of age.
AMOUNT GIVEN: ½ of yearly tuition.
DEADLINE: July 31 or December 15.

Council of International Programs
Youth Worker and Social Worker Exchange Programs
1030 Euclid Ave. #410
Cleveland, OH 44115
216-861-5478
RESTRICTIONS: Summer exchange program in the Federal Republic of Germany or France. Open to graduate students with 1 or more years of professional experience or professional social workers and youth workers. Must be under 40 years of age.
AMOUNT GIVEN: Varies.
DEADLINE: None.

Ecole des Hautes Etudes en Sciences Sociales
54 Boulevard Raspail
75270 Paris, France
RESTRICTIONS: Graduate studies in social sciences. Must have good knowledge of French.
AMOUNT GIVEN: 1,000 francs.
DEADLINE: October 30.

Foundation des Etats Unis
Harriet Hale Wolley Scholarships
15 Boulevard Jourdan
75690 Paris-Cedex 14 France
45-89-35-79
RESTRICTIONS: Art and music scholarships open to U.S. citizens for graduate study in Paris. Must be between 21–30 years of age. Preference given to mature students who have already done graduate study. Must have good knowledge of French and live at Foundation des Etats Unis.
AMOUNT GIVEN: $6,000 stipend + living quarters.
DEADLINE: None.

Institute for American Universities
Scholarships
27 Place de l'Universite
13625 Aix-en-Provence Cedex, France
42-233935
RESTRICTIONS: Scholarships for students enrolled or accepted at the institute for full-time study.
AMOUNT GIVEN: Up to $500.
DEADLINE: None.

Institute of European Studies
875 N. Michigan Ave #1540
Chicago, IL 60611
RESTRICTIONS: Open to any student accepted into one of the institute's programs with proof of financial need.
AMOUNT GIVEN: Tuition, fees, one-way transportation, lodging, board, and books.
DEADLINE: December 10; February 25.

Sweet Briar College
Junior Year in France
Sweet Briar, VA 24595
RESTRICTIONS: Awards open to juniors in accredited U.S. institutions who are proficient in French to study at universities in Paris.
AMOUNT GIVEN: 10–20 awards per year.

North Atlantic Treaty Organization
NATO Science Fellowships for U.S.A. Citizens
B-1110; Science Affairs Division
Brussels, Belgium
2-241-00-40
RESTRICTIONS: Graduate and postdoctoral fellowships for almost all scientific areas, including interdisciplinary areas. Open to U.S. citizens who wish to study/conduct research in another NATO member country. Administered in each country by a national administration.
AMOUNT GIVEN: Amount varies with country.
DEADLINE: January 1–March 1.
APPLICATIONS: Write for address of your country's administration.

GERMANY

Alexander Von Humboldt Foundation
Research Fellowships and Awards
Jean-Paul-Strausse 12
Germany
0228-833-0
RESTRICTIONS: All fields. Open to graduate students under age 40 who wish to do research in Germany. Knowledge of German language necessary for humanities students and helpful for others.
AMOUNT GIVEN: 2,700–3,500 Deutsche Marks per month + expenses. 500 awards per year.
DEADLINE: None.

CDS International Inc.
Robert Bosch Foundation Fellowships

425 Park Ave; 27th floor
New York, NY 10022
212-593-3004
RESTRICTIONS: 9-month fellowship in Germany involving work internships in the federal government and then in regional government or private industry supplemented by special seminars in Berlin, Paris, and Brussels. Must be U.S. citizen with a graduate degree or equivalent professional experience in the fields of business administration, communications, economics, German studies, journalism, law, political science, and public affairs.
AMOUNT GIVEN: 3,000 Deutsche Marks per month + travel expenses.
DEADLINE: October 15.

Christian-Albrechts University
Akademisches Auslandsamt
Olshausenstrasse 40/60
2300 Kiel, Germany
RESTRICTIONS: Scholarships at the university in all fields except medicine, dentistry, and pharmacy. Open to students from universities in the U.S., U.K., Ireland, France, and Denmark that have exchange programs with the University of Kiel. Must have minimum German at Mittelstufe II level.
AMOUNT GIVEN: 16 scholarships of 1-year duration.
DEADLINE: April 1.
CONTACT: Home university.

Council of International Programs
Youth Worker and Social Worker Exchange Programs
1030 Euclid Ave. #410
Cleveland, OH 44115
216-861-5478
RESTRICTIONS: Summer exchange program in Germany or France. Open to graduate students with 1 or more years of professional experience or professional social workers and youth workers. Must be under 40 years of age.
AMOUNT GIVEN: Varies.
DEADLINE: None.

Fredrich Naumann Stiftung Foundation
Educational Scholarships
1M DOL 2-6
1000 Berlin 33 Germany
030-8315071
RESTRICTIONS: All fields. To foreign students living in Germany in master's or Ph.D. programs at German universities.

AMOUNT GIVEN: Approximately 1,000 Deutsche Marks.
DEADLINE: November 30.

Free University Berlin
Altensteinstrasse 40
1000 Berlin 33 Germany
RESTRICTIONS: Exchange scholarships in all fields except medicine, veterinary science, dentistry, pharmacy, biology, chemistry, and psychology. Available to students of the following universities: Duke, Cornwall, Indiana, Minnesota, Stanford, Tulane, Ohio State, Vanderbilt, Wake Forest, Washington, Wisconsin, State University of New York at Albany, Western Michigan, and Texas at Austin (in the U.S.); Laval (in Canada); Copenhagen (in Denmark); London (in the U.K.). Must have equivalent of German Abitur and competent German.
AMOUNT GIVEN: 750–850 Deutsche Marks per month + allowances for lodging, books, and health insurance.
DEADLINE: November 1.
APPLICATIONS: Write to Study Abroad Programs
Institute of International Education
809 United Nations Plaza,
New York, NY 10017

German Academic Exchange Service
Kennedyallee 50
5300 Bonn 2 Germany
RESTRICTIONS: All fields. All nationalities. Graduate students and students with a minimum of 2 years at a university-level institution. Good knowledge of German required. Ages 18–32.
AMOUNT GIVEN: 900–1,490 Deutsche Marks + tuition and allowances for travel, books, and health & accident insurance.
CONTACT: Diplomatic and consular missions of Germany in home country.

Germanistic Society of America
Foreign Study Scholarships
c/o Study Abroad Program
809 U.N. Plaza
New York, NY 10017
212-984-5330
RESTRICTIONS: Must be a U.S. citizen with a bachelor's degree. For graduate study at a West German university in the fields of history, international relations, language, literature, philosophy, political science, public affairs. Selection based on promised project, language fluency, academic achievement, and references.
AMOUNT GIVEN: 4 awards per year. $6,000.
DEADLINE: October 31.

Institute für Europäisch Geschichte
Fellowship Program
Alte Universitässtrasse 19
D-6500 Mainz; Germany
06131-26143 or 06131-24870
RESTRICTIONS: Open to Ph.D. candidates and postdoctoral applicants in European history preferable for completion of dissertation. Also for research in German archives.
AMOUNT GIVEN: Approximately 30 awards. 960–1240 Deutsche Marks.
DEADLINE: Open.

Institute of European Studies
875 N. Michigan Ave. #1540
Chicago, IL 60611
RESTRICTIONS: Open to any student accepted into one of the institute's programs with proof of financial need.
AMOUNT GIVEN: Tuition, fees, one-way transportation, lodging, board, and books.
DEADLINE: December 10; February 25.

Konrad-Adenauer Stiftung
Post-Graduate Awards
Postfach 1260
5205 Sankt Augustin 1 Bei Bonn, Germany
02241 2 46-0
RESTRICTIONS: KAS promotes scientific training of foreign graduate students in Germany at German universities. Should have adequate command of German language.
AMOUNT GIVEN: Monthly grant of 940 Deutsche Marks.
DEADLINE: None.

North Atlantic Treaty Organization
NATO Science Fellowships for U.S.A. Citizens
B-1110; Science Affairs Division
Brussels, Belgium
2-241-00-40
RESTRICTIONS: Graduate and postdoctoral fellowships for almost all scientific areas, including interdisciplinary areas. Open to U.S. citizens who wish to study/conduct research in another NATO member country. Administered in each country by a national administration.
AMOUNT GIVEN: Amount varies with country.
DEADLINE: January 1–March 1.
APPLICATIONS: Write for address of your country's administration.

Radio Free Europe/Radio Liberty
Summer Student Research Internship Program

1201 Connecticut Ave. NW
Washington, DC 20036
RESTRICTIONS: Open to graduate students in the fields of international communications, mass communications, collective behavior or social psychology. For full-time research producing a publishable paper.
AMOUNT GIVEN: Daily stipend of 45 Deutsche Marks + living accommodations.
DEADLINE: February 14.
CONTACT: Mr. Alan Dodds.

Ruprech-Karis-Universitat
Seminarstrasse 2
Postfach 10760
6900 Heidelberg 1 Germany
RESTRICTIONS: Exchange scholarships in all fields available to applicants currently enrolled in universities with exchange programs arranged with the University of Heidelberg: Cornell University, University of Kentucky, Bucknell University, Louisiana State University, Arizona State University, University of Utah (in the United States).
AMOUNT GIVEN: 710–900 Deutsche Marks per month (for 10 months).
CONTACT: Home university.

GREECE

American School of Classical Studies at Athens
Fellowships
41 E. 72nd St.
New York, NY 10021
212-861-0302
RESTRICTIONS: Open to graduate students at American and Canadian universities in fields of classical studies and archaeology for study in Greece.
AMOUNT GIVEN: $4,000 + room and board.
DEADLINE: Varies.

American School of Classical Studies at Athens
Gennadeion Fellowships
41 E. 72nd St.
New York, NY 10021
212-861-0302
RESTRICTIONS: Open to graduate students in the fields of Byzantine and Greek studies to support work and study at the Gennadeion in Athens. Must be U.S. or Canadian citizen.
AMOUNT GIVEN: $4,000 + room and board.
DEADLINE: January 15.

Archaeological Institute of America
Harriet Pomerance Fellowship
675 Commonwealth Ave.
Boston, MA 02215
617-353-9361
RESTRICTIONS: Graduate fellowships to enable work on a scholarly project relating to the Aegean Bronze Age in archeology. Preference to persons whose project requires travel to the Mediterranean. Must be U.S. or Canadian citizen.
AMOUNT GIVEN: $3,000.
DEADLINE: November 15.

Archaeological Institute of America
Olivia James Travelling Fellowship
675 Commonwealth Ave.
Boston, MA 02215
617-353-9361
RESTRICTIONS: For graduate or postgraduate study in Greece, Aegean Islands, Sicily, Southern Italy, Asia Minor, or Mesopotamia. Preference for dissertation or recent Ph.D. research. *Not* for field excavation. Must be U.S. citizen or legal resident for study in fields of archaeology, architecture, classics, history, or sculpture.
AMOUNT GIVEN: $10,000 stipend.
DEADLINE: November 15.

Aristotle University of Thessaloniki
Public Relations Office
Thessaloniki, Greece
RESTRICTIONS: Undergraduate and graduate scholarships at the university. Competitive awards. Some reserved for citizens of certain countries.
AMOUNT GIVEN: 20 awards per year. Stipend, round trip fare, tuition, and fees.

North Atlantic Treaty Organization
NATO Science Fellowships for U.S.A. Citizens
B-1110; Science Affairs Division
Brussels, Belgium
2-241-00-40
RESTRICTIONS: Graduate and postdoctoral fellowships for almost all scientific areas including interdisicplinary areas. Open to U.S. citizens who wish to study/conduct research in another NATO member country. Administered in each country by a national administration.
AMOUNT GIVEN: Amount varies with country.
DEADLINE: January 1–March 1.
APPLICATIONS: Write for address of your country's administration.

Vergilian Society Scholarships
c/o University of Maryland; Classics Dept.
College Park, MD 20742
301-454-2510
RESTRICTIONS: For teachers and graduate students interested in classical civilization as revealed by archaeology, art, and literature in Greece and Italy.
AMOUNT GIVEN: $100–$500.
DEADLINE: February 1.

GRENADA

Inter American Press Association
Scholarships for Study in Latin America and the West Indies
2911 NW 39th St.
Miami, FL 33142
305-634-2465
RESTRICTIONS: For young journalists and graduate students (ages 21–35) for 1 academic year of study/research in a Latin American or West Indian country. Must be a U.S./Canadian citizen. Fluency in the country's language is required.
AMOUNT GIVEN: $10,000.
DEADLINE: August 1.

Organization of American States
Department of Fellowships and Training
OAS PRA Fellowships for U.S.A. Residents
Trainee Selection Division
Washington, DC 20006
202-789-3902
RESTRICTIONS: Graduate fellowships for U.S. citizens/permanent residents who wish to study abroad in an OAS member country. Must have undergraduate degree and have proven ability to pursue studies at advanced level in chosen field. Should be fluent in language of country of intended study. All fields except medicine.
AMOUNT GIVEN: Tuition and fees. Travel expenses and stipend.
DEADLINE: April 30; August 31.

GUATEMALA

Inter American Press Association
Scholarships for Study in Latin America and the West Indies

2911 NW 39th St.
Miami, FL 33142
305-634-2465
RESTRICTIONS: For young journalists and graduate students (ages 21–
35) for 1 academic year of study/research in a Latin American or West
Indian country. Must be a U.S./Canadian citizen. Fluency in the coun-
try's language is required.
AMOUNT GIVEN: $10,000.
DEADLINE: August 1.

GUYANA

Inter American Press Association
Scholarships for Study in Latin America and the West Indies
2911 NW 39th St.
Miami, FL 33142
305-634-2465
RESTRICTIONS: For young journalists and graduate students (ages 21–
35) for 1 academic year of study/research in a Latin American or West
Indian country. Must be a U.S./Canadian citizen. Fluency in the coun-
try's language is required.
AMOUNT GIVEN: $10,000.
DEADLINE: August 1.

HAITI

Inter American Press Association
Scholarships for Study in Latin America and the West Indies
2911 NW 39th St.
Miami, FL 33142
305-634-2465
RESTRICTIONS: For young journalists and graduate students (ages 21–
35) for 1 academic year of study/research in a Latin American or West
Indian country. Must be a U.S./Canadian citizen. Fluency in the coun-
try's language is required.
AMOUNT GIVEN: $10,000.
DEADLINE: August 1.

Organization of American States
Department of Fellowships and Training
OAS PRA Fellowships for U.S.A. Residents
Trainee Selection Division

Washington, DC 20006
202-789-3902
RESTRICTIONS: Graduate fellowships for U.S. citizens/permanent residents who wish to study abroad in an OAS member country. Must have undergraduate degree and have proven ability to pursue studies at advanced level in chosen field. Should be fluent in language of country of intended study. All fields except medicine.
AMOUNT GIVEN: Tuition and fees. Travel expenses and stipend.
DEADLINE: April 30; August 31.

HONDURAS

Inter American Press Association
Scholarships for Study in Latin America and the West Indies
2911 NW 39th St.
Miami, FL 33142
305-634-2465
RESTRICTIONS: For young journalists and graduate students (ages 21–35) for 1 academic year of study/research in a Latin American or West Indian country. Must be a U.S./Canadian citizen. Fluency in the country's language is required.
AMOUNT GIVEN: $10,000.
DEADLINE: August 1.

HUNGARY

Hungarian Academy of Sciences
Roosevelt tér 9
1059 Budapest V, Hungary
RESTRICTIONS: Tertiary scholarships available under bilateral agreements for scientific cooperation. Open to qualified citizens of the U.S., Canada, and other countries for fundamental scientific research and study visits.
AMOUNT GIVEN: 180–450 forints per day (up to 12 months) + lodging, medical care, transportation within Hungary.
CONTACT: Corresponding national institution.

Ministry of Culture and Education
P.O. Box 1
1884 Budapest, Hungary
RESTRICTIONS: Higher-education and postgraduate scholarships available through government and other programs of cultural and scientific

exchange. Open to qualified citizens of the United States, Canada, and many other countries for study and research in all subjects.

AMOUNT GIVEN: 3,000–7,000 forints per month (18-month maximum) + lodging, medical care, and transport within country. Round-trip ticket paid for by applicant's home country.

CONTACT: National authorities in home country.

Organization for International Technical and Scientific Co-operation

U.N. Specialized Agency Fellowships
Nagy Lajos Kiraly Utja 202
1149 Budapest, Hungary

RESTRICTIONS: Fellowships in all major fields open to postgraduate applicants of all nationalities under 50 years of age with proficiency in English, French, or Spanish. Tenable at Hungarian institutions.

DEADLINE: 3 months before desired starting date.

CONTACT: U.N. specialized agency.

ICELAND

American-Scandinavian Foundation

Awards for Study in Scandinavia
127 East 73rd St.
New York, NY 10021
212-879-9779

RESTRICTIONS: All fields. Graduate students. For study or research in Denmark, Norway, or Sweden. Open to U.S. citizens and legal residents who have completed their undergraduate education at time the overseas program begins. Should have some ability in language of country of intended study.

AMOUNT GIVEN: $2,000–$10,000.

DEADLINE: November 1.

Ministry of Culture and Education

Huerfisenta 6
150 Reykjavik, Iceland

RESTRICTIONS: Scholarships available for study in Icelandic language, literature, and history. Open to students from countries chosen yearly or applicants of Icelandic origin from the U.S. or Canada.

AMOUNT GIVEN: Tuition, room and board.

CONTACT: Institute of International Education
              809 United Nations Plaza
              New York, NY 10017
              or concurring department of applicant's country.

North Atlantic Treaty Organization
NATO Science Fellowships for U.S.A. Citizens
B-1110; Science Affairs Division
Brussels, Belgium
2-241-00-40
RESTRICTIONS: Graduate and postdoctoral fellowships for almost all scientific areas, including interdisciplinary areas. Open to U.S. citizens who wish to study/conduct research in another NATO member country. Administered in each country by a national administration.
AMOUNT GIVEN: Amount varies with country.
DEADLINE: January 1–March 1.
APPLICATIONS: Write for address of your country's administration.

INDIA

American Institute of Indian Studies
AIIs Junior Fellowships
c/o University of Chicago
1130 East 59th St.
Foster Hall #212
Chicago, IL 60637
312-702-8638
RESTRICTIONS: Doctoral fellowships for U.S. citizens or foreign nationals in residence at American colleges and universities in the field of Indian studies who wish to complete Ph.D. requirements in India.
AMOUNT GIVEN: Up to $7,000.
DEADLINE: July 1.

American Institute of Indian Studies
Short-Term and Senior Research Fellowships
c/o University of Chicago
1130 East 59th St.
Foster Hall #212
Chicago, IL 60637
312-702-8638
RESTRICTIONS: Postdoctoral fellowships in Indian studies for U.S. citizens or foreign nationals in residence at American colleges and universities. Must have Ph.D. and agree to be formally affiliated with an Indian university while in India.
AMOUNT GIVEN: 40 short-term and 50 senior awards per year. $6,000–$11,000 + travel.
DEADLINE: July 1.

American Institute of Indian Studies
AIIS Language Program

c/o University of Chicago
1130 East 59th St.
Foster Hall #212
Chicago, IL 60637
312-702-8638
RESTRICTIONS: Undergraduate fellowships for research in languages of India open to students who have a minimum of 2 years or 240 hours of classroom instruction in a language of India. Must be U.S. citizen.
AMOUNT GIVEN: 12 awards per year. $3,000 + travel.
DEADLINE: January.

American Institute of Indian Studies
Professional Development Awards
c/o University of Chicago
1130 East 59th St.
Foster Hall #212
Chicago, IL 60637
312-702-8638
RESTRICTIONS: All fields. Graduate students. For professional study in India. Must be U.S. citizen or foreign national in residence at an American college or university. Minimum of a master's degree required.
AMOUNT GIVEN: $11,000 + travel.
DEADLINE: July 1.

Indian Council of Medical Research Fellowships
Post Box 4508
Ansari Nagar New Delhi-110029
India 660235
RESTRICTIONS: For young scientists to research in the field of Biomedical Sciences at the permanent institutes of the council. Maximum tenure for all fellowships is three years, subject to annual review.
AMOUNT GIVEN: Amount varies.

IRAQ

Archaeological Institute of America
Harriet Pomerance Fellowship
675 Commonwealth Ave.
Boston, MA 02215
617-353-9361
RESTRICTIONS: Graduate fellowships to enable work on a scholarly project relating to the Aegean Bronze Age in archeology. Preference to persons whose project requires travel to the Mediterranean. Must be U.S. or Canadian citizen.

AMOUNT GIVEN: $3,000.
DEADLINE: November 15.

Archaeological Institute of America
Olivia James Travelling Fellowship
675 Commonwealth Ave.
Boston, MA 02215
617-353-9361
RESTRICTIONS: For graduate or postgraduate study in Greece, Aegean Islands, Sicily, Southern Italy, Asia Minor, or Mesopotamia. Preference for dissertation or recent Ph.D. research. *Not* for field excavation. Must be U.S. citizen or legal resident for study in fields of archaeology, architecture, classics, history, or sculpture.
AMOUNT GIVEN: $10,000 stipend.

IRELAND

Department of Education
Headquarters Section 3
Marlborough Street
Dublin 1 Ireland
RESTRICTIONS: Postdoctoral fellowships for approved research in the fields of science, engineering, and architecture at Irish universities or colleges. Must be under 30 years of age.
AMOUNT GIVEN: 8,375–10,946 Irish pounds.
DEADLINE: March 31.

Dublin Institute for Advanced Studies   12/29/97 - inquiry
Research Scholarships
10 Burlington Rd.
Dublin 4 Ireland
680748
RESTRICTIONS: Must be Ph.D. or equivalent in an appropriate subject. Also may be available to candidates holding an honors degree or its equivalent. For research in astronomy, Celtic studies, cosmic physics, and theoretical physics at the Dublin Institute. The Dublin Institute is not a university.
AMOUNT GIVEN: $8,600–$12,500. 18 awards per year.
DEADLINE: March 31.

ISRAEL

American Jewish League for Israel
University Scholarship Fund

30 E. 60th St.
New York, NY 10022
212-371-1452
RESTRICTIONS: All fields. Must be Jewish. For Americans who have been accepted for a year of undergraduate or graduate study in Israel at Bar Ilan University, Ben Gurion University, Haifa University, Hebrew University, Jerusalem Technion University, Tel Aviv University, or Weismann Institute of Science.
AMOUNT GIVEN: 5–6 awards per year. $1,000.
DEADLINE: June 1.

European Science Foundation
European Brain Research Fellowships
1 Quay Lezay-Marnesia
67000 Strasbourg, France
88-35-30-63
RESTRICTIONS: For graduate students in the field of science who have some research experience but need further training to broaden their research scopes. Tenable in Europe and Israel. Preference for candidates under 30 years of age.
AMOUNT GIVEN: 7,300 francs per month.
DEADLINE: March 1; September 15.

Hebrew University
Attn: Secretary
Moritz and Charlotte Warburg Prize
Jerusalem, Israel
RESTRICTIONS: Graduate and postgraduate awards available to students of all nationalities in the field of Jewish studies.
AMOUNT GIVEN: $6,500–$7,000 per year.
DEADLINE: November.

Lady Davis Fellowship Trust
Graduate Fellowships
P.O. Box 1255
Jerusalem 91904 Israel
02-663848
RESTRICTIONS: All fields. Graduate students. Open to anyone who demonstrates excellence in their studies, promise of distinction in their chosen fields, and qualities of mind, intellect, and character. Tenable at the Hebrew University of Jerusalem or the Technion Haifa.
AMOUNT GIVEN: Travel, tuition, and reasonable living expenses.
DEADLINE: September 30.

Ministry of Education and Culture
34 Shivley Israel Street
Jerusalem 91911 Israel

RESTRICTIONS: All fields. Postgraduate and graduate scholarships for study at major institutions in Israel available to students of all nationalities. Must be under age 35 with fluent Hebrew or English.
AMOUNT GIVEN: Tuition and registration fees. $1,350.
DEADLINE: December 31.
CONTACT: Nearest embassy or consulate.

ITALY

American Academy in Rome
Rome Prize Fellowships
101 Park Ave.
New York, NY 10017
RESTRICTIONS: Open to U.S. citizens of outstanding achievement for independent research in the fields of architecture, landscape architecture, art history, and classical studies at the American Academy in Rome.
AMOUNT GIVEN: Approximately $4,600 per year + dependents' allowance.
DEADLINE: December 31.

Archaeological Institute of America
Harriet Pomerance Fellowship
675 Commonwealth Ave.
Boston, MA 02215
617-353-9361
RESTRICTIONS: Graduate fellowships to enable work on a scholarly project relating to the Aegean Bronze Age in archeology. Preference to persons whose project requires travel to the Mediterranean. Must be U.S. or Canadian citizen.
AMOUNT GIVEN: $3,000.
DEADLINE: November 15.

Archaeological Institute of America
Olivia James Travelling Fellowship
675 Commonwealth Ave.
Boston, MA 02215
617-353-9361
RESTRICTIONS: For graduate or postgraduate study in Greece, Aegean Islands, Sicily, Southern Italy, Asia Minor, or Mesopotamia. Preference for dissertation or recent Ph.D. research. *Not* for field excavation. Must be U.S. citizen or legal resident for study in fields of archaeology, architecture, classics, history, or sculpture.
AMOUNT GIVEN: $10,000 stipend.
DEADLINE: November 15.

Bologna Center of the Johns Hopkins University
School of Advanced International Studies
Via Belmeloroll
I-40126 Bologna, Italy
051-23-21-85678
RESTRICTIONS: For graduate students with adequate preparation in the social sciences who are interested in the problems confronting European nations and international relations. For study at Johns Hopkins Bologna Center.
AMOUNT GIVEN: 60 awards per year. Tuition + $500–$700 per month stipend.
DEADLINE: March 15.

British School at Rome
Abbey Major Scholarships
c/o Regent's College
Inner Circle
Regent's Park
London NWI 4N5 England
01-935-9576
RESTRICTIONS: Open to postgraduate students who wish to work and study in the field of painting for 1 year at the British School at Rome. Must be a citizen of the U.S. or Great Britain.
AMOUNT GIVEN: Approximately 4,500 British pounds.
DEADLINE: January 15.

European University Institute
Jean Monnet Fellowship
Via de Roccettini 5
San Domenico di Fiesole
50016 Italy
0039-055-50921
RESTRICTIONS: Postdoctoral fellowships in the fields of political science, social sciences, law, economics, and history. Recipients required to make scholarly contribution to research on Europe within one of EUI's research projects or on topics falling within the general interests of the institute. Publication of research is expected.
AMOUNT GIVEN: 25 fellowships per year of $1,400–$2,100 per month + medical and family allowances.
DEADLINE: November 30.

European University Institute
Via de Roccettini 5
San Domenico di Fiesole
50016 Italy
0039-055-50921

RESTRICTIONS: For graduate students in the fields of political science, social sciences, law, economics, and history. Open to qualified candidates with honors and a research project with a European dimension.
AMOUNT GIVEN: $615–$1,000 per month + travel, medical, and family allowances.
DEADLINE: November 30.

Gladys Frieble Delmos Foundation
40 W. 57th St., 27th floor.
New York, NY 10019
RESTRICTIONS: Grants are available for pre-doctoral and postdoctoral research in Venice. Must be U.S. citizen and have some experience in advanced research. Graduate students must have fulfilled all doctoral requirements except dissertation.
AMOUNT GIVEN: $500–$10,000.
DEADLINE: December 15.

Istituto Italiano per gli Studi Storici
Federico Chabod and Adolfo Amodeo Scholarships
12 Via Benedetto
80134 Naples, Italy
081-207704
RESTRICTIONS: For graduate students under 30 years of age for study in the field of European history at the institute.
AMOUNT GIVEN: 5,000,000 lire.
DEADLINE: October.

National Institute for Architectural Education
J. Dinkeloo Traveling Fellowships to Rome
30 W. 22nd St.
New York, NY 10010
212-924-7000
RESTRICTIONS: Travelling fellowship tenable at the American Academy in Rome in the fields of architectural design and technology. Open to U.S. citizens who have or anticipate receiving their first professional degree in architecture between June of the completion year and June 3 years prior.
AMOUNT GIVEN: $5,000.
DEADLINE: April 20.

North Atlantic Treaty Organization
NATO Science Fellowships for U.S.A. Citizens
B-1110; Science Affairs Division
Brussels, Belgium
2-241-00-40
RESTRICTIONS: Graduate and postdoctoral fellowships for almost all scientific areas including interdisciplinary areas. Open to U.S. citizens

who wish to study/conduct research in another NATO member country. Administered in each country by a national administration.
AMOUNT GIVEN: Amount varies with country.
DEADLINE: January 1–March 1.
APPLICATIONS: Write for address of your country's administration.

Scuola Normale Superiore
Post-Graduate Scholarships for Non-Italians
Piazza dei Cavaliere 7
The Director
I-56100 Pisa, Italy
RESTRICTIONS: Scholarships for postgraduate study in the fields of humanities, history, mathematics, physics, biology, and chemistry.
AMOUNT GIVEN: Tuition + 54,300-lire stipend per month.
DEADLINE: November 30.

JAMAICA

Inter American Press Association
Scholarships for Study in Latin America and the West Indies
2911 NW 39th St.
Miami, FL 33142
305-634-2465
RESTRICTIONS: For young journalists and graduate students (ages 21–35) for 1 academic year of study/research in a Latin American or West Indian country. Must be a U.S./Canadian citizen. Fluency in the country's language is required.
AMOUNT GIVEN: $10,000.
DEADLINE: August 1.

Organization of American States
Department of Fellowships and Training
OAS PRA Fellowships for U.S.A. Residents
Trainee Selection Division
Washington, DC 20006
202-789-3902
RESTRICTIONS: Graduate fellowships for U.S. citizens/permanent residents who wish to study abroad in an OAS member country. Must have undergraduate degree and have proven ability to pursue studies at advanced level in chosen field. Should be fluent in language of country of intended study. All fields except medicine.
AMOUNT GIVEN: Tuition and fees. Travel expenses and stipend.
DEADLINE: April 30; August 31.

JAPAN

International University of Japan
I.U.J. Scholarships
Yamato-machi, Minamiuonuma-gun
Niigata-ken 949-72 Japan
RESTRICTIONS: All nationalities. Graduate students in the field of international relations. Master's candidates must show proof of completion of at least 16 years of schooling. Must be proficient in English (TOFEL score of 550 acceptable). Preference for unmarried students.
AMOUNT GIVEN: Scholarship for 1 academic year. Renewable.

Japan Foundation
Japan Foundation Fellowships
Park Building 3-6 Kioi-cho, Chiyodo-ku
Tokyo 102 Japan
RESTRICTIONS: Awards available to students from nations having diplomatic relations with Japan. For studies in all fields relating to Japanese studies (except natural science). Knowledge of Japanese required.
AMOUNT GIVEN: Approximately 190 fellowships.
DEADLINE: November 15.
CONTACT: Japan Foundation New York office for application.

Japan Society for the Promotion of Science
Yamato Bldg. 5-3-1 Kojimachi
Chiyoda-Ku
Tokyo 102 Japan
03-263-1721
RESTRICTIONS: Pre-doctoral and postdoctoral fellowships awarded for study and research in the fields of humanities, math, physics, chemistry, and biology. Tenure for both is 2 years.
AMOUNT GIVEN: 12,300–21,400 yen per month.
DEADLINE: May and October.

Japanese Government
Monbushi Research Scholarships
3-2-2 Kasumigaschi
Chiyoda-Ku
Tokyo 100 Japan
03-581-2164
RESTRICTIONS: All fields. Graduate students.
AMOUNT GIVEN: 965 scholarships available. 175,000 yen monthly, roundtrip airfare, arrival allowance, and housing allowance.
APPLICATION: For information call nearest Japanese embassy or consulate where an explanatory note and the application can be picked up.

Makita Scholarship Foundation
20 Aebeba-cho
Shinjuku-ku
Tokyo 162 Japan
RESTRICTIONS: All fields. All nationalities. Graduate and postgraduate awards available to foreign students studying in Japan at their own expense. Must be under 30 (graduate) or 35 (postgraduate) years of age.
AMOUNT GIVEN: 100,000 yen per month.
DEADLINE: April.

Nihon University
Dean, College of Economics
Nihon Daigaku Heizaigakubu Shogakukin
8-24, Kudan-Minami 4 Chome
Chiyoda-ku
Tokyo 102 Japan
RESTRICTIONS: Scholarships by the school of economics available to undergraduate or graduate foreign students of all nationalities. High grades required.
AMOUNT GIVEN: 150,000 yen per year.
DEADLINE: April.

Nihon University
Dean, College of Commerce
Nihon Daigaku Shogakubu Tokubetsu Kenkyu Shougakukin
8-24, Kudan-Minami 4 Chome
Chiyoda-ku
Tokyo 102 Japan
RESTRICTIONS: Scholarships by the school of commerce available to undergraduate or graduate foreign students of all nationalities. High grades required.
AMOUNT GIVEN: Up to 350,000 yen per year.
DEADLINE: May.

Notre Dame Seishin University
President of the University
2-16-9 Ifukucho
Okayma 700 Japan
RESTRICTIONS: Awards available to foreign female students of all nationalities over the age of 18 for study in the fields of English language and literature, Japanese language and literature, home economics, child welfare, food and human nutrition. Must have completed 12 years of schooling and be proficient in Japanese.
AMOUNT GIVEN: 50,000 yen per month and/or tuition.
DEADLINE: December 31.

Reitaku University
Dean of Students

2-1-1, Hikarigaoka
Kashiwa City
Chiba-pref 277 Japan
RESTRICTIONS: Foreign student scholarships available to applicants of
the university of any nationality for study of Japanese. Must be over 18
years of age.
AMOUNT GIVEN: 400,000–700,000 yen per year + tuition, room and
board.
DEADLINE: November.

Showa Women's University
Dept. of Educational Affairs
1-7 Taishido, Setagaya
Tokyo 154 Japan
RESTRICTIONS: Scholarships in Japanese literature available to foreign
female candidates of all nationalities. Must be over 18 years of age and
of proven financial need.
AMOUNT GIVEN: Tuition + lodging.
DEADLINE: May.

Tokyo Keizai University
Student Office
1-7 Minami-cho
Kokubunju City
Tokyo 185 Japan
RESTRICTIONS: Graduate and undergraduate scholarships in the fields
of economics and business administration available to foreign nationals
with superior scholastic merit. Must be proficient in Japanese.
AMOUNT GIVEN: 25,000 yen per month (undergraduate), 30,000 yen
per month (graduate).

Tokyo Woman's Christian University
Registrar's Office
Tokyo Joshi Daigaku
2-6-1, Zempukuji
Suginami-ku
Tokyo 167 Japan
RESTRICTIONS: Graduate scholarships in the fields of philosophy, Jap-
anese language and literature, English and American literature, history,
and math. Undergraduate scholarships available in these fields as well as
sociology, economics, and psychology. Open to students of all nation-
alities in financial need. Must be proficient in Japanese.
AMOUNT GIVEN: Tuition + Fees.

University of Tokyo
Faculty of Engineering
Committee of the International Cooperation and Exchange

7-3-1 Hongo, Bunkyo-ku
Tokyo 113 Japan
RESTRICTIONS: Scholarships available to foreign nationals of all countries having diplomatic relations with Japan for study in the field of engineering. Must be college or university graduate under the age of 34.
AMOUNT GIVEN: 176,500 yen per month + travel and field study allowances.
DEADLINE: March 31.

JORDAN

Ministry of Education
Amman, Jordan
RESTRICTIONS: All fields. All nationalities in accordance with mutual cultural agreements. Must have secondary school diploma. Knowledge of Arabic and English required. For study at approved institutes in Jordan.
AMOUNT GIVEN: Varies.
APPLICATION: Must be submitted through authority of applicant's home government.

University of Jordan
Attn: President
Amman, Jordan
RESTRICTIONS: Awards available to foreign female students of all nationalities for graduate and undergraduate study in the fields of Arabic language and literature, Arab and Islamic history, and Middle Eastern studies. Must be enrolled in a known university and have a knowledge of Arabic.
AMOUNT GIVEN: Tuition + board.
DEADLINE: August.

KOREA

Academy of Korean Studies
Graduate School
50 Unjung-dong, Seongnam-si
Gyenggi-do, 130-17 Korea
RESTRICTIONS: Scholarships available to students of all nationalities who have graduated from an accredited institution. For study in history, philosophy, political science, economics, sociology, anthropology, edu-

cation, literature, and fine arts. Must speak English, Korean, and one other language.
AMOUNT GIVEN: Tuition, room and board, and stipend.
DEADLINE: April 30–October 30.

Chung-Ang University
Dean
International Education Department
221 Hukusk-dong, Dongjak-ku
Seoul 151 Korea
RESTRICTIONS: Teaching assistantships in the fields of English, Chinese, Japanese, French, and German languages, and Korean studies. Must be 22–30 years of age, hold a B.A., and have a minimum GPA of 3.0 with 2 letters of reference. Must be proficient in Korean.
AMOUNT GIVEN: 5–7 awards per year.
DEADLINE: September 30.

International Cultural Foundation
185 Kahe-dong, Chongro-ku
Seoul, Korea
RESTRICTIONS: Research grants available to foreign students who have an M.A. in Korean studies or intend to major in the field in graduate school.
AMOUNT GIVEN: 1 or 2 grants per year.
DEADLINE: December.

Keimyung University
President
Daegu, Korea
RESTRICTIONS: All fields. All nationalities. For undergraduate or graduate study.
AMOUNT GIVEN: Fellowships at the university.
DEADLINE: November 15.

Korea University
Office of Academic Affairs
1 Anam-dong, Sungbuk-ku
Seoul, Korea
RESTRICTIONS: Scholarships available to foreign graduate students in fields related to Korean studies. Knowledge of Korean required.
AMOUNT GIVEN: 10 awards per year.
DEADLINE: 6 months before the semester begins.

Korean Ministry of Education
Overseas Residents Education Division
Seoul, Korea

RESTRICTIONS: Awards available to citizens of countries having cultural exchange agreements with Korea for study at universities and colleges in Korea in many fields. Must have degree from accredited college or university with master's degree for doctorate program. Must be under 25 and proficient in Korean.
AMOUNT GIVEN: Up to 50 scholarships per year.
CONTACT: Nearest Korean consulate.

Kyungpook National University
Bureau of Student Affairs
370 San Kyuk-dong, uk-gu
Daegu 635 Korea
RESTRICTIONS: Scholarships and loans available to applicants of all nationalities in the fields of humanities, social sciences, natural sciences, economics, commerce, law, engineering, agriculture, teaching, medicine, dentistry, music, and visual arts. Must have completed 12 years of schooling and 2 years of pre-medical or pre-dental courses for study in these fields.
DEADLINE: One semester prior to start of studies.

Yeungnam University
Office of International Affairs
Gyongstan 632 Korea
RESTRICTIONS: All fields. All nationalities. Based on academic record. Must be proficient in Korean.
AMOUNT GIVEN: 50 awards every 2 years.
DEADLINE: November 15.

LUXEMBOURG

North Atlantic Treaty Organization
NATO Science Fellowships for U.S.A. Citizens
B-1110; Science Affairs Division
Brussels, Belgium
2-241-00-40
RESTRICTIONS: Graduate and postdoctoral fellowships for almost all scientific areas, including interdisciplinary areas. Open to U.S. citizens who wish to study/conduct research in another NATO member country. Administered in each country by a national administration.
AMOUNT GIVEN: Amount varies with country.
DEADLINE: January 1–March 1.
APPLICATIONS: Write for address of your country's administration.

MEXICO

American Society for Enology and Viticulture
P.O. Box 1855
Davis, CA 95617
916-753-3142
RESTRICTIONS: Candidate must be enrolled/accepted in an accredited college in North America in curriculum stressing a science basic to the wine and grape industry. Must be North American resident.
AMOUNT GIVEN: $1,000–$3,000.
DEADLINE: March 1.

American Society for Metals
ASM Scholarship Selection Committee
Metals Park, OH 44073
216-338-5151
RESTRICTIONS: Open to undergraduate students in the fields of metallurgy or materials science who have completed at least 1 year of study. For citizens of the U.S., Canada, or Mexico who are enrolled in a recognized college or university.
AMOUNT GIVEN: $500–$2,000.
DEADLINE: June 15.

Council for International Exchange of Scholars
Fulbright Scholar Grant Programs
11 Dupont Circle NW #300
Washington, DC 20036
202-939-5401
RESTRICTIONS: All fields. Graduate students. Designed to increase mutual understanding between people of the U.S. and people of other countries. For U.S. citizens to conduct research and/or lecture abroad. Open to Ph.D's or equivalent.
AMOUNT GIVEN: Varies with country.
DEADLINE: June 15; September 13; January 1; February 1.

Entomology Society of America
4603 Calvert Road
College Park, MD 20740
301-864-1334
RESTRICTIONS: Must be enrolled at a recognized college or university in the U.S. or Canada or Mexico and have accumulated at least 30 semester hours at the time award is presented. For study in fields of entomology, biology, or related science.
AMOUNT GIVEN: $500–$1,000.
DEADLINE: July 1.

Geological Society of America
Research Grants Program
P.O. Box 9140; 3300 Penrose Place
Boulder, CO 80301
303-447-2020
RESTRICTIONS: Open to master's and Ph.D. candidates at colleges and universities in U.S., Canada, Mexico, and Central America in the field of geology. To help support thesis research. GSA membership *not* required.
AMOUNT GIVEN: Approximately 200 awards per year. $500–$1,700.
DEADLINE: February 15.

Institute of International Education
International Fellowships for U.S.A. Residents
809 U.N. Plaza
New York, NY 10017
212-984-5328
RESTRICTIONS: Graduate fellowships for U.S. residents to study/research in a foreign country. All fields. Must be proficient in language of country of intended visit. At least ½ of B.A. must have been completed in the U.S.
AMOUNT GIVEN: Varies with country.
DEADLINE: May 1–October 31.

Inter American Foundation
Doctoral Dissertation Fellowship
1515 Wilson Blvd.
Rosslyn, VA 22209
703-841-3800
RESTRICTIONS: Open to Ph.D. candidates in social sciences and physical sciences enrolled in a U.S. university who have fulfilled all degree requirements other than the dissertation before they travel to their country of intended study. Research themes must deal directly with developing activities among the poor. Candidates must speak the language of the country of intended study.
AMOUNT GIVEN: Approximately $550 per month stipend. Approximately 15 awards per year.
DEADLINE: December 5.

Inter American Foundation
1515 Wilson Blvd.
Rosslyn, VA 22209
703-841-3800
RESTRICTIONS: Open to master's students enrolled in U.S. universities. For 3–6 months of field research in Latin America or the Caribbean. Must speak and write the language of the country of intended study.

AMOUNT GIVEN: 10–15 awards per year. $450 per month stipend.
DEADLINE: November 1; March 1.

Inter American Press Association
Scholarships for Study in Latin America and the West Indies
2911 NW 39th St.
Miami, FL 33142
305-634-2465
RESTRICTIONS: For young journalists and graduate students (ages 21–35) for 1 academic year of study/research in a Latin American or West Indian country. Must be a U.S./Canadian citizen. Fluency in the country's language is required.
AMOUNT GIVEN: $10,000.
DEADLINE: August 1.

Mexican Embassy
Abraham Lincoln/Benito Juarez Scholarship Program
Office of Cultural Affairs
2829 16th St. NW
Washington, DC 20009
202-234-6000
RESTRICTIONS: All fields. Open to master's or doctoral candidates from North America and Latin America. For graduate study or research at Mexican universities required to receive degree in home country. Fluency in Spanish required. Must be between 20 and 35 years of age.
AMOUNT GIVEN: Amount varies.

Organization of American States
Department of Fellowships and Training
OAS PRA Fellowships for U.S.A. Residents
Trainee Selection Division
Washington, D.C. 20006
202-789-3902
RESTRICTIONS: Graduate fellowships for U.S. citizens/permanent residents who wish to study abroad in an OAS member country. Must have undergraduate degree and have proven ability to pursue studies at advanced level in chosen field. Should be fluent in language of country of intended study. All fields except medicine.
AMOUNT GIVEN: Tuition and fees. Travel expenses and stipend.
DEADLINE: April 30; August 31.

Rotary Foundation of Rotary International
Graduate Study Abroad Scholarships
One Rotary Center
1560 Sherman Ave
Evanston, IL. 60201
312-866-3000

RESTRICTIONS: Open to graduate students 18 to 30 years of age who received their bachelor's degree in the U.S. and wish to complete 1 academic year of study in a foreign country where rotary clubs exist. Rotary members and employees not eligible.
AMOUNT GIVEN: Full tuition, travel + living expenses.
DEADLINE: January 1–July 1.
APPLICATIONS: Do not write to above address. Applications must be obtained through local chapter of rotary club listed in phone directory.

Rotary Foundation of Rotary International
Undergraduate Study Abroad Scholarships
One Rotary Center
1560 Sherman Ave
Evanston, IL. 60201
312-866-3000
RESTRICTIONS: Open to unmarried undergraduate students age 18 to 24 who have completed 2 years of study in the U.S. and wish to complete their junior and senior year in a foreign country where rotary clubs are located.
AMOUNT GIVEN: Full tuition, travel + living expenses.
DEADLINE: January 1–July 1.
APPLICATIONS: Do not write to above address. Applications must be obtained through local chapter of rotary club listed in phone directory.

NETHERLANDS

Hubrecht Laboratory
International Embryological Institute
Deputy Director
Uppsalalaan 8
3584 CT Utrecht, Netherlands
RESTRICTIONS: Awards available to students of all nationalities for study in developmental biology of amphibians and mammals. Must have research experience and English proficiency. Research projects must meet with approval of Hubrecht Laboratory program.
DEADLINE: January 1; July 1.

International Agricultural Centre (IAC)
P.O. Box 88
6700 AB Wageningen, Netherlands
RESTRICTIONS: Fellowships available to students holding an M.S. or B.S. degree with experience in their field of study. Must be at least 25 years old.
AMOUNT GIVEN: Room and board. Daily allowance of 16 florins + health insurance, study tours and book allowance.
DEADLINE: 6 months prior to beginning studies.

North Atlantic Treaty Organization
NATO Science Fellowships for U.S.A. Citizens
B-1110; Science Affairs Division
Brussels, Belgium
2-241-00-40
RESTRICTIONS: Graduate and postdoctoral fellowships for almost all scientific areas, including interdisciplinary areas. Open to U.S. citizens who wish to study/conduct research in another NATO member country. Administered in each country by a national administration.
AMOUNT GIVEN: Amount varies with country.
DEADLINE: January 1; March 1.
APPLICATIONS: Write for address of your country's administration.

NEW ZEALAND

British Federation of University Women
Johnstone & Florence Stoney Studentship
Crosby Hall; Cheyne Walk
London SW3 5BA England
01-352-5354
RESTRICTIONS: Open to members of the British and Irish Federations of University Women for postgraduate research in Australia, New Zealand, or South Africa. Study in biological, geological, meteorological and radiological sciences.
AMOUNT GIVEN: Up to 3,000 British pounds.
DEADLINE: September 15.

Lincoln College
MacMillian Brown Agricultural Scholarships
Registrar
Christchurch 252 811 New Zealand
RESTRICTIONS: For Ph.D. candidates who wish to research some problem bearing on agriculture or horticulture.
AMOUNT GIVEN: NZ $1,000.
DEADLINE: February 1.

Lincoln College
U.G.C. Post-Doctoral Fellowships
Registrar
Christchurch 252 811 New Zealand
RESTRICTIONS: All fields. Open to applicants who have a Ph.D. and are under 35 years of age. Fellowships tenable for 2 years.
AMOUNT GIVEN: 6 awards per year. NZ $35,000.
DEADLINE: March 30.

Lincoln College
Sir John Ormand Post-Graduate Scholarships

Registrar
Christchurch 252 811 New Zealand
RESTRICTIONS: Scholarships in marketing for graduate students who
wish to undertake research at Lincoln College on some aspect of mar-
keting. May be expected to teach on a limited basis.
AMOUNT GIVEN: NZ $3,000.
DEADLINE: February 1.

Massey University
Research Awards Office
Palmerston North
New Zealand 69-099
RESTRICTIONS: All fields. Fellowships open to applicants with Ph.D.
tenable at a New Zealand university.
AMOUNT GIVEN: NZ $6,000.
DEADLINE: July 31.

Medical Research Council of New Zealand
Post-Doctoral Fellowships
P.O. Box 5541; Wellesley St.
Auckland, New Zealand
798-227
RESTRICTIONS: Scholarships for biomedical research open to appli-
cants with Ph.D. or equivalent degree based on academic standing and
research capabilities. Applicants should be under 35 years of age.
AMOUNT GIVEN: NZ $30,500.
DEADLINE: April 1; October 1.

University of Canterbury
William and Ina Cartwright Scholarship
Christchurch, New Zealand
64-3-488-489
RESTRICTIONS: All fields. Open to graduates of not less than 3 years'
standing. Tenable at the university for up to 2 years at doctoral or 1
year at master's level.
AMOUNT GIVEN: NZ $2,652–NZ $5,304. 2 awards per year (mas-
ter's), 1 award per year (doctoral).
DEADLINE: October 1.

NICARAGUA

Inter American Press Association
Scholarships for Study in Latin America and the West Indies
2911 NW 39th St.

Miami, FL 33142
305-634-2465
RESTRICTIONS: For young journalists and graduate students (ages 21–35) for 1 academic year of study/research in a Latin American or West Indian country. Must be a U.S./Canadian citizen. Fluency in the country's language is required.
AMOUNT GIVEN: $10,000.
DEADLINE: August 1.

NIGERIA

International Institute of Tropical Agriculture
Training Programs
Oyo Road PMB 5320
Ibadan, Nigeria
413244-413315-413440
RESTRICTIONS: The main objective of the various training programs is to build up the agricultural capacity of the professional personnel of developing countries. Participants for training range from secondary school levels to holders of advanced degrees.
AMOUNT GIVEN: Varies.

NORWAY

American-Scandinavian Foundation
Awards for Study in Scandinavia
127 East 73rd St.
New York, NY 10021
212-879-9779
RESTRICTIONS: All fields. Graduate students. For study or research in Denmark, Norway, or Sweden. Open to U.S. citizens and legal residents who have completed their undergraduate education by the time the overseas program begins. Should have some familiarity with language of country of intended study.
AMOUNT GIVEN: $2,000–$10,000.
DEADLINE: November 1.

International Peace Research Institute, Oslo
Fuglehaugsgt 11
0260 Oslo 2 Norway
RESTRICTIONS: Awards available to postgraduate researchers of all nationalities in the field of peace research. Must be proficient in English.

AMOUNT GIVEN: 8,000 kroner per month.
CONTACT: Tor Andreas Gitlesen, Adm. Director.

North Atlantic Treaty Organization
NATO Science Fellowships for U.S.A. Citizens
B-1110; Science Affairs Division
Brussels, Belgium
2-241-00-40
RESTRICTIONS: Graduate and postdoctoral fellowships for almost all
scientific areas, including interdisciplinary areas. Open to U.S. citizens
who wish to study/conduct research in another NATO member coun-
try. Administered in each country by a national administration.
AMOUNT GIVEN: Amount varies with country.
DEADLINE: January 1; March 1.
APPLICATIONS: Write for address of your country's administration.

Norwegian Ministry of Foreign Affairs
P.O. Box 8115 DEP
Press and Cultural Relations Dept.
0032 Oslo 1 Norway
02-20-41-70
RESTRICTIONS: Scholarships available to postgraduate students in all
fields for specialized study in Norway. Should be under 40 years of age.
Working ability of Norwegian or English required. For citizens of coun-
tries with which Norway has a bilateral cultural agreement.
AMOUNT GIVEN: 4100 kroner per month.
DEADLINE: April 1.

Royal Norwegian Council for Scientific and Industrial Research
P.O. Box 70 Tasen
N-0801 Oslo 8 Norway
47-2-23-76-85
RESTRICTIONS: Postdoctoral fellowships in the fields of applied sciences and engineering open to foreign scientists under the age of 36
who wish to do research work in Norway. Qualifications must be equivalent to at least a British or American Ph.D. in applied science or engineering.
AMOUNT GIVEN: 20 awards per year. 9,000 kroner if single, 11,000
kroner if married + expenses.
DEADLINE: March 1; September 1.

PANAMA

Inter American Press Association
Scholarships for Study in Latin America and the West Indies
2911 NW 39th St.

Miami, FL 33142
305-634-2465
RESTRICTIONS: For young journalists and graduate students (ages 21–35) for 1 academic year of study/research in a Latin American or West Indian country. Must be a U.S./Canadian citizen. Fluency in the country's language is required.
AMOUNT GIVEN: $10,000.
DEADLINE: August 1.

PARAGUAY

Inter American Press Association
Scholarships for Study in Latin America and the West Indies
2911 NW 39th St.
Miami, FL 33142
305-634-2465
RESTRICTIONS: For young journalists and graduate students (ages 21–35) for 1 academic year of study/research in a Latin American or West Indian country. Must be a U.S./Canadian citizen. Fluency in the country's language is required.
AMOUNT GIVEN: $10,000.
DEADLINE: August 1.

PERU

Inter American Press Association
Scholarships for Study in Latin America and the West Indies
2911 NW 39th St.
Miami, FL 33142
305-634-2465
RESTRICTIONS: For young journalists and graduate students (ages 21–35) for 1 academic year of study/research in a Latin American or West Indian country. Must be a U.S./Canadian citizen. Fluency in the country's language is required.
AMOUNT GIVEN: $10,000.
DEADLINE: August 1.

PHILIPPINES

Centro Escolar University
Chairman, Scholarship Committee

Mendiola Street
Manila, Philippines
RESTRICTIONS: All fields. All nationalities. Must be under 23 years old. Sufficient score on competitive exam and proof of graduation in top 25% of class is mandatory. Must be proficient in English.
AMOUNT GIVEN: Tuition and miscellaneous fees.
DEADLINE: April.

De La Salle University
Admissions Director
2401 Taft Avenue
Manila, Philippines
RESTRICTIONS: Scholarships available to students of all nationalities with a secondary school diploma. English required. Must be 18 to 22 years of age. For study in fields of liberal arts, commerce, engineering, natural sciences and computer science.
DEADLINE: October.

POLAND

Kosciuszko Foundation
Grants and Study Programs for North Americans in Poland
15 E. 65th St.
New York, NY 10021
212-734-2130
RESTRICTIONS: All fields. For U.S. and Canadian citizens who wish to do graduate study or research in Poland. Fluency in Polish required.
AMOUNT GIVEN: Tuition + monthly living allowance.
DEADLINE: November 15.

PORTUGAL

Fundaco Calouste Gulbenkian
International Department
Avenida de Berna 45
Lisbon 1, Portugal
RESTRICTIONS: Postgraduate research awards in sciences and arts. Tenable in Portugal. Research project must be approved by the institution where applicant intends to study.
AMOUNT GIVEN: Maintenance awards + dependents fees.
DEADLINE: May 31; October 31.

North Atlantic Treaty Organization
NATO Science Fellowships for U.S.A. Citizens
B-1110; Science Affairs Division
Brussels, Belgium
2-241-00-40
RESTRICTIONS: Graduate and postdoctoral fellowships for almost all scientific areas, including interdisciplinary areas. Open to U.S. citizens who wish to study/conduct research in another NATO member country. Administered in each country by a national administration.
AMOUNT GIVEN: Amount varies with country.
DEADLINE: January 1–March 1.
APPLICATIONS: Write for address of your country's administration.

PUERTO RICO

University of Puerto Rico
Biology Department
College of Natural Sciences
Rio Piedras Campos
Rio Piedras, Puerto Rico 00931
RESTRICTIONS: Assistantships open to undergraduate and graduate students in the field of biology. Spanish proficiency required.
DEADLINE: April 15.

SOUTH AFRICA

British Federation of University Women
Johnstone & Florence Stoney Studentship
Crosby Hall; Cheyne Walk
London SW3 5BA England
01-352-5354
RESTRICTIONS: Open to members of the British and Irish Federations of University Women for postgraduate research in Australia, New Zealand, or South Africa. Study in biological, geological, meteorological, and radiological sciences.
AMOUNT GIVEN: Up to 3,000 British pounds.
DEADLINE: September 15.

Human Sciences Research Council Merit Bursary
Private Bag X41
Pretoria, South Africa 0001
012-28-3944

RESTRICTIONS: Open to graduate students in the fields of sociology and history. Must obtain at least 65% in the graduate exam for sociology or history. Award must be used in South Africa. Enrollment in a full-time program required.
AMOUNT GIVEN: 3600 rand per year. 6–10 awards per year.
DEADLINE: January 15.

Rhodes University
Hugh Le May Fellowship
P.O. Box 94
Grahamstown 6140 South Africa
RESTRICTIONS: Graduate fellowships available for students qualified to pursue advanced study in philosophy, theology, classics, history, languages, politics, and law.
AMOUNT GIVEN: 2,800 rand + room and board.
DEADLINE: July 31.

Rhodes University
Director
University Fellowship
P.O. Box 94
Grahamstown 6140 South Africa
RESTRICTIONS: Fellowships available to mature scholars in the field of social sciences with preference to research pertaining to South Africa. Must speak English.
AMOUNT GIVEN: 20,406 rand per year.

South African Association of University Women
Bertha Stoneman Award for Botany
P.O. Box 2163
Grahamstown 6140 South Africa
0461-22818
RESTRICTIONS: Open to female graduate students for use in South Africa. Preference for (but not limited to) association members. For study in the field of botany.
AMOUNT GIVEN: 400 rand.
DEADLINE: October 31.

South African Association of University Women
Isie Smuts Award
P.O. Box 2163
Grahamstown 6140 South Africa
0461-22818
RESTRICTIONS: Open to female graduate students in all fields who are working on their theses. Award should be used in South Africa. Preference for (but not limited to) association members.

AMOUNT GIVEN: 400 rand.
DEADLINE: October 31.

South African Association of University Women
Student Aid Award
P.O. Box 2163
Grahamstown 6140 South Africa
0461-22818
RESTRICTIONS: Open to female students in all fields seeking a bachelor's degree who have successfully completed their first year of study. Preference to association members.
AMOUNT GIVEN: 15 awards per year. 150 rand.
DEADLINE: October 31.

South African Department of National Education
Directorate of Culture Scholarships
Private Bag X122
Pretoria 0001 South Africa
012-314-6089
RESTRICTIONS: All fields. Open to graduate students who wish to research a thesis they are working on for a home university. Tenable for one year in South Africa.
AMOUNT GIVEN: Approximately 22 awards per year. Stipend + expenses.

SPAIN

Institute of European Studies
875 N. Michigan Ave #1540
Chicago, IL 60611
RESTRICTIONS: Open to any student accepted into one of the institute's program with proof of financial need.
AMOUNT GIVEN: Tuition, fees, one-way transportation, lodging, board, and books.
DEADLINE: December 10th; February 25th.

Ministerio de Asuntos Esteriores
Dirección Gen'l de Relaciones
Culturales y Científicas
28071 Madrid, Spain
441-90-44
RESTRICTIONS: All fields. Undergraduate. Tenable at centers of higher education in Spain under the Ministry of Education and Science. Should have a good working knowledge of Spanish.
AMOUNT GIVEN: Free tuition, medical expenses, and life insurance.
CONTACT: Spanish embassy in home country.

North Atlantic Treaty Organization
NATO Science Fellowships for U.S.A. Citizens
B-1110; Science Affairs Division
Brussels, Belgium
2-241-00-40
RESTRICTIONS: Graduate and postdoctoral fellowships for almost all scientific areas, including interdisciplinary areas. Open to U.S. citizens who wish to study/conduct research in another NATO member country. Administered in each country by a national administration.
AMOUNT GIVEN: Amount varies with country.
DEADLINE: January 1; March 1.
APPLICATIONS: Write for address of your country's administration.

ST. LUCIA

Inter American Press Association
Scholarships for Study in Latin America and the West Indies
2911 NW 39th St.
Miami, FL 33142
305-634-2465
RESTRICTIONS: For young journalists and graduate students (ages 21–35) for 1 academic year of study/research in a Latin American or West Indian country. Must be a U.S./Canadian citizen. Fluency in the country's language is required.
AMOUNT GIVEN: $10,000.
DEADLINE: August 1.

Organization of American States
Department of Fellowships and Training
OAS PRA Fellowships for U.S.A. Residents
Trainee Selection Division
Washington, DC 20006
202-789-3902
RESTRICTIONS: Graduate fellowships for U.S. citizens/permanent residents who wish to study abroad in an OAS member country. Must have undergraduate degree and have proven ability to pursue studies at advanced level in chosen field. Should be fluent in language of country of intended study. All fields except medicine.
AMOUNT GIVEN: Tuition and fees. Travel expenses and stipend.
DEADLINE: April 30; August 31.

ST. VINCENT/GRENADINES

Inter American Press Association
Scholarships for Study in Latin America and the West Indies

2911 NW 39th St.
Miami, FL 33142
305-634-2465
RESTRICTIONS: For young journalists and graduate students (ages 21–35) for 1 academic year of study/research in a Latin American or West Indian country. Must be a U.S./Canadian citizen. Fluency in the country's language is required.
AMOUNT GIVEN: $10,000.
DEADLINE: August 1.

SURINAME

Inter American Press Association
Scholarships for Study in Latin America and the West Indies
2911 NW 39th St.
Miami, FL 33142
305-634-2465
RESTRICTIONS: For young journalists and graduate students (ages 21–35) for 1 academic year of study/research in a Latin American or West Indian country. Must be a U.S./Canadian citizen. Fluency in the country's language is required.
AMOUNT GIVEN: $10,000.
DEADLINE: August 1.

Organization of American States
Department of Fellowships and Training
OAS PRA Fellowships for U.S.A. Residents
Trainee Selection Division
Washington, DC 20006
202-789-3902
RESTRICTIONS: Graduate fellowships for U.S. citizens/permanent residents who wish to study abroad in an OAS member country. Must have undergraduate degree and have proven ability to pursue studies at advanced level in chosen field. Should be fluent in language of country of intended study. All fields except medicine.
AMOUNT GIVEN: Tuition and fees. Travel expenses and stipend.
DEADLINE: April 30; August 31.

SWEDEN

American-Scandinavian Foundation
Awards for Study in Scandinavia
127 East 73rd St.

New York, NY 10021
212-879-9779
RESTRICTIONS: All fields. Graduate students. For study or research in
Denmark, Norway, or Sweden. Open to U.S. citizens and legal residents
who have completed their undergraduate education at time the overseas program begins. Should have some ability in language of country
of intended study.
AMOUNT GIVEN: $2,000–$10,000.
DEADLINE: November 1.

Svenska Handelsbanken Foundations for Social Science Research
Secretary of the Board
10328 Stockholm, Sweden.
RESTRICTIONS: Graduate research grants in the fields of economics
and social sciences. Area of interest must concern international payments and capital movement, domestic payments, markets, and economic planning. Tenable in Sweden for up to 1 year at Swedish research
institute.
AMOUNT GIVEN: Stipend + expenses.
DEADLINE: March 10.

Swedish Institute
Scholarships for Study or Research in Sweden
P.O. Box 7434
S-103 91 Stockholm, Sweden
RESTRICTIONS: All fields. Open to graduate students and researchers
who are not Swedish citizens. For study or research in Sweden when it
cannot be done equally well in another country. 1–3 years' duration.
Knowledge of Swedish or English required.
AMOUNT GIVEN: 3,880 kronor per month.
DEADLINE: September 1–December 1.

Texas Swedish Cultural Foundation
Scholarships for Study in Sweden
c/o Mrs. Gudrun Wallgren Merrill
2234 Inwood Dr.
Houston, TX 77019
713-522-7154
RESTRICTIONS: All fields. Open to graduate or postgraduate students
who are Texas residents or Swedish citizens who are outstanding graduates of a recognized Texas college or university for study, research, or
professional training in Sweden.
AMOUNT GIVEN: $2,500.
DEADLINE: April 15.

University of Stockholm
International Graduate Scholarships

S-106 Stockholm, Sweden
08-16-34-66
RESTRICTIONS: One-year graduate diploma program with emphasis on Scandinavia. Open to foreign students of all nationalities who have completed an academic degree in a field of social science. Minimum of a "B" average and fluency in English required.
AMOUNT GIVEN: Tuition + $350.
DEADLINE: March 1.

SWITZERLAND

Graduate Institute of International Studies
132 Rud de Lausanne
P.O. Box 36 1211
Geneva 21 Switzerland
31-17-30
RESTRICTIONS: Open to graduate students in the field of international relations. Must have solid background in discipline of specialization and sufficient knowledge of French and English.
AMOUNT GIVEN: 350 Swiss francs per month.
DEADLINE: June 1.

Institute of International Education
Scholarships for Study in Switzerland
809 United Nations Plaza
New York, NY 10017
212-883-8200 or 212-984-5328
RESTRICTIONS: All fields. Postgraduate scholarships offered by the Swiss government for study/research at a Swiss university.
AMOUNT GIVEN: $1,250 per month.
DEADLINE: May 1–October 31.
CONTACT: U.S. citizens should address inquires to the attention of "U.S. Student Programs Division" at above address.

THAILAND

Thailand Ministry of Education
Commission for UNESCO
Bangkok 10300 Thailand
281-6370
RESTRICTIONS: All fields. Fellowships, scholarships, and junior scholarships open to students from foreign countries who wish to study in Thailand. Working knowledge of Thai required.

AMOUNT GIVEN: Varies.
CONTACT: Nearest Thai embassy for initial inquiries.

Thailand–United States Educational Foundation
Fulbright Scholarship for American Nationals
127 South Sathorn Road
Bangkok 10120 Thailand
RESTRICTIONS: Available to U.S. citizens with exceptional undergraduate record. For study in the fields of business administration, economics and Thai studies. Preference given to students currently enrolled in graduate studies. Knowledge of Thai required.
AMOUNT GIVEN: $11,000–$13,000.
DEADLINE: September 15.
CONTACT: Americans Abroad Program
              IIE, United Nations Plaza
              New York, NY 10017

TRINIDAD/TOBAGO

Inter American Press Association
Scholarships for Study in Latin America and the West Indies
2911 NW 39th St.
Miami, FL 33142
305-634-2465
RESTRICTIONS: For young journalists and graduate students (ages 21–35) for 1 academic year of study/research in a Latin American or West Indian country. Must be a U.S./Canadian citizen. Fluency in the country's language is required.
AMOUNT GIVEN: $10,000.
DEADLINE: August 1.

Organization of American States
Department of Fellowships and Training
OAS PRA Fellowships for U.S.A. Residents
Trainee Selection Division
Washington, DC 20006
202-789-3902
RESTRICTIONS: Graduate fellowships for U.S. citizens/permanent residents who wish to study abroad in an OAS member country. Must have undergraduate degree and have proven ability to pursue studies at advanced level in chosen field. Should be fluent in language of country of intended study. All fields except medicine.
AMOUNT GIVEN: Tuition and fees. Travel expenses and stipend.
DEADLINE: April 30; August 31.

TUNISIA

Institut Pasteur de Tunis
Bourses Charles Nicolle
13 Place Pasteur
1002 Tunis Belvedere-Tunisie
283-022
RESTRICTIONS: Graduate awards for study in Tunisia in the fields of medicine and biology.
AMOUNT GIVEN: 2,000 Tunisian dinars.
CONTACT: Nearest Tunisian embassy for more information.

TURKEY

American Research Institute in Turkey
c/o University Museum 33rd and Spruce St.
Philadelphia, PA 19104
215-898-3474
RESTRICTIONS: Open to Ph.D. candidates at U.S. and Canadian institutes who have completed all coursework except dissertation. For doctoral dissertation research in Turkey in the fields of humanities and social sciences.
AMOUNT GIVEN: $1,000–$4,000.
DEADLINE: November 15.

Archaeological Institute of America
Olivia James Travelling Fellowship
675 Commonwealth Ave.
Boston, MA 02215
617-353-9361
RESTRICTIONS: For graduate or postgraduate study in Greece, Aegean Islands, Sicily, Southern Italy, Asia Minor, or Mesopotamia. Preference for dissertation or recent Ph.D. research. Not for field excavation. Must be U.S. citizen or legal resident for study in fields of archaeology, architecture, classics, history, or sculpture.
AMOUNT GIVEN: $10,000 stipend.
DEADLINE: November 15.

Archaeological Institute of America
Harriet Pomerance Fellowship
675 Commonwealth Ave.
Boston, MA 02215
617-353-9361

RESTRICTIONS: Graduate fellowships to enable work on a scholarly project relating to the Aegean Bronze Age in archeology. Preference to persons whose project requires travel to the Mediterranean. Must be U.S. or Canadian citizen.
AMOUNT GIVEN: $3,000.
DEADLINE: November 15.

North Atlantic Treaty Organization
NATO Science Fellowships for U.S.A. Citizens
B-1110; Science Affairs Division
Brussels, Belgium
2-241-00-40
RESTRICTIONS: Graduate and postdoctoral fellowships for almost all scientific areas, including interdisciplinary areas. Open to U.S. citizens who wish to study/research in another NATO member country. Administered in each country by a national administration.
AMOUNT GIVEN: Amount varies with country.
DEADLINE: January 1–March 1.
APPLICATIONS: Write for address of your country's administration.

UNION OF SOVIET SOCIALIST REPUBLICS

Soviet Ministry of Higher and Secondary Specialized Education
USSR
RESTRICTIONS: All fields. Undergraduate and graduate scholarships for study in institutions of higher learning in the USSR. Open to non-Soviet citizens selected by the IUS and approved by the Soviet government.
AMOUNT GIVEN: Tuition, cost of living, and travel expenses to and from the USSR.
DEADLINE: November 1.
CONTACT: International Research and Exchanges Board
              110 E. 59th St.
              New York, NY 10022

Soviet Ministry of Higher and Secondary Specialized Education
Moscow, USSR
RESTRICTIONS: All fields. Scholarships to foreign nationals for post-graduate studies at Soviet universities and institutions. Students must be currently engaged in teaching, study, or research at an approved institution, under 35 years of age with proficiency in the Russian language.
AMOUNT GIVEN: Tuition and maintenance fees.
DEADLINE: April 1.
APPLICATION: Through applicant's home government.

UNITED KINGDOM

American Friends of the London School of Economics
AFLSE Scholarship Program
1025 Thomas Jefferson St. NW
#400 East Lobby
Washington, DC 20007
202-944-3640
RESTRICTIONS: All fields. Graduate awards open to U.S. citizens or legal residents for one year of study at the London School of Economics. Preference to students who have not previously studied in Great Britain. For newly enrolled students only.
AMOUNT GIVEN: 8 scholarships per year. $2500.
DEADLINE: March 1.

American Heart Association
Division of Research Awards
British-American Research Fellowships
7320 Greenville Ave.
Dallas, TX 75231
214-706-1453
RESTRICTIONS: Postdoctoral awards open to U.S. citizens who seek research training in the United Kingdom.
AMOUNT GIVEN: $22,000 stipend.
DEADLINE: July 1.

Animal Health Trust
Blount Memorial Fund Scholarship
Lanwades Hall; General Secretary
Newmarket
Suffolk CB8 7PN England
RESTRICTIONS: Scholarships to study all aspects of animal health. For graduate study at agreed centers in the U.K.
AMOUNT GIVEN: 2,000 British pounds.
DEADLINE: March 1.

Association of Commonwealth Universities
Marshall Scholarships
36 Gordon Square
London WC1H OPF England
01-387-8572
RESTRICTIONS: All fields. Open to graduate and undergraduate students who are U.S. citizens under 26 years of age. Minimum requirement of 3.7 GPA. Tenable for two years of study in the U.K. at an approved university.

AMOUNT GIVEN: Approximately 30 awards. 11,000 British pounds per year.
DEADLINE: October 22.
CONTACT: British Embassy
             Marshall Scholarship Program
             Education Office
             3100 Massachusetts Avenue, NW
             Washington, DC 20008
             202-462-1340.

British Council
10 Spring Gardens
London SW1A 2BN England
RESTRICTIONS: Graduate fellowships for advanced study or research at institutions in the United Kingdom available to citizens of countries in which the British Council is represented. Preference to applicants between the ages of 25 and 35.
AMOUNT GIVEN: Varies.
DEADLINE: August.
CONTACT: The British Council office in home country.

British Dental Association
The Dentsply Scholarship Fund
64 Wimpole St.
London W1M 8AL England
01-935-0875
RESTRICTIONS: Scholarships to provide financial assistance towards the special education and training for a career in dentistry. U.K. citizens may study at any accredited institution in any country. Non-U.K. citizens must study at a U.K. institution.
AMOUNT GIVEN: 15 awards per year. 200–500 British pounds.
DEADLINE: May 1.

British Federation of University Women
Theodora Bosanquet Bursary
Crosby Hall; Cheyne Walk
London SW3 5BA England
01-352-5354
RESTRICTIONS: Open to female undergraduate and graduate students who are carrying out research in the field of English literature or English history requiring use of reference libraries or other sources of information in London.
AMOUNT GIVEN: Residential fees and board for up to 6 weeks.
DEADLINE: November 23.

British University Summer Schools
c/o University of Oxford; Dept. of External Studies

1 Wellington Square
Oxford OX1 2JA England
0865-270378
RESTRICTIONS: For U.S. graduate students between the ages of 20 and 35 who wish to study in England.
AMOUNT GIVEN: Approximately 15 scholarships covering ⅓ of program costs excluding travel.
DEADLINE: March 15.
CONTACT: U.S. Student Programs Division
Institute of International Education
809 U.N. Plaza
New York, NY 10017

English Speaking Union
Lucy Dalbiac Luard Scholarship
16 E. 69th St.
New York, NY 10021
212-879-6800
RESTRICTIONS: Open to students attending a United Negro College or Howard University. Scholarship to spend undergraduate junior year at a U.K. university. Must be U.S. citizen.
AMOUNT GIVEN: Full tuition + expenses.
DEADLINE: December 1.

Girton College Fellowships *12/29/97*
Secretary to the Council *inquiry*
Cambridge CB3 OJG England
338-999
RESTRICTIONS: Research fellowships in the areas of humanities and science open to graduate students of any university. Tenable at Girton College.
AMOUNT GIVEN: Up to 9,200 British pounds per year.
DEADLINE: October 14.

Charles and Julia Henry Fund
c/o University of Cambridge
The Old Schools
Cambridge CB2 1TN England
RESTRICTIONS: Awards for U.S. citizens to study in the U.K. (at Cambridge or Oxford) or U.K. citizens to study in the U.S. (at Harvard or Yale). U.S. citizens must be enrolled at Harvard or Yale at time of application. For single students who will have already obtained their B.A. at the time they take up the award with a preference for applicants in their last year of undergraduate studies.
AMOUNT GIVEN: Full-maintenance grant + fees.
DEADLINE: Late autumn.

APPLICATION: U.S. citizens write to Harvard University c/o the secretary.

Institute of Chartered Secretaries and Administrators
16 Park Crescent
London W1N 4AH England
01-580-4741
RESTRICTIONS: Applications accepted for final year undergraduate students, graduate students, members of the institute and others who are eligible for admission to postgraduate work at a university or polytechnic or its equivalent in the United Kingdom in the fields of law, business administration, economics and public administration.
AMOUNT GIVEN: 2,000 British pounds.
DEADLINE: April 30.

Institute of European Studies
875 N. Michigan Ave. #1540
Chicago, IL 60611
RESTRICTIONS: Open to any student accepted into one of the institute's programs with proof of financial need.
AMOUNT GIVEN: Tuition, fees, one-way transportation, lodging, board, and books.
DEADLINE: December 10; February 25.

Institute of Mechanical Engineers
Manville Fellowship
P.O. Box 23 Northgate Ave.
Bury St. Edmunds
Suffolk IP32 6BN England
0284-63277
RESTRICTIONS: Awards for postgraduate studies or approved research in automobile engineering at the institution. Must be a member of IMECHE. Applicants should normally have received an approved engineering degree and had at least one year of acceptable training in auto engineering.
AMOUNT GIVEN: 1,000 British pounds.
DEADLINE: U.K.—January 31; overseas—February 28.

Institution of Mechanical Engineers
Bramah Scholarship
P.O. Box 23; Northgate Ave.
Bury St. Edmonds, Suffolk IP32 6BN England
0284-63277
RESTRICTIONS: Awards for undergraduate and graduate students to study hydraulic mechanisms, particularly hydrostatic transmissions and servo mechanisms. Tenable at the institution.
AMOUNT GIVEN: 1,000 British pounds.
DEADLINE: U.K.—January 31; overseas—February 28.

Institution of Mining and Metallurgy
Stanley Moore Fellowships
44 Portland Place
London W1N 4BR England
01-580-3802
RESTRICTIONS: For graduate research into all branches of extractive metallurgy and mineral processing. Tenable at U.K. universities. Preference given to members of institution.
AMOUNT GIVEN: 1,500–6,000 British pounds.
DEADLINE: March 16.

Institution of Mining and Metallurgy
G. Vernon Hobson Bequest
44 Portland Place
London W1N 4BR England
01-580-3802

RESTRICTIONS: Awards for the advancement of teaching geology as applied to mining. Open to graduate students. Preference to institution members.
AMOUNT GIVEN: 1,500 British pounds.
DEADLINE: March 16.

Institution of Mining and Metallurgy
Bosworth Smith Trust Fund
44 Portland Place
London W1N 4BR England
01-580-3802
RESTRICTIONS: Grants available for postgraduate research in metal mining, nonferrous extraction, metallurgy, or mineral dressing. For use towards working expenses and costs of visits to mines. Preference given to members of the institution.
AMOUNT GIVEN: 3,500 British pounds.
DEADLINE: March 16.
CONTACT: The secretary of the institution.

Kings College London
Cleave Cocherill Post-Graduate Studentship
Office of the Dean
The Strand, London WC2R 2LS England
01-836-5454
RESTRICTIONS: Awarded to a candidate for holy orders in the Church of England who wishes to proceed to a higher degree in theology. Preference given to graduates of Kings College.
AMOUNT GIVEN: 500 British pounds.
DEADLINE: None.

London Chamber of Commerce and Industry Examinations Board (LCCIEB)

Centenary Scholarships
Marlowe House
Station Road
Sidcup, Kent DA15 7BJ England
RESTRICTIONS: Scholarships open to students of any nationality for studies in commerce or business at approved central London institutions. Overseas applicants may be asked to attend an interview in their home country. Must be at least 18 years of age.
AMOUNT GIVEN: 750 British pounds per year.
DEADLINE: December 31.

London School of Economics and Political Science
Houghton St. Scholarships Office
London WC2A 2AE England
01-955-7163
RESTRICTIONS: Open to graduate students who wish to undertake either contemporary or historical research at the school in a socio-legal area of Law.
AMOUNT GIVEN: Varies.
DEADLINE: September 1.

London School of Economics and Political Science
Houghton St. Scholarships Office
London WC2A 2AE England
01-955-7163
RESTRICTIONS: Awards and prizes available to students wishing to attend the university as graduate or undergraduate students in the fields of accounting; economics; finance and political science.
AMOUNT GIVEN: Amount varies.

London School of Economics and Political Science
Houghton St. Scholarships Office
London WC2A 2AE England
01-955-7163
RESTRICTIONS: Open to applicants who register as full-time students of the school and pursue graduate work in the social sciences.
AMOUNT GIVEN: 600 British pounds.
DEADLINE: September 1.

London School of Economics and Political Science
Roseberry Studentships
Houghton St. Scholarships Office
London WC2A England
01-955-7163
RESTRICTIONS: For graduate work at the school in the social sciences. Preference to students studying some aspect of transport.

AMOUNT GIVEN: 300 British pounds minimum.
DEADLINE: September 1.

Newberry Library
Newberry-British Academy Fellowship for Study in Great Britain
60 West Walton St.
Chicago, IL 60610
312-943-9090
RESTRICTIONS: Exchange fellowships open to established postdoctoral scholars, readers, and staff members of the Newberry Library for research in the humanities.
AMOUNT GIVEN: $6,000.
DEADLINE: March 1.

Newnham College *12/29/97 ongoing*
College Secretary
Cambridge CB3 9DF England
0223-335700
RESTRICTIONS: Research fellowships open only to women. Evidence of the ability to conduct independent research of at least Ph.D. standard is required.
AMOUNT GIVEN: 5,052–5,601 British pounds.
DEADLINE: February.

North Atlantic Treaty Organization
NATO Science Fellowships for U.S.A. Citizens
B-1110; Science Affairs Division
Brussels, Belgium
2-241-00-40
RESTRICTIONS: Graduate and postdoctoral fellowships for almost all scientific areas including interdisciplinary areas. Open to U.S. citizens who wish to study/research in another NATO member country. Administered in each country by a national administration.
AMOUNT GIVEN: Amount varies with country.
DEADLINE: January 1–March 1.
APPLICATIONS: Write for address of your country's administration.

Norwich Jubilee Esperanto Foundation
37 Granville Court
Oxford OX3 OHS England
0865-245509
RESTRICTIONS: Scholarships for anyone to travel to the U.K. to improve their use of Esperanto. Candidates should be competent in the use of the language.
AMOUNT GIVEN: Maximum of 25 awards per year. Up to 1,000 British pounds.
DEADLINE: None.

Queen's University of Belfast *14/29/97 inquiry*
Visiting Studentships
Newforge Lane, Belfast BT9 5PX Northern Ireland
Belfast-6661166
RESTRICTIONS: All fields. Graduate scholarships available for good honors graduates of another university who already have research experience to undertake postgraduate research.
AMOUNT GIVEN: Value equivalent to government studentship + 20% per annum + travel allowance and fees.
DEADLINE: February 1.

Queen's University of Belfast
Harold Barbour/MacGeough Bond Scholarship
Newforge Lane, Belfast BT9 5PX Northern Ireland
Belfast-6661166
RESTRICTIONS: Postgraduate scholarship for training or research in agriculture, especially application of science to Northern Irish agriculture. Must be graduate of a U.K. university.
AMOUNT GIVEN: 2,430 British pounds.
DEADLINE: May 1.

Queen's University of Belfast *12/29/97 inquiry*
Junior Research Fellowships
Secretary to Academic Council
Belfast BT7 INN Northern Ireland
245-133 ext. 3006
RESTRICTIONS: Fellowships for graduate students with honors degree and research experience. For 1 year of study at the university in the field of Irish studies.
AMOUNT GIVEN: 3,548 British pounds + fees.
DEADLINE: January 22.

Rhodes Scholarship Trust
c/o Pomona College
Claremont, CA 91711
714-621-8138
RESTRICTIONS: All fields. For unmarried U.S. citizens ages 17–23. Grants tenable only at Oxford University. Bachelor's degree required before taking up award. Based on scholarship, character, leadership, and physical vigor.
AMOUNT GIVEN: 32 awards per year. Tuition + stipend.
DEADLINE: October.

Royal Academy of Dramatic Art
Scholarships and Grants
62-64 Gower St.

London WC1E 6ED England
01-636-7076
RESTRICTIONS: Open to U.K. and overseas candidates. Audition and fluency in English required. Auditions held in New York and England.
AMOUNT GIVEN: Partial or full tuition.
DEADLINE: February 1.

Royal College of Veterinary Surgeons
Sir Fredrick Smith and Miss Aleen Cust Research Fellowships
32 Belgrave Square
London SW1X 8QP England
01-235-4971
RESTRICTIONS: Postgraduate fellowships available for research at an approved institution in the field of veterinary science.
AMOUNT GIVEN: $1,000 per annum + 200 pounds.

Royal Society
Executive Secretary
Pinkering Research Fellowship
6 Carlton House Terrace
London SW1Y 5AG England
RESTRICTIONS: Fellowships in chemistry, horticulture, or botany available to students of all nationalities who have proven ability to do independent scientific research. Preference for applicants under the age of 26.
AMOUNT GIVEN: 10,670 British pounds per year.

Royal Society
Executive Secretary
Rosenhein Research Fellowship
6 Carlton House Terrace
London SW1Y 5AG England
RESTRICTIONS: Fellowships in biochemistry of plants and simpler forms of animal life available to students of all nationalities who have proven ability to do independent scientific research. Preference for applicants under the age of 26.
AMOUNT GIVEN: 10,670 British pounds per year.

Saint Andrew's Society of the State of New York
281 Park Ave. South
New York, NY 10010
212-473-6912
RESTRICTIONS: All fields. Open to undergraduate seniors at accredited U.S. institutions who are of Scottish ancestry and residents of Pennsylvania, New Jersey, New York, or the New England states. Must be U.S. citizens. Preference to applicants who have not had a previous

opportunity to study in Great Britain. Tenable at an approved Scottish university.
AMOUNT GIVEN: Tuition + stipend.
DEADLINE: October.

School of Oriental and African Studies
J. T. Bishop Registrar
London WC1E 7HP England
01-637-2388
RESTRICTIONS: Scholarships open to master's degree students in the areas of Oriental and African studies. For study in London.
AMOUNT GIVEN: 10 awards per year. Approximately 4,600 British pounds.
DEADLINE: May 1.

Smith and Nephew Foundation
Research Fellowships
2 Temple Place
Victoria Embankment
London WC2R 3BP England
RESTRICTIONS: Postdoctoral research fellowships open to citizens of any country between the ages of 25 and 35 who have had 2 years of general clinical experience. Awards tenable in the U.K. in the fields of surgery research and internal medicine. Fellows must return to their home country after completion of studies.
AMOUNT GIVEN: 14,000 British pounds.
DEADLINE: April.

Social Science Research Council
Fellowships Coordinator
605 Third Ave.
New York, NY 10158
212-661-0280
RESTRICTIONS: Doctoral dissertation research fellowships for Ph.D. candidates of all nationalities at U.S. institutions or U.S. citizens or legal residents enrolled at any accredited institution in the U.S. or abroad. For research in the fields of social sciences, humanities, demography, urban planning, education.
AMOUNT GIVEN: 50–100 fellowships per year.
DEADLINE: November 1.

Society for the Protection of Ancient Buildings
Memorial Trust Scholarships
37 Spital Square
London E1 6DY England
01-377-1644

RESTRICTIONS: 9-month traveling scholarship open to both under-graduate and graduate students for conservation architecture to be used in the U.K. Emphasis on practical training, traditional building, modern and traditional repairs.
AMOUNT GIVEN: 2–3 awards per year. 3,200 British pounds.
DEADLINE: December 31.

University of Aberdeen
Regent Walk
Aberdeen AB9 1FX Scotland
RESTRICTIONS: Postgraduate studentships available to applicants of all nationalities accepted at the university in the fields of social sciences, science, engineering, agriculture, forestry, divinity, law, and medicine. Must have a minimum of first-class honors degree and a TOEFL score of at least 500 or equivalent. Provision for handicapped.
AMOUNT GIVEN: 10 awards per year.
DEADLINE: July 31.

University of Aberdeen
C. B. Davidson Scholarships
Clerk to the Faculty of Law
University Office
Regent Walk
Aberdeen AB9 1FX Scotland
RESTRICTIONS: Scholarships in comparative law available to appli-cants of all nationalities with an honors degree in law.
AMOUNT GIVEN: Standard research council rates.

University of Aberdeen
Clerk to the Faculty of Divinity
University Office
Regent Walk
Aberdeen AB9 1FX Scotland
RESTRICTIONS: Scholarships open to applicants of all nationalities with an honors degree in Hebrew or a Semitic language for study at the university.
AMOUNT GIVEN: Standard research council rates.

University of Birmingham
Hugh Morton Scholarships
The Registry; P.O. Box 363
Birmingham B15 2TT England
RESTRICTIONS: Scholarships for students enrolled in the faculty of law, pursuing an approved course of study for the higher degree of Ph.D. or LL.D. Applicants must be nominated by the faculty of law and have taken or qualified for the LL.B. degree with honors. Recipients will remain, in

regards to study and discipline, under the control of the Dean of the Faculty.
AMOUNT GIVEN: Tuition and fees.
DEADLINE: None.

University of Cambridge
Hughes Hall Studentship
Senior Tutor; Hughes Hall
Cambridge CB12 EW England
02223-334893
RESTRICTIONS: Studentships are open to students who are accepted for graduate studies in the areas of medicine, law and education at Cambridge University.
AMOUNT GIVEN: 15–20 studentships per year. 750 British pounds.
DEADLINE: July.

University of Cambridge—Christ's College
Senior Tutor
Cambridge CB2 1RH England
RESTRICTIONS: All fields. All nationalities. Available to students who have graduated from another university before October 1 of award year with minimum of a first-class honors degree or equivalent. Must be under 30 years of age. Scholarships for research degree programs only.
AMOUNT GIVEN: Full maintenance award + fees and allowances.
DEADLINE: April 1.

University of Cambridge—Churchill College
Tutor for Advanced Students
Cambridge CB3 ODS England
RESTRICTIONS: All fields. For graduate students who intend to register for a degree of Ph.D. at the University of Cambridge. Must hold a first-class degree.
AMOUNT GIVEN: 2,756 British pounds + fees.
DEADLINE: January 15.

University of Cambridge—Corpus Christi College
Tutor for Advanced Studies
Cambridge CB2 1RH England
0223-338-006
RESTRICTIONS: All fields. Open to postgraduate students accepted at Corpus Christi College by the Board of Graduate Studies.
AMOUNT GIVEN: Tuition + 2,806 British pounds stipend.
DEADLINE: None.

University of Cambridge—Kings College
External Studentships

Kings College Head Tutor for Graduate Studies
Cambridge CB2 1ST England
RESTRICTIONS: All fields. All nationalities. For graduate research/study at Kings College.
AMOUNT GIVEN: Fees + maintenance.
DEADLINE: April.

University of Cambridge—Sidney Sussex College
Tutor for Graduate Studies
Cambridge CB2 3HU England
0223-338200
RESTRICTIONS: All fields. All nationalities. Open to new Ph.D. candidates for study at the University of Cambridge. Preference to students who nominate Sidney Sussex as their college of first choice.
AMOUNT GIVEN: Up to 3,125 British pounds per year + fees.
DEADLINE: March 1.

University of Cambridge—St. John's College
Harper-Wood Studentship
Cambridge CB2 1TP England
RESTRICTIONS: Studentship available in field of creative writing in English poetry and literature. Open to graduate students in country of choice sponsored by St. John's. Must be a graduate of any university of the U.K./the Commonwealth or the U.S. Must be under 30 years of age.
AMOUNT GIVEN: up to 2,815 British pounds.
DEADLINE: June 30.

University of Cambridge—St. Johns College
Norman Laski Senior Studentship
Master; St. Johns College
Cambridge CB2 1TP England
RESTRICTIONS: Awards available to graduate students from any country for study in the fields of economics, engineering and applied mathematics. Preference for study or research related to business or management. Must not be working for postgraduate qualification at the beginning of tenure. Must be over 23 years of age.
AMOUNT GIVEN: up to 7,530 British pounds.
DEADLINE: March 31.

University of Cambridge—Trinity College
Overseas fees Bursaries
Cambridge CB2 1TQ England
RESTRICTIONS: All fields. Graduate and undergraduate awards. Open to overseas students who are liable for overseas rates for university fees.
AMOUNT GIVEN: Varies.
APPLICATION: Undergraduates apply to the Tutor for Admissions. Graduates apply to the Tutor for Advanced Studies.

University of Dundee
Postgraduate Office
Dundee DD1 4HN Scotland
RESTRICTIONS: Awards available to foreign nationals in the fields of medicine, dentistry, science, law, engineering, arts, social sciences, environmental studies, and education. Applicants must have a minimum of an upper second-class honors degree or equivalent.
AMOUNT GIVEN: Up to 2,860 British pounds.
DEADLINE: March 31.

University of Durham
Old Shire Hall
Durham DH1 3HP
RESTRICTIONS: Fellowships available to senior researchers from any country with Ph.D. standing. For research in arts and social sciences.
AMOUNT GIVEN: 6,070–10,575 British pounds.
DEADLINE: Announced yearly.

University of Edinburgh
Old College South Bridge
Edinburgh EH8 9YL Scotland
031-667-1011
RESTRICTIONS: All fields. All nationalities. Postgraduate study at the university. Competitive awards.
AMOUNT GIVEN: 10–20 awards per year. 2,664 British pounds + fees.
DEADLINE: April 15.

University of Glasgow
Post-Graduate Awards in Law and Financial Studies
Glasgow 912 8QQ Scotland
041-339-8855
RESTRICTIONS: For graduate students for research in topic specified by applicant and approved by the school of law. Must have honors degree. Tenable at the university.
AMOUNT GIVEN: 2 awards per year.
DEADLINE: February 28.
CONTACT: Mrs. A. E. Wilson, Clerk of the Faculty, for more information.

University of Keele
Scholarships for Overseas Students
The Senior Tutor
Keele Straffordshire ST5 5BG England
0782-621-111 ext. 372/362
RESTRICTIONS: All fields. Undergraduate and graduate students from overseas who are required to pay the higher tuition fees set by the U.K. government. Based on academic merit.

AMOUNT GIVEN: 10 awards per year. 500 British pounds per year.
DEADLINE: August.

University of Lancaster

Peel Studentship and Grants/Cartmel College
Bursaries/County College J.C.R. Award
Office of Colleges and Welfare Services
University House
Lancaster LA1 4YW England
RESTRICTIONS: All fields. All nationalities. Open to students admitted
to the university who cannot obtain other financial assistance.
DEADLINE: June 2.

University of Lancaster

Senate Studentships/Philip Andrew Memorial
Fellowship/County College Supplementary Award
c/o Miss C. J. Martin, Administrative Officer
Office of Colleges and Welfare Services
University House
Lancaster LA1 4YW England
RESTRICTIONS: All fields. All nationalities. Open to postgraduate students admitted to the University who cannot obtain other financial assistance.
DEADLINE: June 2.

University of Leeds

Scholarships for Overseas Students
Head Tutor
Leeds LS2 9JT England
471-751
RESTRICTIONS: All fields. Overseas students of high academic standard who are accepted for admission by the university as full-time graduate or undergraduate students.
AMOUNT GIVEN: 70 awards per year. 1,400 British pounds.
DEADLINE: June 1.

University of London

Warburg Institute
Frances A. Yates Fellowships
Weburn Square; Head Tutor
London WC1H OAB England
01-580 9663
RESTRICTIONS: Postgraduate fellowships to study any aspect of cultural and intellectual history. Preference is given to those with special interest in the study of medieval and renaissance history, to which Dame Frances Yates contributed.

AMOUNT GIVEN: Short-term—500–1,200 British pounds. Long-term—5,000–8,500 British pounds.
DEADLINE: Early December.

University of London
Pfeiffer Fellowship
Warden
College Hall
London WCIE 7H2 England
RESTRICTIONS: All fields. Open to female graduate students for study at College Hall.
AMOUNT GIVEN: 1 award every four years.
DEADLINE: March 1.

University of London
JFH Knight Fellowship
Senate House; Room 21A
Malet Street
London, WC1E 7HU England
RESTRICTIONS: For postgraduate research into the social epidemilogical or preventive aspects of diseases of adult life, with special reference to the problems of venereal disease; alcohol; drugs of addiction and similar matters. Open to university graduates who are registered medical practitioners or of equivalent qualifications. Tenable at the London School of Hygiene & Tropical Medicine.
AMOUNT GIVEN: 2,995 British pounds.
DEADLINE: March 1.

University of London
Carlo Campolin Postgraduate Scholarship
Senate House; Room 21A
Malet Street
London, W1CE 7HU England
RESTRICTIONS: Award for research in biology or astronomy offered for an approved program of research as an internal student leading to a research degree at the University of London.
AMOUNT GIVEN: Stipend + expenses.
DEADLINE: March 1.

University of London—Bedford
Postgraduate Office
Engham Hill
Engham, Surney TW20 OEX England
RESTRICTIONS: Awards available to foreign nationals in the fields of medicine, dentistry, science, law, engineering, arts, social sciences, environmental studies, and education. Applicants must have a minimum of upper second-class honors degree or equivalent.

AMOUNT GIVEN: Up to 2,860 British pounds.

University of London—Bedford
Attn: Registrar
Engham Hill
Engham, Surrey TW20 OEX England
RESTRICTIONS: Awards available to students of any nationality holding a higher degree in English or who have completed a minimum of 2 years of research towards a higher degree.
AMOUNT GIVEN: Equivalent to a British Academy Major scholarship.

University of London—Bedford College
Lady Huggins Scholarship
Attn: Registrar
Engham Hill
Engham, Surrey TW20 OEX England
RESTRICTIONS: Scholarship in the field of sociology available to women graduate students of all nationalities. Preference to applicants with honors degrees in philosophy, psychology, economics, or sociology.
AMOUNT GIVEN: As funds permit.
DEADLINE: May 1.

University of Manchester
Institute of Science and Technology
Mohn Research Fellowships
P.O. Box 88
Manchester M60 1QD England
061-236-3311
RESTRICTIONS: Postgraduate fellowships for persons who wish to pursue research in the faculty of technology. Preference given to studies in the areas of metallurgy, material science, and chemical engineering.
AMOUNT GIVEN: Approximately 4,000 British pounds.
DEADLINE: None.

University of Manchester
Institute of Science and Technology
William Jones Scholarships
P.O. Box 88
Manchester M60 1QD England
061-236-3311
RESTRICTIONS: Awarded to undergraduate or postgraduate students for study or research in the technology of fibers.
GIVEN: Approximately 4,000 British pounds.
DEADLINE: None.

University of Nottingham
University Park
Nottingham NG7 2RD England
RESTRICTIONS: Postgraduate research studentships in all fields awarded to students of sufficient promise.
AMOUNT GIVEN: 2,730 British pounds per annum.
DEADLINE: May 1.

University of Oxford
Squire and Marriott Bursaries
University Office; Wellington Square
Oxford OX1 2JD England
0865-270001
RESTRICTIONS: Undergraduate and graduate scholarships. Applicants must intend to offer themselves for ordination in the Church of England or any church in communion therewith. Must show financial need.
AMOUNT GIVEN: 6 awards per year.
DEADLINE: March or September.

University of Oxford
Hall-Houghton Studentship
University Office; Wellington Square
Oxford OX1 2JD England
0865-270001
RESTRICTIONS: For postgraduate study at the University of Oxford in the field of theology, with emphasis on the Greek New Testament or Septuagint version of the Hebrew scriptures in its relation to the Bible and the Greek testament or the Syriac versions of the Holy Scriptures.
AMOUNT GIVEN: 500 British pounds.
DEADLINE: Early February.

University of Oxford
Denyer and Johnson Studentships
University Office; Wellington Square
Oxford OX1 2JD England
0865-270001
RESTRICTIONS: For postgraduate study at the University of Oxford. Applicants for higher degrees under the Board of the Faculty at the university.
AMOUNT GIVEN: Up to 1,300 British pounds.
DEADLINE: February 1.

University of Oxford—Somerville College
Janet Watson Bursary
Somerville College Secretary
Oxford OX2 6HD England
0865-57595

RESTRICTIONS: All fields. For a U.S. woman graduate wishing to research for a further degree at Oxford as a member of Somerville College.
AMOUNT GIVEN: 2,400 British pounds.
DEADLINE: April 1.

University of Oxford—St. Catherine's College
Manor Road; Attn: Senior Tutor
Oxford OX1 3UJ England
0865-249541
RESTRICTIONS: All fields. Competitive scholarships available to non-British citizens for graduate study at St. Catherine's College.
AMOUNT GIVEN: 1,500 British pounds.
DEADLINE: April 30.

University of Oxford—St. Cross College
St. Cross College
Oxford OXI 3L2 England
0865-278490
RESTRICTIONS: Supplementary awards open to students intending to undertake postgraduate research at Oxford University in the fields of biochemistry, chemistry, and engineering.
AMOUNT GIVEN: 700 British pounds.
DEADLINE: May 12.

University of Oxford—St. Hilda's College
Overseas Bursaries for Women
St. Hilda's College Secretary
Oxford OX4 1DY England
086-270001
RESTRICTIONS: All fields. Open to women who are not British citizens for graduate or undergraduate study at St. Hilda's College.
AMOUNT GIVEN: 1,500 British pounds.
DEADLINE: May 22.

University of Oxford—St. Hilda's College
Graduate Studentships for Women
St. Hilda's College Secretary
Oxford OX4 1DY England
086-270001
RESTRICTIONS: All fields. Open to women for their undergraduate senior year at St. Hilda's College.
AMOUNT GIVEN: 250 British pounds.
DEADLINE: May 22.

University of Oxford—St. Hughes College
University Offices; Wellington Square

Oxford OX1 2JD England
0865-270001
RESTRICTIONS: All fields. Open to graduate students who are admitted to a full-time course of study leading to a higher degree at St. Hugh's College.
AMOUNT GIVEN 1,000 British pounds.
DEADLINE: March 14.

University of Reading
Whiteknights; P.O. Box 217
Reading Berkshire RG6 2AH England
RESTRICTIONS: All fields. Postgraduate studentships available to students who are admitted to the university for a full-time course leading to the award of a higher degree.
AMOUNT GIVEN: 2,756 British pounds per year.
DEADLINE: March 31.

University of Sheffield
Registrar
Sheffield S10 2TN England
RESTRICTIONS: Awards available in the areas of arts, economics, social studies, law, and architecture. Open to graduate students of all nationalities.
AMOUNT GIVEN: 2 studentships and 1 fellowship per year.
DEADLINE: June 1.

University of Sheffield
Medical Research Fellowships.
Attn: Registrar
Sheffield S10 2TN England
RESTRICTIONS: Awards in all branches of medicine approved by the faculty open to graduate students of all nationalities.
AMOUNT GIVEN: Varies.

University of Southampton
Highfield; Attn: Registrar
Southampton S09 5NH England
0703-559-122 ext. 3623
RESTRICTIONS: All fields. Research scholarships at the master's or Ph.D. level.
AMOUNT GIVEN: 8 awards per year. Approx. 2,800 British pounds + tuition and fees.
DEADLINE: June.

University of Strathclyde
John Anderson Studentships
McCance Building

16 Richmond St.
Glasgow G1 1XQ Scotland
041-552-4400
RESTRICTIONS: All fields. All nationalities. Studentships for postgraduate training at the university.
AMOUNT GIVEN: Up to 2,756 British pounds.
DEADLINE: June 16.

URUGUAY

Inter American Press Association
Scholarships for Study in Latin America and the West Indies
2911 NW 39th St.
Miami, FL 33142
305-634-2465
RESTRICTIONS: For young journalists and graduate students (ages 21–35) for 1 academic year of study/research in a Latin American or West Indian country. Must be a U.S./Canadian citizen. Fluency in the country's language is required.
AMOUNT GIVEN: $10,000.
DEADLINE: August 1.

VENEZUELA

Inter American Press Association
Scholarships for Study in Latin America and the West Indies
2911 NW 39th St.
Miami, FL 33142
305-634-2465
RESTRICTIONS: For young journalists and graduate students (ages 21–35) for 1 academic year of study/research in a Latin American or West Indian country. Must be a U.S./Canadian citizen. Fluency in the country's language is required.
AMOUNT GIVEN: $10,000.
DEADLINE: August 1.

YUGOSLAVIA

Archaeological Institute of America
Harriet Pomerance Fellowship
675 Commonwealth Ave.

Boston, MA 02215
617-353-9361
RESTRICTIONS: Graduate fellowships to enable work on a scholarly project relating to the Aegean Bronze Age in archeology. Preference to persons whose project requires travel to the Mediterranean. Must be U.S. or Canadian citizen.
AMOUNT GIVEN: $3,000.
DEADLINE: November 15.

Archaeological Institute of America
Olivia James Travelling Fellowship
675 Commonwealth Ave.
Boston, MA 02215
617-353-9361
RESTRICTIONS: For graduate or postgraduate study in Greece, Aegean Islands, Sicily, Southern Italy, Asia Minor, or Mesopotamia. Preference for dissertation or recent Ph.D. research. Not for field excavation. Must be U.S. citizen or legal resident for study in fields of archaeology, architecture, classics, history, or sculpture.
AMOUNT GIVEN: $10,000 stipend.
DEADLINE: November 15.

Australian Dept. of Education
Yugoslav Government Fellowships
P.O. Box 926; International Education Branch
Woden ACT 2602 Australia
062-837-777
RESTRICTIONS: All fields. Postgraduate fellowship for study at various tertiary institutions in Yugoslavia during the academic year (October 1–June 30). Must hold a bachelor's degree.
AMOUNT GIVEN: Living allowance + book allowance + travel expenses.
DEADLINE: None.

Subject Listings

AERONAUTICS

Von Karman Institute for Fluid Dynamics
Diploma Course Scholarship
72 Chaussée de Waterloo
1640 Rhode-St-Genese, Belgium
02-358-1901
RESTRICTIONS: For aeronautics, aerospace, turbomachinery, or industrial fluid dynamics. Must be citizen of NATO country. For postgraduate study at the Von Karman Institute.
AMOUNT GIVEN: 21,500 Belgian francs per month. 35 scholarships per year.
DEADLINE: May 31.
CONTACT: J. J. Gineux, Director.

AGRICULTURE

American Society for Enology and Viticulture
P.O. Box 1855
Davis, CA 95617
916-753-3142
RESTRICTIONS: Candidate must be enrolled/accepted in an accredited college in North America in curriculum stressing a science basic to the wine and grape industry. Must be a North American resident.
AMOUNT GIVEN: $1,000–$3,000.
DEADLINE: March 1.

Farrer Memorial Trust
Farrer Memorial Research Scholarship
Secretary
c/o N.S.W. Dept. of Agriculture
P.O. Box K 220
Haymarket, New South Wales 2000 Australia

RESTRICTIONS: Open to graduate students for research into agricultural problems. Selected by trustees on the basis of demonstrated superior ability after graduation.
AMOUNT GIVEN: 1-year scholarships, available at irregular intervals. Possible extension.

International Agricultural Centre (IAC)
P.O. Box 88
6700 AB Wageningen Netherlands
RESTRICTIONS: Fellowships available to students holding an M.S. or B.S. degree with experience in their field of study. Must be at least 25 years old.
AMOUNT GIVEN: Room and Board. Daily allowance of 16 florins + health insurance, study tours and book allowance.
DEADLINE: 6 months prior to beginning studies.

International Institute of Tropical Agriculture
Training Programs
Oyo Road PMB 5320
Ibadan, Nigeria
413244-413315-413440
RESTRICTIONS: The main objective of the various training programs is to build up the agricultural capacity of the professional personnel of developing countries. Participants for training range from secondary school levels to holders of advanced degrees.
AMOUNT GIVEN: Varies.

Kyungpook National University
Bureau of Student Affairs
370 San Kyuk-dong, uk-gu
Daegu 635 Korea
RESTRICTIONS: Scholarships and loans available to applicants of all nationalities in the fields of humanities, social sciences, natural sciences, economics, commerce, law, engineering, agriculture, teaching, medicine, dentistry, music, and visual arts. Must have completed 12 years of schooling and 2 years of pre-medical or pre-dental courses for study in these fields.
DEADLINE: One semester prior to start of studies.

La Trobe University
Registrar
Attn: Scholarships officer
Bundoora, Victoria 3083 Australia
RESTRICTIONS: Research scholarships for master's and Ph.D. candidates. Available to students from any country holding the equivalent to a 4-year, first-class honors degree from an Australian university. Proof of

significant written work required. Must be efficient in English. Renewable if progress is satisfactory.
AMOUNT GIVEN: Aus. $7,000 + possible spousal and dependents' allowance. Thesis allowance up to Aus. $800 and possible general service fee and travel allowance. 2 yrs. (master's); 4 yrs. (Ph.D.).
DEADLINE: July 31.

Lincoln College
MacMillian Brown Agricultural Scholarships
Registrar
Christchurch 252 811 New Zealand
RESTRICTIONS: For graduate students studying for Ph.D. who wish to research some problem bearing on agriculture or horticulture.
AMOUNT GIVEN: NZ $1,000.
DEADLINE: February 1.

Natural Sciences and Engineering Research Council of Canada
Science and Engineering Scholarships
200 Kent Street
Ottawa, Ontario K1A 1H5 Canada
613-996-2009
RESTRICTIONS: For graduate students in the fields of agriculture, biology, chemistry, computer science, engineering, food science, forestry, and geography with superior scholastic or research ability for study and research in Canada leading to Ph.D.
AMOUNT GIVEN: 60 awards per year of $17,500.
DEADLINE: December 8.

Natural Sciences and Engineering Research Council of Canada
Undergraduate Student Research Awards
200 Kent Street
Ottawa, Ontario K1A 1H5 Canada
613-996-2009
RESTRICTIONS: Open to Canadian citizens or legal residents for undergraduate research at universities or industrial labs in fields of agriculture, biology, computer science, engineering, food science, forestry, geography, and geology to encourage students to undertake graduate studies. Tenable during summer or may be used during academic year.
AMOUNT GIVEN: Canadian $750 for a maximum of 4 months.
DEADLINE: Set by university.

Queen's University of Belfast
Harold Barbour/MacGeough Bond Scholarship
Newforge Lane, Belfast BT9 5PX Northern Ireland
Belfast-6661166

RESTRICTIONS: Postgraduate scholarship for training or research in agriculture, especially application of science to Northern Irish agriculture. Must be graduate of a U.K. university.
AMOUNT GIVEN: 2,430 British pounds.
DEADLINE: May 1.

University of Aberdeen
Regent Walk
Aberdeen AB9 1FX Scotland
RESTRICTIONS: Postgraduate studentships available to applicants of all nationalities accepted at the university in the fields of social sciences, science, engineering, agriculture, forestry, divinity, law, and medicine. Must have minimum of first-class honors degree and a TOEFL score of at least 500 or equivalent. Provision for handicapped.
AMOUNT GIVEN: 10 awards per year.
DEADLINE: July 31.

University of Guelph
Dean of Graduate Studies
Guelph, Ontario N1G 2WI Canada
RESTRICTIONS: Awards for postgraduate study in fields of agriculture, arts, biological science, physical sciences, social sciences, veterinary sciences. Open to students of all nationalities having graduated from a recognized university.
AMOUNT GIVEN: Canadian $2,400–$3,000 per year.
CONTACT: Desired department.

University of Saskatchewan
College of Graduate Studies and Research
Saskatoon, Saskatchewan
Canada
RESTRICTIONS: Graduates of all nationalities with B.A. (honors) or equivalent from recognized university. Scholarships available in fields of agriculture, education, engineering, health sciences, humanities, physical education, science, and social sciences.
AMOUNT GIVEN: Up to Canadian $8,800 for eight months with possible addition of Canadian $4,400 for summer semester.
DEADLINE: February 1.

ANTHROPOLOGY

Academy of Korean Studies
Graduate School
50 Unjung-dong, Seongnam-si
Gyenggi-do, 130-17 Korea

RESTRICTIONS: Scholarships available to students of all nationalities who have graduated from an accredited institution. For study in fields of history, philosophy, political science, economics, sociology, anthropology, education, literature, and fine arts. Must speak English, Korean, and one other language.
AMOUNT GIVEN: Tuition, room and board, and stipend.
DEADLINE: April 30; October 30.

Trent University
Graduate Teaching/Research Assistantships
P.O. Box 4800; Graduate Studies & Research Officer
Peterborough, Ontario K9J 7B8 Canada
705-748-1245
RESTRICTIONS: Open to Master's candidates in the fields of anthropology, archaeology, biology, Canadian studies, and geography. For teaching/research assistantships at the university.
AMOUNT GIVEN: 28 awards of Canadian $2,140 per year for up to 2 years of study.

ARCHAEOLOGY

American School of Classical Studies at Athens
Fellowships
41 E. 72nd St.
New York, NY 10021
212-861-0302
RESTRICTIONS: Open to graduate students at American and Canadian universities in fields of classical studies and archaeology for study in Greece.
AMOUNT GIVEN: $4,000 + room and board.
DEADLINE: Varies.

Archaeological Institute of America
Harriet Pomerance Fellowship
675 Commonwealth Ave.
Boston, MA 02215
617-353-9361
RESTRICTIONS: Graduate fellowships to enable work on a scholarly project relating to the Aegean Bronze Age in archaeology. Preference to persons whose project requires travel to the Mediterranean. Must be U.S. or Canadian citizen.
AMOUNT GIVEN: $3,000.
DEADLINE: November 15.

Archaeological Institute of America
Olivia James Travelling Fellowship

675 Commonwealth Ave.
Boston, MA 02215
617-353-9361
RESTRICTIONS: For graduate or postgraduate study in Greece, Aegean Islands, Sicily, Southern Italy, Asia Minor or Mesopotamia. Preference for dissertation or recent Ph.D. research. Not for field excavation. Must be U.S. citizen or legal resident for study in fields of archaeology, architecture, classics, history, or sculpture.
AMOUNT GIVEN: $10,000 stipend.
DEADLINE: November 15.

La Trobe University
Registrar
ATTN: Scholarships officer
Bundoora, Victoria 3083 Australia
RESTRICTIONS: Research scholarships for master's and Ph.D. candidates. Available to students from any country holding the equivalent to a 4-year, first-class honors degree from an Australian university. Proof of significant written work required. Must be proficient in English. Renewable if progress is satisfactory.
AMOUNT GIVEN: Aus. $7,000 + possible spousal and dependents' allowance. Thesis allowance up to $800 and possible general service fee and travel allowance. 2 yrs. (master's); 4 yrs. (Ph.D.).
DEADLINE: July 31.

Trent University
Graduate Teaching/Research Assistantships
P.O. Box 4800; Graduate Studies & Research Officer
Peterborough, Ontario K9J 7B8 Canada
705-748-1245
RESTRICTIONS: Open to master's candidates in the fields of anthropology, archeology, biology, Canadian studies, and geography. For teaching/research assistantships at the university.
AMOUNT GIVEN: 28 awards of Canadian $2,140 per year for up to 2 years of study.

United Chapters of Phi Beta Kappa
Mary Isabel Sibley Fellowship
1811 Q St., NW
Washington, DC 20009
RESTRICTIONS: Postdoctoral fellowships for study in the fields of Greek language, literature, history, or archaeology open to single women ages 25–30 who have proved ability to carry on original research. Must have Ph.D. or have completed all requirements except dissertation. Must research full-time during fellowship. Tenable anywhere.
AMOUNT GIVEN: $6,000. One fellowship per year.

University of Calgary
Department of Archaeology
2920 24th Avenue NW
Calgary, Alberta T2N 1N4 Canada
RESTRICTIONS: Research Assistantships and Teaching Assistantships available to graduate students of all nationalities for study in archeology.
AMOUNT GIVEN: 33 assistantships awarded yearly.
DEADLINE: February 1.

Vergilian Society Scholarships
c/o University of Maryland; Classics Dept.
College Park, MD 20742
301-454-2510
RESTRICTIONS: For teachers and graduate students interested in classical civilization as revealed by archaeology, art, and literature in Greece and Italy.
AMOUNT GIVEN: $100–$500.
DEADLINE: February 1.

ARCHITECTURE

American Academy in Rome
Rome Prize Fellowships
101 Park Avenue
New York, NY 10017
RESTRICTIONS: Open to U.S. citizens with outstanding ability for independent research in the fields of architecture, landscape architecture, art history, and classical studies at the American Academy in Rome.
AMOUNT GIVEN: Approximately $4,600 per year + dependents' allowance.
DEADLINE: December 31.

American Institute of Architects Foundation
1735 New York Avenue NW
Washington, DC 20006
202-626-7349
RESTRICTIONS: For graduate students and undergraduate students in their final 2 years pursuing their master's degree for study at institutes in Canada and the U.S. in the field of architecture.
AMOUNT GIVEN: $500–$2,500.
DEADLINE: February 1.

Archaeological Institute of America
Olivia James Travelling Fellowship
675 Commonwealth Ave.

Boston, MA 02215
617-353-9361
RESTRICTIONS: For graduate or postgraduate study in Greece, Aegean
Islands, Sicily, Southern Italy, Asia Minor, or Mesopotamia. Preference
for dissertation or recent Ph.D. research. Not for field excavation. Must
be U.S. citizen or legal resident. For study in fields of archaeology, architecture, classics, history, or sculpture.
AMOUNT GIVEN: $10,000 stipend.
DEADLINE: November 15.

Department of Education
Headquarters Section 3
Marlborough Street
Dublin 1 Ireland
RESTRICTIONS: Postdoctoral fellowships for approved research in the
fields of science, engineering, and architecture at Irish universities or
colleges. Must be under 30 years of age.
AMOUNT GIVEN: 8,375–10,946 Irish pounds.
DEADLINE: March 31.

National Institute for Architectural Education
J. Dinkeloo Traveling Fellowships to Rome
30 W. 22nd St.
New York, NY 10010
212-924-7000
RESTRICTIONS: Traveling fellowship tenable at the American Academy in Rome in the fields of architectural design and technology. Open
to U.S. citizens who have or anticipate receiving their first professional
degree in architecture between June of the completion year and June 3
years prior.
AMOUNT GIVEN: $5,000.
DEADLINE: April 20.

National Institute for Architectural Education
Van Alen Architect Memorial Fellowship
30 W. 22nd St.
New York, NY 10010
212-924-7000
RESTRICTIONS: Design competition for travel and study abroad open
to undergraduate or master's students enrolled in an accredited archi-
tectural or engineering program in the U.S. or Canada.
AMOUNT GIVEN: Up to $6,000.
DEADLINE: April 6.

Society for the Protection of Ancient Buildings
Memorial Trusts Scholarships
37 Spital Square

London E1 6DY England
01-377-1644
RESTRICTIONS: 9-month traveling scholarship open to both undergraduate and graduate students for conservation architecture to be used in the U.K. Emphasis on practical training, traditional building, modern and traditional repairs.
AMOUNT GIVEN: 2–3 awards per year. 3,200 British pounds.
DEADLINE: December 31.

University of Adelaide
Clive E. Boyce Fellowship
Registrar
G.P.O. Box 498
Adelaide, South Australia 5001
RESTRICTIONS: Fellowships in architecture or urban and regional planning open to students of all nationalities with proper degree from a recognized university. Tenable at the University of Adelaide.
AMOUNT GIVEN: Minimum of Aus. $5,000. Awarded as available.

University of Sheffield
Registrar
Sheffield S10 2TN England
RESTRICTIONS: Awards available in the areas of arts, economics, social studies, law, and architecture. Open to graduate students of all nationalities.
AMOUNT GIVEN: 2 studentships and 1 fellowship per year.
DEADLINE: June 1.

ART HISTORY

American Academy in Rome
Rome Prize Fellowships
101 Park Avenue
New York, NY 10017
RESTRICTIONS: Open to U.S. citizens with outstanding qualifications for independent research in the fields of architecture, landscape architecture, art history, and classical studies at the American Academy in Rome.
AMOUNT GIVEN: Approximately $4,600 per year + dependents' allowance.
DEADLINE: December 31.

American College in Paris
French Nationality Scholarships
Attn: Director of Financial Aid

Office of Admission
31 Avenue Bosquet
75007 Paris, France
RESTRICTIONS: Scholarships for students of all nationalities in the fields of art history, comparative literature, computer science, European cultural studies, French studies, international affairs, international business administration, and international economics who have demonstrated English proficiency and established need.
AMOUNT GIVEN: Full tuition.
DEADLINE: July 31 or December 15.

American College in Paris
Work/Study and Tuition reductions
Attn: Director of Financial Aid
Office of Admission
31 Avenue Bosquet
75007 Paris, France
RESTRICTIONS: Scholarships for students of all nationalities in the fields of art history, comparative literature, computer science, European cultural studies, French studies, international affairs, international business administration, and international economics who have demonstrated English proficiency and established need. Must be 18 years of age.
AMOUNT GIVEN: ½ of yearly tuition.
DEADLINE: July 31 or December 15.

La Trobe University
Registrar
ATTN: Scholarships officer
Bundoora, Victoria 3083 Australia
RESTRICTIONS: Research scholarships for master's and Ph.D. candidates. Available to students from any country holding the equivalent to a 4-year first-class honors degree from an Australian university. Proof of significant written work required. Must be proficient in English. Renewable if progress is satisfactory.
AMOUNT GIVEN: Aus. $7,000 + possible spousal and dependents' allowance. Thesis allowance up to Aus. $800 and possible general service fee and travel allowance. 2 yrs. (master's); 4 yrs. (Ph.D.).
DEADLINE: July 31.

Vergilian Society Scholarships
c/o University of Maryland; Classics Dept.
College Park MD 20742
301-454-2510
RESTRICTIONS: For teachers and graduate students interested in classical civilization as revealed by archaeology, art, and literature in Greece and Italy.

AMOUNT GIVEN: $100–$500.
DEADLINE February 1.

ASIAN STUDIES

American Institute of Indian Studies
AIIS Junior Fellowships
c/o University of Chicago
1130 East 59th Street
Foster Hall, #212
Chicago, IL 60637
312-702-8638
RESTRICTIONS: Doctoral fellowships for U.S. citizens or foreign nationals in residence at American colleges and universities in the field of Indian studies who wish to complete Ph.D. requirements in India.
AMOUNT GIVEN: up to $7,000.
DEADLINE: July 1.

American Institute of Indian Studies
Short-term and Senior Research Fellowships
c/o University of Chicago
1130 East 59th Street
Foster Hall, #212
Chicago, IL 60637
312-702-8638
RESTRICTIONS: Postdoctoral fellowships in Indian studies for U.S. citizens or foreign nationals in residence at American colleges and universities. Must have Ph.D. and agree to be formally affiliated with an Indian university while in India.
AMOUNT GIVEN: 40 short-term and 50 senior awards per year. $6,000–$11,000 + travel.
DEADLINE: July 1.

American Institute of Indian Studies
AIIS Language Program
c/o University of Chicago
1130 East 59th Street
Foster Hall, #212
Chicago, IL 60637
312-702-8638
RESTRICTIONS: Undergraduate fellowships for research in languages of India. Open to students who have a minimum of 2 years or 240 hours of classroom instruction in a language of India. Must be U.S. citizen.
AMOUNT GIVEN: 12 awards per year. $3,000 + travel.
DEADLINE: January.

American Institute of Indian Studies
Professional Development Awards
c/o University of Chicago
1130 East 59th Street
Foster Hall, #212
Chicago, IL 60637
312-702-8638
RESTRICTIONS: All fields. Graduate students. For professional study in India. Must be U.S. citizen or foreign national in residence at an American college or university. Minimum of a master's degree required.
AMOUNT GIVEN: $11,000 + travel.
DEADLINE: July 1.

AUCC
Awards Division
People's Republic of China Graduate Scholarships
151 Slater Street; Enquiries Clerk
Ottawa, Ontario K1P 5N1 Canada
613-563-1236
RESTRICTIONS: Graduate scholarships and doctoral research scholarships in the field of Chinese studies open to Canadian citizens who have obtained a first degree from a recognized university. Awards tenable in China. Knowledge of Chinese language is preferred.
AMOUNT GIVEN: Tuition, accommodations, medical service.
DEADLINE: October 31.

Australian National University
Master's Degree Scholarships
Registrar
B.P.O. Box 4
Canberra ACT 2601 Australia
49-5111
RESTRICTIONS: Open to students holding a first degree with a minimum level of second-class honors (upper division) or equivalent for study in arts, Asian studies, economics, law, or science.
AMOUNT GIVEN: Aus. $7,375 per year + possible dependents' allowance. One-year duration, possibly renewable.
DEADLINE: October 31.

Chung-Ang University
Dean
International Education Department
221 Hukusk-dong, Dongjak-ku
Seoul 151 Korea
RESTRICTIONS: Teaching assistantships in the fields of English, Chinese, Japanese, French, and German languages, as well as Korean studies. Must

be 22–30 years of age, hold a B.A., have a minimum GPA of 3.0, and submit 2 letters of reference. Must be proficient in Korean.
AMOUNT GIVEN: 5–7 awards per year.
DEADLINE: September 30.

International Cultural Foundation
185 Kahe-dong, Chongro-ku
Seoul, Korea
RESTRICTIONS: Research grants available to foreign students who have an M.A. in Korean studies or who intend to major in the field in graduate school.
AMOUNT GIVEN: 1 or 2 grants per year.
DEADLINE: December.

Korea University
Office of Academic Affairs
1 Anam-dong, Sungbuk-ku
Seoul, Korea
RESTRICTIONS: Scholarships available to foreign graduate students in fields related to Korean studies. Knowledge of Korean required.
AMOUNT GIVEN: 10 awards per year.
DEADLINE: 6 months before semester begins.

School of Oriental and African Studies
J. T. Bishop Registrar
London WC1E 7HP England
01-637-2388
RESTRICTIONS: Scholarships open to master's degree students in the areas of Oriental and African studies. For study in London.
AMOUNT GIVEN: 10 awards per year. Approximately $4,600.
DEADLINE: May 1.

Taiwan Ministry of Education
Scholarships for Foreign Students
5 South Chung-Shan Road
Taipei, Taiwan
321-6375
RESTRICTIONS: Undergraduate and graduate scholarships for foreign students wishing to study in Taiwan. Must study full-time in Chinese studies.
AMOUNT GIVEN: 7,000 New Taiwan dollars.
DEADLINE: Between February 1 and April 30.

Thailand United States Educational Foundation
Fulbright Scholarship for American Nationals
127 South Sathorn Road
Bangkok 10120 Thailand

RESTRICTIONS: Available to U.S. citizens with exceptional undergraduate record. For study in the fields of business administration, economics, and Thai studies. Preference to students currently enrolled in graduate studies. Knowledge of Thai required.
AMOUNT GIVEN: $11,000–$13,000.
DEADLINE: September 15.
CONTACT: Americans Abroad Program
           IIE United National Plaza
           New York, NY 10017

ASTRONOMY

Dublin Institute for Advanced Studies
Research Scholarships
10 Burlington Road
Dublin 4 Ireland
(DUBLIN) 680748
RESTRICTIONS: Must hold a Ph.D. or equivalent in an appropriate subject. Also may be available to candidates holding an honors degree or its equivalent. For research in astronomy, Celtic studies, cosmic physics and theoretical physics at the Dublin Institute. The Dublin Institute is not a university.
AMOUNT GIVEN: 8,600–12,500 Irish pounds. 18 awards per year.
DEADLINE: March 31.

University of London
Carlo Campolin Postgraduate Scholarship
Senate House; Room 21A
Malet Street
London W1CE 7HU England
RESTRICTIONS: Awards for research in biology or astronomy offered for an approved program of research as an internal student leading to a research degree at the University of London.
AMOUNT GIVEN: Stipend + expenses.
DEADLINE: March 1.

BIOCHEMISTRY

La Trobe University
Registrar
Attn: Scholarships Officer
Bundoora, Victoria 3083 Australia

RESTRICTIONS: Research scholarships for master's and Ph.D. candidates. Available to students from any country holding the equivalent to a 4-year first-class honors degree from an Australian university. Proof of significant written work required. Must be efficient in English. Renewable if progress is satisfactory.
AMOUNT GIVEN: Aus. $7,000 + possible spousal and dependents' allowance. Thesis allowance up to $800 and possible general service fee and travel allowance. 2 yrs. (master's); 4 yrs. (Ph.D.).
DEADLINE: July 31.

Royal Society
Executive Secretary
Rosenhein Research Fellowship
6 Carlton House Terrace
London SW1Y 5AG England
RESTRICTIONS: Fellowships in biochemistry of plants and simpler forms of animal life available to students of all nationalities who have proven ability to do independent scientific research. Preference for applicants under the age of 26.
AMOUNT GIVEN: 10,670 British pounds per year.

University of Oxford
St. Cross College
Oxford OX1 3L2 England
0865-278-490
RESTRICTIONS: Supplementary award for students intending to undertake postgraduate research at Oxford University in the fields of biochemistry, chemistry, or engineering.
AMOUNT GIVEN: 700 British pounds.
DEADLINE: May 12.

BIOLOGY

Acadia University
Graduate Fellowship in Biology
Welfville NS BOP 1XO Canada
902-542-2201
RESTRICTIONS: Candidate must meet requirements for entrance to the M.S. course in biology at Acadia University. The fellow will work half-time as graduate assistant in the department and study half-time in graduate classes.
AMOUNT GIVEN: Canadian $5,000.
DEADLINE: None.
CONTACT: Dr. M. E. Peach

Entomology Society of America
4603 Calvert Road
College Park, MD 20740
301-864-1334
RESTRICTIONS: Must be enrolled at a recognized college or university in the U.S., Canada, or Mexico and have accumulated at least 30 semester hours at the time award is presented. For study in fields of entomology, biology, or related science.
AMOUNT GIVEN: $500–$1,000
DEADLINE: July 1.

Hubrecht Laboratory
International Embryological Institute
Deputy Director
Uppsalalaan 8
3584 CT Utrecht, Netherlands
RESTRICTIONS: Awards available to students of all nationalities for study in developmental biology of amphibians and mammals. Must have research experience and English proficiency. Research projects must meet with approval of Hubrecht Laboratory program.
DEADLINE: January 1; July 1.

Institut Pasteur de Tunis
Bourses Charles Nicolle
13 Place Pasteur
1002 Tunis Belvedere, Tunisia
283-022
RESTRICTIONS: Graduate awards for study in Tunisia in the fields of medicine and biology.
AMOUNT GIVEN: 2,000 Tunisian dinars.
CONTACT: Nearest Tunisian embassy for more information.

Japan Society for the Promotion of Science
Yamato Bldg. 5-3-1 Kojimachi
Chiyoda-Ku
Tokyo 102 Japan
03-263-1721
RESTRICTIONS: Pre-doctoral and postdoctoral fellowships awarded for study and research in the fields of humanities, math, physics, chemistry, and biology. Tenure for both is 2 years.
AMOUNT GIVEN: 12,300–21,400 yen per month.
DEADLINE: May and October.

Natural Sciences and Engineering Research Council of Canada
Science and Engineering Scholarships
200 Kent Street

Ottawa, Ontario K1A 1H5 Canada
613-996-2009
RESTRICTIONS: For graduate students in the fields of agriculture, biology, chemistry, computer science, engineering, food science, forestry, and geography with superior scholastic or research ability for study and research in Canada leading to Ph.D.
AMOUNT GIVEN: 60 awards per year of Canadian $17,500.
DEADLINE: December 8.

Natural Sciences and Engineering Research Council of Canada
Undergraduate Student Research Awards
200 Kent Street
Ottawa, Ontario K1A 1H5 Canada
613-996-2009
RESTRICTIONS: Open to Canadian citizens or legal residents for undergraduate research at universities or industrial labs in the fields of agriculture, biology, computer science, engineering, food science, forestry, geography, and geology to encourage students to undertake graduate studies. Tenable during summer or may be used during academic year.
AMOUNT GIVEN: Canadian $750 for a maximum of 4 months.
DEADLINE: Set by university.

Scuola Normale Superiore
Post-Graduate Scholarships for Non-Italians
Piazza dei Cavaliere 7
The Director
I-56100 Pisa, Italy
RESTRICTIONS: Scholarships for postgraduate study in the fields of humanities, history, mathematics, physics, biology and chemistry.
AMOUNT GIVEN: Tuition + 54,300 lire stipend per month.
DEADLINE: November 30.

Trent University
Graduate Teaching/Research Assistantships
P.O. Box 4800; Graduate Studies & Research Officer
Peterborough, Ontario K9J 7B8 Canada
705-748-1245
RESTRICTIONS: Open to master's candidates in the fields of anthropology, archaeology, biology, Canadian studies, and geography. For teaching/research assistantships at the university.
AMOUNT GIVEN: 28 awards of Canadian $2,140 per year for up to 2 years of study.

University of Guelph
Dean of Graduate Studies
Guelph, Ontario N1G 2WI Canada

RESTRICTIONS: Awards for postgraduate study in fields of agriculture, arts, biological science, physical sciences, social sciences, veterinary sciences. Open to students of all nationalities having graduated from a recognized university.
AMOUNT GIVEN: Canadian $2,400–$3,000 per year.
CONTACT: Desired department.

University of London
Carlo Campolin Postgraduate Scholarship
Senate House; Room 21A
Malet Street
London, W1CE 7HU England
RESTRICTIONS: Awards for research in biology or astronomy offered for an approved program of research as an internal student leading to a research degree at the University of London.
AMOUNT GIVEN: Stipend + expenses.
DEADLINE: March 1.

University of Puerto Rico
Biology Department
College of Natural Sciences
Rio Piedras Campos
Rio Piedras, Puerto Rico 00931
RESTRICTIONS: Assitantships open to undergraduate and graduate students in the field of biology. Spanish proficiency required.
DEADLINE: April 15.

University of Queensland
F. G. Meade Post-Graduate Scholarship
Academic Registrar; Scholarships Section
St. Lucia QLD 4067 Australia
617-377-3512
RESTRICTIONS: Applicants must hold the equivalent of an Australian first-class honors or master's degree. Awards renewable if satisfactory progress is made in the first year.
AMOUNT GIVEN: Aus. $12,000 per year. Scholarships for full-time graduate study in the biological sciences at the University of Queensland.
DEADLINE: October 31.

BOTANY

La Trobe University
Registrar
Attn: Scholarships Officer
Bundoora, Victoria 3083 Australia

RESTRICTIONS: Research scholarships for master's and Ph.D. candidates. Available to students from any country holding the equivalent to a 4-year, first-class honors degree from an Australian university. Proof of significant written work required. Must be efficient in English. Renewable if progress is satisfactory.
AMOUNT GIVEN: Aus. $7,000 + possible spousal and dependents allowance. Thesis allowance up to Aus. $800 and possible general service fee and travel allowance. 2 yrs. (master's); 4 yrs. (Ph.D.).
DEADLINE: July 31.

Mycological Society of America
Graduate Fellowships
c/o P.O. Box 5130; Forest Products Lab
Center for Forest Mycology Research
Madison, WI 53705
608-264-5634
RESTRICTIONS: Scholarships in the field of mycology available to Ph.D. candidates at accredited U.S. or Canadian universities. Can't be previous fellowship recipient.
AMOUNT GIVEN: $1,000.
DEADLINE: March 1.

Royal Society
Executive Secretary
Pinkering Research Fellowship
6 Carlton House Terrace
London SW1Y 5AG England
RESTRICTIONS: Fellowships in chemistry, horticulture, or botany available to students of all nationalities who have proven ability to do independent scientific research. Preference for applicants under the age of 26.
AMOUNT GIVEN: 10,670 British pounds per year.

South African Association of University Women
Bertha Stoneman Award for Botany
P.O. Box 2163
Grahamstown 6140 South Africa
0461-22818
RESTRICTIONS: Open to female graduate students for use in South Africa. Preference for (but not limited to) association members. For study in the field of botany.
AMOUNT GIVEN: 400 rand.
DEADLINE: October 31.

BUSINESS ADMINISTRATION AND MANAGEMENT

American Assembly of Collegiate Schools of Business
Doctoral Fellowship in Business Administration

605 Old Ballas Rd. #220
St. Louis, MO 63141
314-872-8481
RESTRICTIONS: Fellowships for Ph.D. candidates in the above fields who plan to pursue faculty careers at U.S. or Canadian schools of business. Awards tenable at colleges and universities accredited by AACSB. Must be Canadian or U.S. citizen.
AMOUNT GIVEN: Tuition + $10,000 stipend.
DEADLINE: January 1.

American College in Paris
French Nationality Scholarships
Attn: Director of Financial Aid
Office of Admission
31 Avenue Bosquet
75007 Paris, France
RESTRICTIONS: Scholarships for students of all nationalities in the fields of art history, comparative literature, computer science, European cultural studies, French studies, international affairs, international business administration, and international economics who have demonstrated English proficiency and established need.
AMOUNT GIVEN: Full tuition.
DEADLINE: July 31 or December 15.

American College in Paris
Work/Study and Tuition Reductions
Attn: Director of Financial Aid
Office of Admission
31 Avenue Bosquet
75007 Paris, France
RESTRICTIONS: Scholarships for students of all nationalities in the fields of art history, comparative literature, computer science, European cultural studies, French studies, international affairs, international business administration, and international economics who have demonstrated English proficiency and established need. Must be 18 years of age.
AMOUNT GIVEN: ½ of yearly tuition.
DEADLINE: July 31 or December 15.

AUCC
Awards Division
Emergency Planning Canada Research Fellowship
151 Slater St.; Enquiries Clerk
Ottawa, Ontario K1P 5N1 Canada
613-563-1236
RESTRICTIONS: For graduate research fellowships. Open to Canadian citizens or legal residents who have a first Canadian degree or equivalent. Particularly to encourage applicants in planning; geography; risk

analysis; system science; sociology; business administration; health administration to develop ongoing interest in emergency planning. Preference to Ph.D. candidates, but Master's candidates are considered.
AMOUNT GIVEN: Tuition fees + Canadian $10,810 stipend. Awards tenable for 4 years at a Canadian institution.
DEADLINE: February 1.

AUCC
Awards Division
Petro Canada, Inc. Graduate Research Program
151 Slater St., Enquiries Clerk
Ottawa, Ontario K1P 5N1 Canada
613-563-1236
RESTRICTIONS: For full-time graduate study at an accredited Canadian institution. Granted primarily on the basis of academic standing and demonstrated potential for advanced study/research. Must be Canadian citizen or legal resident.
AMOUNT GIVEN: Canadian $10,000. Possibly renewable pending satisfactory progress.
DEADLINE: February 1.

CDS International Inc.
Robert Bosch Foundation Fellowships
425 Park Ave; 27th Floor
New York, NY 10022
212-593-3004
RESTRICTIONS: 9-month fellowship in Germany involving work internships in the federal government and then in regional government or private industry, supplemented by special seminars in Berlin, Paris, and Brussels. Must be U.S. citizen with a graduate degree or equivalent professional experience in the fields of business administration, communications, economics, German studies, journalism, law, political science, and public affairs.
AMOUNT GIVEN: 3,000 Deutsche Marks per month + travel expenses.
DEADLINE: October 15.

Concordia University
Alcan Doctoral Fellowship
in Commerce and Administration
Attn: Graduate Admissions
1455 de Maisonneuve Boulevard West
Montreal, Quebec H3G 1M8 Canada
514-848-3809
RESTRICTIONS: For graduate students who are Canadian citizens or legal residents. For full-time study in Ph.D. administration program at Concordia University in business administration.

AMOUNT GIVEN: Canadian $10,000.
DEADLINE: February 1.

Concordia University
Shell Canada Ltd. Doctoral Fellowship
1455 de Maisonneuve Boulevard West
Montreal, Quebec H3G 1M8 Canada
RESTRICTIONS: Doctoral fellowship in commerce and administration open to qualified students of all nationalities. Based on academic record.
AMOUNT GIVEN: Canadian $7,500 per year.
DEADLINE: February 1.
CONTACT: Director of the graduate program to which you are applying.

De La Salle University
Admissions Director
2401 Taft Avenue
Manila, Philippines
RESTRICTIONS: Scholarships available to students of all nationalities with a secondary school diploma. English required. Must be 18–22 years of age. For study in fields of liberal arts, commerce, engineering, natural sciences, and computer science.
DEADLINE: October.

Institute of Chartered Secretaries and Administrators
16 Park Crescent
London W1N 4AH England
01-580-4741
RESTRICTIONS: Applications accepted from final year undergraduate students, graduate students, members of the institute, and others who are eligible for admission to postgraduate work at a university of polytechnic or its equivalent in the United Kingdom in the fields of law, business administration, economics, and public administration.
AMOUNT GIVEN: 2,000 British pounds.
DEADLINE: April 30.

Richard D. Irwin Foundation
1818 Ridge Road
Homewood, IL 60430
708-798-6000
RESTRICTIONS: For Ph.D. candidates in the fields of business administration or economics who have completed all coursework except dissertation. Awards tenable at U.S. and Canadian institutions. Preference given to those who plan to teach in the U.S. or Canada.
AMOUNT GIVEN: 20 awards per year of $2,000–$2,500.
DEADLINE: February 1.

Kyungpook National University
Bureau of Student Affairs
370 San Kyuk-dong, uk-gu
Daegu 635 Korea
RESTRICTIONS: Scholarships and loans available to applicants of all nationalities in the fields of humanities, social sciences, natural sciences, economics, commerce, law, engineering, agriculture, teaching, medicine, dentistry, music, and visual arts. Must have completed 12 years of schooling and 2 years of pre-medical or pre-dental courses for study in those fields.
DEADLINE: One semester prior to start of studies.

Lincoln College
Sir John Ormand Post-Graduate Scholarships
Registrar
Christchurch 252 811 New Zealand
RESTRICTIONS: Scholarships in marketing for graduate students who wish to undertake research at Lincoln College on some aspect of marketing. May be expected to teach on a limited basis.
AMOUNT GIVEN: NZ$3,000.
DEADLINE: February 1.

London Chamber of Commerce and Industry
Examinations Board (LCCIEB)
Centenary Scholarships
Marlowe House
Station Road
Sidcup, Kent DA15 7BJ England
RESTRICTIONS: Scholarships open to students of any nationality for studies in commerce or business at approved central London institutions. Overseas applicants may be asked to attend an interview in their home country. Must be at least 18 years of age.
AMOUNT GIVEN: 750 British pounds per year.
DEADLINE: December 31.

Nihon University
Dean, College of Commerce
Nihon Daigaku Shogakubu Tokubetsu Kenkyu Shougakukin
8-24, Kudan-Minami 4 Chome
Chiyoda-ku
Tokyo 102 Japan
RESTRICTIONS: Scholarships to the school of commerce available to undergraduate and graduate foreign students of all nationalities. High grades required.
AMOUNT GIVEN: up to 350,000 yen per year.
DEADLINE: May.

Thailand–United States Educational Foundation
Fulbright Scholarships for American Nationals
127 South Sathorn Road
Bangkok 10120 Thailand
RESTRICTIONS: Available to U.S. citizens with exceptional undergraduate records. For study in the fields of business administration, economics and Thai studies. Preference to students currently enrolled in graduate studies. Knowledge of Thai required.
AMOUNT GIVEN: $11,000–$13,000.
DEADLINE: September 15.
CONTACT: Americans Abroad Program
                 IIE, United Nations Plaza
                 New York, NY 10017

Tokyo Keizai University
Student Office
1-7 Minami-cho
Kokubunju City
Tokyo 185 Japan
RESTRICTIONS: Graduate and undergraduate scholarships in the fields of economics and business administration available to foreign nationals with superior scholastic merit. Must be proficient in Japanese.
AMOUNT GIVEN: 25,000 yen per month (undergraduate); 30,000 yen per month (graduate).

CHEMISTRY

Electrochemical Society
Summer Research Fellowships
10 South Main St.
Pennington, NJ 08534
609-737-7882
RESTRICTIONS: Summer Fellowships open to graduate students at accredited colleges in universities in the U.S. and Canada for research of interest to the electrochemical society and research aimed at reducing energy consumption.
AMOUNT GIVEN: $2,000–$6,000.
DEADLINE: January 15.

Japan Society for the Promotion of Science
Yamato Bldg. 5-3-1 Kojimachi
Chiyoda-ku
Tokyo 102 Japan
03-263-1721

RESTRICTIONS: Pre-doctoral and postdoctoral fellowships awarded for study and research in the fields of humanities, math, physics, chemistry, and biology. Tenure for both is 2 years.
AMOUNT GIVEN: 12,300–21,400 yen per month.
DEADLINE: May and October.

La Trobe University
Registrar
Attn: Scholarships officer
Bundoora, Victoria 3083 Australia
RESTRICTIONS: (Inorganic, analytical, organic and physical chemistry) research scholarships for master's and Ph.D. candidates. Available to students from any country holding the equivalent to a 4-year, first-class honors degree from an Australian university. Proof of significant written work required. Must be proficient in English. Renewable if progress is satisfactory.
AMOUNT GIVEN: Aus. $7,000 + possible spousal and dependents allowance. Thesis allowance up to Aus. $800 and possible general service fee and travel allowance. 2 yrs. (master's); 4 yrs. (Ph.D.).
DEADLINE: July 31.

Natural Sciences and Engineering Research Council of Canada
Science and Engineering Scholarships
200 Kent Street
Ottawa, Ontario K1A 1H5 Canada
613-996-2009
RESTRICTIONS: For graduate students in the fields of agriculture, biology, chemistry, computer science, engineering, food science, forestry, and geography with superior scholastic or research ability for study and research in Canada leading to Ph.D.
AMOUNT GIVEN: 60 awards per year of Canadian $17,500.
DEADLINE: December 8.

Pulp and Paper Research Institute
McGill University
Harold Hibbert Fellowship
Attn: Chairman, Education Committee
Montreal, Quebec
Canada
RESTRICTIONS: Fellowship in chemistry, chemical engineering, mechanical engineering in relation to the pulp and paper industry. Open to students of all nationalities who have a Ph.D. or equivalent in chemistry or physics from an approved university. Full-time study and research in department of chemistry at McGill and in the Pulp and Paper Research Institute of Canada is required.
AMOUNT GIVEN: Canadian $20,000.
DEADLINE: February 1.

Pulp and Paper Research Institute
McGill University
F. L. Mitchell Fellowship
Attn: Chairman, Education Committee
Montreal, Quebec
Canada
RESTRICTIONS: Fellowship open to applicants from the U.S. or from the Commonwealth for research in chemistry, chemical engineering, mechanical engineering in relation to the pulp and paper industry.
AMOUNT GIVEN: Canadian $11,000.
DEADLINE: February 1.

Pulp and Paper Research Institute of Canada
Fowler Fellowships; Papricorn Fellowships
570 St. John's Blvd.
Pointe Claire, Quebec H9R 3J9 Canada
514-630-4100
RESTRICTIONS: Open to graduate and postdoctorate students in mechanical engineering, chemical engineering and electrical engineering to research topics relevant to the pulp and paper industry.
AMOUNT GIVEN: Up to Canadian $20,000.
DEADLINE: February 1.

Royal Society
Executive Secretary
Pinkering Research Fellowship
6 Carlton House Terrace
London SW1Y 5AG England
RESTRICTIONS: Fellowships in chemistry, horticulture, or botany available to students of all nationalities who have proven ability to do independent scientific research. Preference for applicants under the age of 26.
AMOUNT GIVEN: 10,670 British pounds per year.

Scuola Normale Superiore
Post-Graduate Scholarships for Non-Italians
Piazza dei Cavaliere 7
The Director
I-56100 Pisa, Italy
RESTRICTIONS: Scholarships for postgraduate study in the fields of humanities, history, mathematics, physics, biology, and chemistry.
AMOUNT GIVEN: Tuition + 54,300 lire stipend per month.
DEADLINE: November 30.

University of Manchester
Institute of Science and Technology
Mohn Research Fellowships

P.O. Box 88
Manchester M60 1QD England
061-236-3311
RESTRICTIONS: Postgraduate fellowships for persons who wish to pursue research in the faculty of technology. Preference given to studies in the areas of metallurgy, materials science, and chemical engineering.
AMOUNT GIVEN: Approximately 4,000 British pounds.
DEADLINE: None.

University of Oxford—St. Cross College
Oxford OX1 3L2 England
0865-278-490
RESTRICTIONS: Supplementary award for student intending to undertake postgraduate research at Oxford University in the fields of biochemistry, chemistry, or engineering.
AMOUNT GIVEN: 700 British pounds.
DEADLINE: May 12.

CLASSICS

American Academy in Rome
Rome Prize Fellowships
101 Park Avenue
New York, NY 10017
RESTRICTIONS: Open to U.S. citizens of outstanding ability for independent research in the fields of architecture, landscape architecture, art history, and classical studies at the American Academy in Rome.
AMOUNT GIVEN: Approximately $4,600 per year + dependents' allowance.
DEADLINE: December 31.

American School of Classical Studies at Athens Fellowships
41 E. 72nd St.
New York, NY 10021
212-861-0302
RESTRICTIONS: Open to graduate students at American and Canadian universities in fields of classical studies and archaeology for study in Greece.
AMOUNT GIVEN: $4,000 + room and board.
DEADLINE: Varies.

Archaeological Institute of America
Olivia James Travelling Fellowship
675 Commonwealth Ave.

Boston, MA 02215
617-353-9361
RESTRICTIONS: For graduate or postgraduate study in Greece, Aegean Islands, Sicily, Southern Italy, Asia Minor, or Mesopotamia. Preference for dissertation or recent Ph.D. research *not* for field excavation. Must be U.S. citizen or legal resident for study in fields of archaeology, architecture, classics, history, or sculpture.
AMOUNT GIVEN: $10,000 stipend.
DEADLINE: November 15.

Rhodes University
Hugh Le May Fellowship
P.O. Box 94 Grahamstown 6140
South Africa
RESTRICTIONS: Graduate fellowships available for students qualified to pursue advanced study in philosophy, theology, classics, history, languages, politics, and law.
AMOUNT GIVEN: 2,800 rand + room and board.
DEADLINE: July 31.

United Chapters of Phi Beta Kappa
Mary Isabel Sibley Fellowship
1811 Q Street, NW
Washington, DC 20009
RESTRICTIONS: Postdoctoral fellowships for study in the fields of Greek language, literature, history, or archaeology, open to single women ages 25–30 who have proved ability to carry on original research. Must have Ph.D. or have completed all requirements except dissertation. Must research full-time during fellowship. Tenable anywhere.
AMOUNT GIVEN: $6,000. One fellowship per year.

Vergilian Society Scholarships
c/o University of Maryland; Classics Dept.
College Park MD 20742
301-454-2510
RESTRICTIONS: For teachers and graduate students interested in classical civilization as revealed by archaeology, art, and literature in Greece and Italy.
AMOUNT GIVEN: $100–$500.
DEADLINE: February 1.

COMMUNICATIONS

AUCC
Awards Division

Telecommunications Research Fellowship
151 Slater St.; Enquiries Clerk
Ottawa, Ontario K1P 5N1 Canada
613-563-1236
RESTRICTIONS: Open to master's or Ph.D. candidates for thesis research relating to engineering of broadbench communications systems. Must be Canadian citizen or legal resident.
AMOUNT GIVEN: Canadian $5,000.
DEADLINE: February 1.

AUCC
Awards Division
Teleglobe Canada
151 Slater St.; Enquiries Clerk
Ottawa, Ontario K1P 5N1 Canada
613-563-1236
RESTRICTIONS: Open to graduates of a Canadian university. Must have achieved a high level of academic excellence and exhibited superior intellectual ability and judgment. Must be a Canadian citizen or legal resident.
AMOUNT GIVEN: Canadian $7,500.
DEADLINE: February 1.

Australian Telecommunications and Electronics Research Board
P.O. Box 76
Epping NSW 2121 Australia
02-868-0459
RESTRICTIONS: Postdoctoral research fellowships open to young scientists and engineers of all nationalities. Preference for students under 30.
AMOUNT GIVEN: Aus. $55,000. 2 years of research at an approved Australian institute.
DEADLINE: July 30.

CDS International Inc.
Robert Bosch Foundation Fellowships
425 Park Ave; 27th Floor
New York, NY 10022
212-593-3004
RESTRICTIONS: 9-month fellowship in Germany involving work internships in the federal government and then in regional government or private industry, supplemented by special seminars in Berlin, Paris, and Brussels. Must be U.S. citizen with a graduate degree or equivalent professional experience in the fields of business administration, communications, economics, German studies, journalism, law, political science, and public affairs.

AMOUNT GIVEN: 3,000 Deutsche Marks per month + travel expenses.
DEADLINE: October 15.

Radio Free Europe/Radio Liberty
Summer Student Research Internship Program
1201 Connecticut Ave. NW
Washington, DC 20036
RESTRICTIONS: Open to graduate students in the fields of international communications, mass communications, collective behavior, or social psychology. For full-time research producing a publishable paper.
AMOUNT GIVEN: Daily stipend of 45 marks + living accommodations.
DEADLINE: February 14.
CONTACT: Mr. Alan Dodds.

Society for Technical Communication
Graduate Scholarships
815 15th St. NW
Washington, DC 20005
202-737-0035
RESTRICTIONS: Open to full-time undergraduate students or graduate students who are enrolled in an accredited master's or doctoral degree program for a career in any area of technical communications. Tenable at recognized colleges and universities in the U.S. and Canada.
AMOUNT GIVEN: $1,500.
DEADLINE: February 15.

COMPARATIVE LITERATURE

American College in Paris
French Nationality Scholarships
Attn: Director of Financial Aid
Office of Admission
31 Avenue Bosquet
75007 Paris, France
RESTRICTIONS: Scholarships for students of all nationalities in the fields of art history, comparative literature, computer science, European cultural studies, French studies, international affairs, international business administration, international economics who have demonstrated English proficiency and established need.
AMOUNT GIVEN: Full tuition.
DEADLINE: July 31 or December 15.

American College in Paris
Work/Study and Tuition Reductions

Attn: Director of Financial Aid
Office of Admission
31 Avenue Bosquet
75007 Paris, France
RESTRICTIONS: Scholarships for students of all nationalities in the fields of art history, comparative literature, computer science, European cultural studies, French studies, international affairs, international business administration, and international economics who have demonstrated English proficiency and established need. Must be 18 years of age.
AMOUNT GIVEN: ½ of yearly tuition.
DEADLINE: July 31 or December 15.

COMPUTER SCIENCE

American College in Paris
French Nationality Scholarships
Attn: Director of Financial Aid
Office of Admission
31 Avenue Bosquet
75007 Paris, France
RESTRICTIONS: Scholarships for students of all nationalities in the fields of art history, comparative literature, computer science, European cultural studies, French studies, international affairs, international business administration, and international economics who have demonstrated English proficiency and established need.
AMOUNT GIVEN Full tuition.
DEADLINE: July 31 or December 15.

American College in Paris
Work/Study and Tuition reductions
Attn: Director of Financial Aid
Office of Admission
31 Avenue Bosquet
75007 Paris, France
RESTRICTIONS: Scholarships for students of all nationalities, in the fields of art history, comparative literature, computer science, European cultural studies, French studies, international affairs, international business administration, international economics who have demonstrated English proficiency and established need. Must be 18 years of age.
AMOUNT GIVEN: ½ of yearly tuition.
DEADLINE: July 31 or December 15.

De La Salle University
Admissions Director

2401 Taft Avenue
Manila, Philippines
RESTRICTIONS: Scholarships available to students of all nationalities with a secondary school diploma. English required. Must be 18–22 years of age. For study in fields of liberal arts, commerce, engineering, natural sciences, and computer science.
DEADLINE: October.

La Trobe University
Registrar
ATTN: Scholarships Officer
Bundoora, Victoria 3083 Australia
RESTRICTIONS: Research scholarships for master's and Ph.D. candidates. Available to students from any country holding the equivalent of a 4-year, first-class honors degree from an Australian university. Proof of significant written work required. Must be proficient in English. Renewable if progress is satisfactory.
AMOUNT GIVEN: Aus. $7,000 + possible spousal and dependents allowance. Thesis allowance up to Aus. $800 and possible general service fee and travel allowance. 2 yrs. (master's); 4 yrs. (Ph.D.).
DEADLINE: July 31.

Natural Sciences and Engineering Research Council of Canada
Science and Engineering Scholarships
200 Kent Street
Ottawa, Ontario K1A 1H5 Canada
613-996-2009
RESTRICTIONS: For graduate students in the fields of agriculture, biology, chemistry, computer science, engineering, food science, forestry, and geography with superior scholastic or research ability for study and research in Canada leading to Ph.D.
AMOUNT GIVEN: 60 awards per year of Canadian $17,500.
DEADLINE: December 8.

Natural Sciences and Engineering Research Council of Canada
Undergraduate Student Research Awards
200 Kent Street
Ottawa, Ontario K1A 1H5 Canada
613-996-2009
RESTRICTIONS: Open to Canadian citizens or legal residents for undergraduate research at universities or industrial labs in fields of agriculture, biology, computer science, engineering, food science, forestry, geography, and geology to encourage students to undertake graduate studies. Tenable during summer or may be used during academic year.
AMOUNT GIVEN: Canadian $750 for a maximum of 4 months.
DEADLINE: Set by university.

University of New Brunswick
School of Graduate Studies and Research
P.O. Box 4400
Fredericton, New Brunswick E3B 5A3 Canada
RESTRICTIONS: Graduate assistantships and teaching assistantship in the fields of computer science, education, engineering, forestry, humanities, mathematics, physical education and recreation, science, and social sciences. Available to students of all nationalities who fulfill requirements for admission as higher degree candidates in the School of Graduate Studies and Research.
AMOUNT GIVEN: up to Canadian $12,000 per year.
DEADLINE: March 1.
CONTACT: Director of appropriate department.

DENTISTRY

British Dental Association
The Dentsply Scholarship Fund
64 Wimpole St.
London W1M 8AL England
01-935-0875
RESTRICTIONS: Scholarships to provide financial assistance toward the special education and training for a career in dentistry. U.K. citizens may study at any accredited institution in any country. Non-U.K. citizens must study at a U.K. institution.
AMOUNT GIVEN: 15 awards per year. 200–500 British pounds.
DEADLINE: May 1.

Kyungpook National University
Bureau of Student Affairs
370 San Kyuk-dong, uk-gu
Daegu 635 Korea
RESTRICTIONS: Scholarships and loans available to applicants of all nationalities in the fields of humanities, social sciences, natural sciences, economics, commerce, law, engineering, agriculture, teaching, medicine, dentistry, music, and visual arts. Must have completed 12 years of schooling and 2 years of pre-medical or pre-dental courses for study in these fields.
DEADLINE: One semester prior to start of studies.

University of Adelaide
G.O. Lawrence Scholarship
Registrar
G.P.O. Box 498
Adelaide, South Australia 5001

RESTRICTIONS: For students of all nationalities with a degree of B.D.S. or equivalent qualifications for study in dentistry at the University of Adelaide.
AMOUNT GIVEN: 1-year scholarship renewable to 2 years. Not offered yearly, but when vacancy occurs.

University of Dundee
Postgraduate Office
Dundee DD1 4HN Scotland
RESTRICTIONS: Awards available to foreign nationals in the fields of medicine, dentistry, science, law, engineering, arts, social sciences, environmental studies, and education. Applicants must have a minimum of an upper second-class honors degree or equivalent.
AMOUNT GIVEN: up to 2,860 British pounds.
DEADLINE: March 31.

University of Sheffield
Medical Research Fellowships
Attn: Registrar
Sheffield S10 2TN England
RESTRICTIONS: Awards in all branches of medicine approved by the faculty open to graduate students of all nationalities.
AMOUNT GIVEN: Varies.

ECONOMICS AND FINANCE

Academy of Korean Studies
Graduate School
50 Unjung-dong, Seongnam-si
Gyenggi-do, 130-17 Korea
RESTRICTIONS: Scholarships available to students of all nationalities who have graduated from an accredited institution. For study in fields of history, philosophy, political science, economics, sociology, anthropology, education, literature, and fine arts. Must speak English, Korean, and one other language.
AMOUNT GIVEN: Tuition, room and board, and stipend.
DEADLINE: April 30–October 30.

American College in Paris
French Nationality Scholarships
Attn: Director of Financial Aid
Office of Admission
31 Avenue Bosquet
75007 Paris, France

RESTRICTIONS: Scholarships for students of all nationalities in the fields of Art History, Comparative Literature, Computer Science, European Cultural Studies, French Studies, International Affairs, International Business Administration, International Economics who have demonstrated English proficiency and established need.
AMOUNT GIVEN: Full tuition.
DEADLINE: July 31 or December 15.

American College in Paris
Work/Study and Tuition reductions
Attn: Director of Financial Aid
Office of Admission
31 Avenue Bosquet
75007 Paris, France
RESTRICTIONS: Scholarships for students of all nationalities in the fields of art history, comparative literature, computer science, European cultural studies, French studies, international affairs, international business administration, international economics who have demonstrated English proficiency and established need. Must be 18 years of age.
AMOUNT GIVEN: ½ of yearly tuition.
DEADLINE: July 31 or December 15.

American Friends of the London School of Economics
AFLSE Scholarship Program
1025 Thomas Jefferson Street, NW
#400 East Lobby
Washington, DC 20007
202-944-3640
RESTRICTIONS: All fields. Graduate awards open to U.S. citizens or legal residents for one year of study at the London School of Economics. Preference to students who have not previously studied in Great Britain. For newly enrolled students only.
AMOUNT GIVEN: 8 scholarships per year. $2,500.
DEADLINE: March 1.

Australian National University
Master's Degree Scholarships
Registrar
G.P.O. Box 4
Canberra ACT 2601 Australia
49-5111
RESTRICTIONS: Open to students holding a first degree with a minimum level of second-class honors (upper division) or equivalent for study in arts, Asian studies, economics, law, and science.
AMOUNT GIVEN: Aus. $7,375 per year + possible dependents' allowance. 1-year duration, possibly renewable.
DEADLINE: October 31.

CDS International Inc.
Robert Bosch Foundation Fellowships
425 Park Ave; 27th Floor
New York, NY 10022
212-593-3004
RESTRICTIONS: 9-month fellowship in Germany involving work internships in the federal government and then in regional government or private industry, supplemented by special seminars in Berlin, Paris, and Brussels. Must be U.S. citizen with a graduate degree or equivalent professional experience in the fields of business administration, communications, economics, German studies, journalism, law, political science and public affairs.
AMOUNT GIVEN: 3,000 Deutsche Marks per month + travel expenses.
DEADLINE: October 15th.

European University Institute
Via de Roccettini 5
San Domenico di Fiesole
50016 Italy
0039-055-50921
RESTRICTIONS: For graduate students in the fields of political science, social sciences, law, economics, and history. Open to qualified candidates with good honors and a research project with a European dimension.
AMOUNT GIVEN: $615–$1,000 per month + travel, medical, and family allowances.
DEADLINE: November 30.

European University Institute
Jean Monnet Fellowship
Via de Roccettini 5
San Domenico di Fiesole
50016 Italy
0039-055-50921
RESTRICTIONS: Postdoctoral fellowships in the fields of political science, social sciences, law, economics and history. Recipients required to make scholarly contribution to research on Europe within one of EUI's research projects or on topics falling within the general interests of the institute. Publication of research is expected.
AMOUNT GIVEN: 25 fellowships per year of $1,400–$2,100 per month + medical and family allowances.
DEADLINE: November 30.

Institute of Chartered Secretaries and Administrators
16 Park Crescent

London W1N 4AH England
01-580-4741
RESTRICTIONS: Applications accepted for final year undergraduate students, graduate students, members of the institute, and others who are eligible for admission to postgraduate work at a university or polytechnic or its equivalent in the United Kingdom in the fields of law, business administration, economics and public administration.
AMOUNT GIVEN: 2,000 British pounds.
DEADLINE: April 30.

Richard D. Irwin Foundation
1818 Ridge Road
Homewood, IL 60430
RESTRICTIONS: For Ph.D. candidates in the fields of business administration or economics who have completed all coursework except dissertation. Awards tenable at U.S. and Canadian institutions. Preference given to those who plan to teach in the U.S. or Canada.
AMOUNT GIVEN: 20 awards per year of $2,000–$2,500.
DEADLINE: February 1.

Kyungpook National University
Bureau of Student Affairs
370 San Kyuk-dong, uk-gu
Daegu 635 Korea
RESTRICTIONS: Scholarships and loans available to applicants of all nationalities in the fields of humanities, social sciences, natural sciences, economics, commerce, law, engineering, agriculture, teaching, medicine, dentistry, music, and visual arts. Must have completed 12 years of schooling and 2 years of pre-medical or pre-dental courses for study in these fields.
DEADLINE: One semester prior to start of studies.

La Trobe University
Registrar
Attn: Scholarships Officer
Bundoora, Victoria 3083 Australia
RESTRICTIONS: Research scholarships for master's and Ph.D. candidates. Available to students from any country holding the equivalent to a 4-year, first-class honors degree from an Australian university. Proof of significant written work required. Must be proficient in English. Renewable if progress is satisfactory.
AMOUNT GIVEN: Aus. $7,000 + possible spousal and dependents' allowance. Thesis allowance up to Aus. $800 and possible general service fee and travel allowance. 2 yrs. (master's); 4 yrs. (Ph.D.).
DEADLINE: July 31.

London School of Economics and Political Science
Houghton St. Scholarships Office

London WC2A 2AE England
01-955-7163
RESTRICTIONS: Awards and prizes available to students wishing to attend the university as graduate or undergraduate students in the fields of accounting, economics, finance, and political science.
AMOUNT GIVEN: Amount varies.

Nihon University
Dean, College of Economics
Nihon Daigaku Heizaigakubu Shogakukin
8-24, Kudan-Minami 4 Chome
Chiyoda-ku
Tokyo 102 Japan
RESTRICTIONS: Scholarships by the school of economics available to undergraduate or graduate foreign students of all nationalities. High grades required.
AMOUNT GIVEN: 150,000 yen per year.
DEADLINE: April.

Svenska Handelsbanken Foundations for Social Science Research
Secretary of the Board
10328 Stockholm, Sweden
RESTRICTIONS: Graduate research grants in the fields of economics and social sciences. Area of interest must concern international payments and capital movement, domestic payments, markets and economic planning. Tenable in Sweden for up to 1 year at Swedish research institute.
AMOUNT GIVEN: Stipend + expenses.
DEADLINE: March 10.

Thailand-United States Educational Foundation
Fulbright Scholarship for American Nationals
127 South Sathorn Road
Bangkok 10120 Thailand
RESTRICTIONS: Available to U.S. citizens with exceptional undergraduate record. For study in the fields of business administration, economics, and Thai studies. Preference to students currently enrolled in graduate studies. Knowledge of Thai required.
AMOUNT GIVEN: $11,000–$13,000.
DEADLINE: September 15.
CONTACT: Americans Abroad Program
             IIE, United Nations Plaza
             New York, NY 10017

Tokyo Keizai University
Student Office
1-7 Minami-cho

Kokubunju City
Tokyo 185 Japan
RESTRICTIONS: Graduate and undergraduate scholarships in the fields of economics and business administration available to foreign nationals with superior scholastic merit. Must be proficient in Japanese.
AMOUNT GIVEN: 25,000 yen per month (undergraduate); 30,000 yen per month (graduate).

Tokyo Women's Christian University
Registrar's Office
Tokyo Joshi Daigaku
2-6-1, Zempukuji
Suginami-ku
Tokyo 167
RESTRICTIONS: Graduate scholarships in the fields of philosophy, Japanese language and literature, English and American literature, history, and math. Undergraduate scholarships available in these fields as well as sociology, economics, and psychology. Open to students of all nationalities in financial need. Must be proficient in Japanese.
AMOUNT GIVEN: Tuition + fees.

University of Cambridge—St. Johns College
Norman Laski Senior Studentship
Master; St. Johns College
Cambridge CB2 1TP England
RESTRICTIONS: Awards available to graduate students from any country for study in the fields of economics, engineering, and applied mathematics. Preference for study or research related to business or management. Must not be working for postgraduate qualification at the beginning of tenure. Must be over 23 years of age.
AMOUNT GIVEN: Up to 7,530 British pounds.
DEADLINE: March 31.

University of Sheffield
Registrar
Sheffield S10 2TN England
RESTRICTIONS: Awards available in the areas of arts, economics, social studies, law, and architecture. Open to graduate students of all nationalities.
AMOUNT GIVEN: 2 studentships and 1 fellowship per year.
DEADLINE: June 1.

University of Tasmania
Post-Graduate Course Awards
GPO Box 252 C
Hobart, Tasmania 7001 Australia

RESTRICTIONS: For graduate study at the university in the fields of educational studies, environmental studies, financial studies, fine arts, humanities, music, psychology, social science, special education, and welfare law. Open to postgraduate students from Australia and overseas who hold first- or second-class honors degree or equivalent qualifications from recognized institutions or other universities.
AMOUNT GIVEN: Aus. $7,000. Renewable for 2 years maximum or length of degree, whichever is lesser.
DEADLINE: October 31.

EDUCATION

Academy of Korean Studies
Graduate School
50 Unjung-dong, Seongnam-si
Gyenggi-do, 130-17 Korea
RESTRICTIONS: Scholarships available to students of all nationalities who have graduated from an accredited institution. For study in fields of history, philosophy, political science, economics, sociology, anthropology, education, literature, and fine arts. Must speak English, Korean, and one other language.
AMOUNT GIVEN: Tuition, room and board, and stipend.
DEADLINE: April 30–October 30.

Jewish Welfare Board
JWB Scholarship Program
Grants Coordinator
15 E. 26th St.
New York, NY 10010
212-532-4949
RESTRICTIONS: Open to U.S. and Canadian citizens of the Jewish faith. For master's degree programs only in fields of adult education, early childhood education, physical education and social work. Should have a strong desire to enter and work in the Jewish Community Center field.
AMOUNT GIVEN: $7,500. 18 awards per year.
DEADLINE: February 1.

Kyungpook National University
Bureau of Student Affairs
370 San Kyuk-dong, uk-gu
Daegu 635 Korea
RESTRICTIONS: Scholarships and loans available to applicants of all nationalities in the fields of humanities, social sciences, natural sciences, economics, commerce, law, engineering, agriculture, teaching, medi-

cine, dentistry, music, and visual arts. Must have completed 12 years of schooling and 2 years of pre-medical or pre-dental courses for study in these fields.
DEADLINE: One semester prior to start of studies.

La Trobe University
Registrar
Attn: Scholarships officer
Bundoora, Victoria 3083 Australia
RESTRICTIONS: Research scholarships for master's and Ph.D. candidates. Available to students from any country holding the equivalent to a 4-year, first-class honors degree from an Australian university. Proof of significant written work required. Must be efficient in English. Renewable if progress is satisfactory.
AMOUNT GIVEN: Aus. $7,000 + possible spousal and dependents allowance. Thesis allowance up to Aus. $800 and possible general service fee and travel allowance. 2 yrs. (master's); 4 yrs. (Ph.D.).
DEADLINE: July 31.

Murdoch University
Attn: Secretary, Board of Research and Post-Graduate Studies
Murdoch, Western Australia 6150 Australia
RESTRICTIONS: Postgraduate students of all nationalities not already holding a Ph.D. For study leading to a master's degree in the fields of applied psychology, education, or public policy.
AMOUNT GIVEN: 4 scholarships per year. Aus. $7,000 + dependents, incidentals, thesis, and fares allowances.
DEADLINE: September 30.

Social Science Research Council
Fellowships Coordinator
605 Third Ave.
New York, NY 10158
212-661-0280
RESTRICTIONS: Doctoral dissertation research fellowships for Ph.D. candidates of all nationalities at U.S. institutions or U.S. citizens or legal residents enrolled at any accredited institution in the U.S. or abroad. For research in the fields of social sciences, humanities, demography, urban planning, education.
AMOUNT GIVEN: 50–100 fellowships per year.
DEADLINE: November 1.

University of Cambridge
Hughes Hall Studentship
Senior Tutor; Hughes Hall
Cambridge CB12 EW England
02223-334893

RESTRICTIONS: Studentships are open to students who are accepted for graduate studies in the areas of medicine, law, and education at Cambridge University.
AMOUNT GIVEN: 15–20 studentships per year. 750 British pounds.
DEADLINE: July.

University of Dundee
Postgraduate Office
Dundee DD1 4HN Scotland
RESTRICTIONS: Awards available to foreign nationals in the fields of medicine, dentistry, science, law, engineering, arts, social sciences, environmental studies, and education. Applicants must have a minimum of an upper second-class honors degree or equivalent.
AMOUNT GIVEN: Up to 2,860 British pounds.
DEADLINE: March 31.

University of New Brunswick
School of Graduate Studies and Research
P.O. Box 4400
Fredericton, New Brunswick E3B 5A3 Canada
RESTRICTIONS: Graduate assistantships and teaching assistantships in the fields of computer science, education, engineering, forestry, humanities, mathematics, physical education and recreation, science, and social sciences. Available to students of all nationalities who fulfill requirements for admission as higher degree candidates in the School of Graduate Studies and Research.
AMOUNT GIVEN: Up to Canadian $12,000 per year.
DEADLINE: March 1.
CONTACT: Director of appropriate department.

University of Regina
Teaching Assistantships
Dean of Graduate Studies and Research
Regina, Saskatchewan S4S OA2 Canada
RESTRICTIONS: Teaching assistantships in education, engineering, fine arts, humanities, science, and social science available to students of all nationalities.
AMOUNT GIVEN: 35 awards of up to Canadian $3,310 per semester (limit of 2 semesters).
DEADLINE: April 1.

University of Regina
Graduate Scholarships
Dean of Graduate Studies and Research
Regina, Saskatchewan S4S OA2 Canada
RESTRICTIONS: Scholarships for graduate students accepted by the graduate faculty as fully qualified participants in the master's or Ph.D.

programs in the fields of education, fine arts, humanities, interdisciplinary sciences, science, and social science. Available to students of all nationalities.
AMOUNT GIVEN: 11 awards of up to Canadian $3,100 per semester (limit of 3 semesters).
DEADLINE: April 1.

University of Saskatchewan
College of Graduate Studies and Research
Saskatoon, Saskatchewan
Canada
RESTRICTIONS: Graduates of all nationalities with B.A. (honors) or equivalent from recognized universities. Scholarships available in fields of agriculture, education, engineering, health sciences, humanities, physical education, science, and social sciences.
AMOUNT GIVEN: Up to Canadian $8,800 for eight months with possible addition of Canadian $4,400 for summer semester.
DEADLINE: February 1.

University of Tasmania
Post-Graduate Course Awards
GPO Box 252 C
Hobart, Tasmania 7001 Australia
RESTRICTIONS: For graduate study at the university in the fields of educational studies, environmental studies, financial studies, fine arts, humanities, music, psychology, social science, special education, and welfare law. Open to postgraduate students from Australia and overseas who hold a first- or second-class honors degree or equivalent qualifications from a recognized institution or other university.
AMOUNT GIVEN: Aus. $7,000. Renewable for 2 years maximum or length of degree (whichever is lesser).
DEADLINE: October 31.

ENGINEERING

AUCC
Awards Division
Petro Canada Inc. Graduate Research Program
151 Slater St.; Enquiries Clerk
Ottawa Ontario K1P 5N1 Canada
613-563-1236
RESTRICTIONS: For Full-time graduate study at an accredited Canadian institution. Granted primarily on the basis of academic standing and demonstrated potential for advanced study/research. Must be Canadian citizen or legal resident.

AMOUNT GIVEN: Canadian $10,000. Possibly renewable pending satisfactory progress.
DEADLINE: February 1.

Canada Roads and Transportation Association
RTAC Scholarships
1765 St. Laurent Boulevard
Ottawa, Ontario K19 3V4 Canada
613-521-4052
RESTRICTIONS: To financially assist graduate students displaying high promise of future achievement in the field of transportation. Award can be used in Canada or U.S.A. Must be Canadian citizen or legal resident.
AMOUNT GIVEN: Canadian $3,000. 3 awards per year. Possibly renewable.
DEADLINE: March 1.

De La Salle University
Admissions Director
2401 Taft Avenue
Manila, Philippines
RESTRICTIONS: Scholarships available to students of all nationalities with a secondary school diploma. English required. Must be 18–22 years of age. For study in fields of liberal arts, commerce, engineering, natural sciences, and computer science.
DEADLINE: October.

Department of Education
Headquarters Section 3
Marlborough Street
Dublin 1 Ireland
RESTRICTIONS: Postdoctoral fellowships for approved research in the fields of science, engineering, and architecture at Irish universities or colleges. Must be under 30 years of age.
AMOUNT GIVEN: 8,375–10,946 Irish pounds.
DEADLINE: March 31.

Institute of Mechanical Engineers
Manville Fellowship
P.O. Box 23 Northgate Ave
Bury St. Edmunds
Suffolk IP32 6BN England
0284-63277
RESTRICTIONS: Awards for postgraduate studies or approved research in automobile engineering at the institution. Must be a member of IMECHE. Applicants should normally have received an approved engineering degree and had at least one year of acceptable training in auto engineering.

AMOUNT GIVEN: 1,000 British pounds.
DEADLINE: U.K.—January 31. Overseas—February 28.

Kyungpook National University
Bureau of Student Affairs
370 San Kyuk-dong, uk-gu
Daegu 635 Korea
RESTRICTIONS: Scholarships and loans available to applicants of all nationalities in the fields of humanities, social sciences, natural sciences, economics, commerce, law, engineering, agriculture, teaching, medicine, dentistry, music, and visual arts. Must have completed 12 years of schooling and 2 years of pre-medical or pre-dental courses for study in these fields.
DEADLINE: One semester prior to start of studies.

National Academy of Sciences
Post-Doctoral Visiting Scholar Exchange Program
2101 Constitution Ave. NW
Washington, DC 20418
202-334-2718
RESTRICTIONS: Postdoctoral grants to support research in the People's Republic of China by U.S. scholars and research in the U.S. by Chinese scholars. Open to U.S. or PRC citizens in the fields of engineering, humanities, natural sciences, and social sciences. For 1–3 month research visits only; does not support study leading to academic degree.
AMOUNT GIVEN: Amount varies.
DEADLINE: October 10.

National Institute for Architectural Education
Van Alen Architect Memorial Fellowship
30 W. 22nd St.
New York, NY 10010
212-924-7000
RESTRICTIONS: Design competition for travel and study abroad open to undergraduate or master's students enrolled in an accredited architectural or engineering program in the U.S. or Canada.
AMOUNT GIVEN: Up to $6,000.
DEADLINE: April 6.

National Research Council of Canada
Research Associateships
Research Associates Office
Ottawa, Ontario K1A 1H5 Canada
RESTRICTIONS: Open to recent Ph.D.s in natural sciences or recent M.A.s or Ph.D.s in engineering. Tenable at NRCC Laboratories throughout Canada. 2–5 years duration. Preference to Canadian citizens or legal residents.

AMOUNT GIVEN: Up to Canadian $31,423 stipend.
DEADLINE: November 30.

Natural Sciences and Engineering Research Council of Canada
200 Kent St.
Visiting Fellowships in Canadian Government Laboratories
Ottawa, Ontario K1A 1H5 Canada
RESTRICTIONS: Fellowships for research in science and engineering available to applicants of all nationalities who meet all Canadian immigration requirements. Must possess a Ph.D. from an accepted university or a master's degree with a minimum of two years of post-master's experience. Must have proven ability to successfully conduct independent research. No more than five years may have passed since applicant received his or her doctorate.
AMOUNT GIVEN: Canadian $28,992 per year + travel allowances.
DEADLINE: December 15.

Natural Sciences and Engineering Research Council of Canada
Undergraduate Student Research Awards
200 Kent Street
Ottawa, Ontario K1A 1H5 Canada
613-996-2009
RESTRICTIONS: Open to Canadian citizens or legal residents for undergraduate research at universities or industrial labs in fields of agriculture, biology, computer science, engineering, food science, forestry, geography, and geology to encourage students to undertake graduate studies. Tenable during summer or may be used during academic year.
AMOUNT GIVEN: Canadian $750 for a maximum of 4 months.
DEADLINE: Set by University

Pulp and Paper Research Institute
McGill University
Harold Hibbert Fellowship
Attn: Chairman, Education Committee
Montreal, Quebec
Canada
RESTRICTIONS: Fellowships in chemistry, chemical engineering, and mechanical engineering in relation to the pulp and paper industry. Open to students of all nationalities who have a Ph.D. or equivalent in chemistry or physics from an approved university. Full-time study and research in department of chemistry at McGill and in the Pulp and Paper Research Institute of Canada is required.
AMOUNT GIVEN: Canadian $20,000.
DEADLINE: February 1.

Pulp and Paper Research Institute
McGill University

F.L. Mitchell Fellowship
Attn: Chairman, Education Committee
Montreal, Quebec
Canada
RESTRICTIONS: Fellowship open to applicants from the U.S. or from the Commonwealth for research in chemistry, chemical engineering, mechanical engineering in relation to the pulp and paper industry.
AMOUNT GIVEN: Canadian $11,000.
DEADLINE: February 1.

Queen's University at Kingston
W.W. King Graduate Fellowships
School of Graduate Studies and Research
Kingston, Ontario
Canada
RESTRICTIONS: Fellowships in engineering for applicants of all nationalities who are candidates for the Master of Science degree.
AMOUNT GIVEN: Canadian $4,500 per year. Not renewable.
DEADLINE: March 1.

Royal Norwegian Council for Scientific and Industrial Research
P.O. Box 70 Tasen
N-0801 Oslo 8 Norway
47-2-23-76-85
RESTRICTIONS: Postdoctoral fellowships in the fields of applied sciences and engineering open to foreign scientists under the age of 36 who wish to do research work in Norway. Qualifications must be equivalent to at least a British or American Ph.D. in applied science or engineering.
AMOUNT GIVEN: 20 awards per year. 9,000 Norwegian kroner if single, 11,000 Norwegian kroner if married + expenses.
DEADLINE: March 1; September 1.

University of Aberdeen
Regent Walk
Aberdeen AB9 1FX Scotland
RESTRICTIONS: Postgraduate studentships available to applicants of all nationalities accepted at the university in the fields of social sciences, science, engineering, agriculture, forestry, divinity, law, and medicine. Must have a minimum of first-class honors degree and a TOEFL score of at least 500 or equivalent. Provision for handicapped.
AMOUNT GIVEN: 10 awards per year.
DEADLINE: July 31.

University of Alberta
Killam Scholarships
Director of Student Awards
Edmonton, Alberta T6G 2EI Canada

RESTRICTIONS: Doctoral students. All fields. All nationalities. English proficiency required.
AMOUNT GIVEN: 10 scholarships yearly.
DEADLINE: February 1.

University of Cambridge—St. Johns College
Norman Laski Senior Studentship
Master; St. Johns College
Cambridge CB2 1TP England
RESTRICTIONS: Awards available to graduate students from any country for study in the fields of economics, engineering, and applied mathematics. Preference for study or research related to business or management. Must not be working for postgraduate qualification at the beginning of tenure. Must be over 23 years of age.
AMOUNT GIVEN: Up to 7,530 British pounds.
DEADLINE: March 31.

University of Dundee
Postgraduate Office
Dundee DD1 4HN Scotland
RESTRICTIONS: Awards available to foreign nationals in the fields of medicine, dentistry, science, law, engineering, arts, social sciences, environmental studies, and education. Applicants must have a minimum of an upper second-class honors degree or equivalent.
AMOUNT GIVEN: Up to 2,860 British pounds.
DEADLINE: March 31.

University of New Brunswick
School of Graduate Studies and Research
P.O. Box 4400
Fredericton, New Brunswick E3B 5A3 Canada
RESTRICTIONS: Graduate assistantships and teaching assistantship in the fields of computer science, education, engineering, forestry, humanities, mathematics, physical education and recreation, science, and social sciences. Available to students of all nationalities who fulfill requirements for admission as higher degree candidates in the School of Graduate Studies and Research.
AMOUNT GIVEN: Up to Canadian $12,000 per year.
DEADLINE: March 1.
CONTACT: Director of appropriate department.

University of Ottawa
Merit Graduate Research Scholarships in Sciences and Engineering
Graduate Studies Scholarships
School of Graduate Studies
115 Wilbrod
Ottawa, Ontario K1N 6N5 Canada

RESTRICTIONS: Scholarships for study at the University of Ottawa in fields of sciences and engineering available to qualified applicants of all nationalities. Fluency in English or French required.
AMOUNT GIVEN: Canadian $1,000–2,000.
DEADLINE: Fall session by July 1. Winter session by December 1. Summer session by April 1.

University of Ottawa
Research Excellence Scholarships in Sciences and Engineering
School of Graduate Studies
115 Wilbrod
Ottawa, Ontario K1N 6N5 Canada
RESTRICTIONS: Scholarships for study at the University of Ottawa in fields of sciences and engineering available to qualified applicants of all nationalities. Fluency in English or French required.
AMOUNT GIVEN: Canadian $3,500 per year. Renewable for one year at Canadian $2,500.
DEADLINE: Fall session by July 1. Winter session by December 1. Summer session by April 1.

University of Ottawa
Entrance Scholarships
in Sciences and Engineering
Graduate Studies Scholarships
School of Graduate Studies
115 Wilbrod
Ottawa, Ontario K1N 6N5 Canada
RESTRICTIONS: Scholarships for study at the University of Ottawa in fields of sciences and engineering available to qualified applicants of all nationalities. Fluency in English or French required.
AMOUNT GIVEN: Canadian $1,500.
DEADLINE: Fall session by July 1. Winter session by December 1. Summer session by April 1.

University of Oxford
St. Cross College
Oxford OX1 3L2 England
0865-278-490
RESTRICTIONS: Supplementary award for student intending to undertake postgraduate research at Oxford University in the fields of biochemistry, chemistry or engineering.
AMOUNT GIVEN: 700 British pounds.
DEADLINE: May 12.

University of Regina
Teaching Assistantships

Dean of Graduate Studies and Research
Regina, Saskatchewan S4S OA2 Canada
RESTRICTIONS: Teaching assistantships in education, engineering, fine arts, humanities, science, and social science available to students from all nationalities.
AMOUNT GIVEN: 35 awards of up to Canadian $3,310 per semester (limit of 2 semesters).
DEADLINE: April 1.

University of Saskatchewan
College of Graduate Studies and Research
Saskatoon, Saskatchewan
Canada
RESTRICTIONS: Graduates of all nationalities with B.A. (honors) or equivalent from recognized university. Scholarships available in fields of agriculture, education, engineering, health sciences, humanities, physical education, science and social sciences.
AMOUNT GIVEN: Up to Canadian $8,800 for eight months with possible addition of Canadian $4,400 for summer semester.
DEADLINE: February 1.

University of Tokyo
Faculty of Engineering
Committee of the International Cooperation and Exchange
7-3-1 Hongo, Bunkyo-ku
Tokyo 113 Japan
RESTRICTIONS: Scholarships available to foreign nationals of all countries having diplomatic relations with Japan for study in the field of engineering. Must be college or university graduate under the age of 34.
AMOUNT GIVEN: 176,500 yen per month + arrival and field study allowances.
DEADLINE: March 31.

ELECTRICAL ENGINEERING

Australian Telecommunication and Electronics Research Board
P.O. Box 76
Epping NSW 2121 Australia
02-868-0459
RESTRICTIONS: Postdoctoral research fellowships open to young scientists and engineers of all nationalities. Preference for students under 30 years old.
AMOUNT GIVEN: Aus. $55,000. Two years of research at an approved Australian institution.
DEADLINE: July 30.

Electrochemical Society
Summer Research Fellowships
10 South Main St.
Pennington, NJ 08534
609-737-7882
RESTRICTIONS: Summer fellowships open to graduate students at accredited colleges or universities in the U.S. and Canada for research of interest to the electrochemical society and research aimed at reducing energy consumption.
AMOUNT GIVEN: $2,000–$6,000.
DEADLINE: January 15.

Institute of Electrical & Electronics Engineers
Charles Le Geyt Fortescue Fellowship
345 East 47th St.
New York, NY 10017
212-705-7882
RESTRICTIONS: For first-year graduate students in field of electrical engineering at recognized engineering schools in the U.S. or Canada.
AMOUNT GIVEN: $24,000.
DEADLINE: January 31.

Pulp and Paper Research Institute of Canada
Fowler Fellowships; Papricorn Fellowships
570 St. John's Blvd.
Pointe Claire, Quebec H9R 3J9 Canada
514-630-4100
RESTRICTIONS: Open to graduate and postdoctorate students in mechanical engineering, chemical engineering, and electrical engineering to research topics relevant to the pulp and paper industry.
AMOUNT GIVEN: Up to Canadian $20,000.
DEADLINE: February 1.

MECHANICAL ENGINEERING

Institution of Mechanical Engineers
Bramah Scholarship
P.O. Box 23; Northgate Avenue
Bury St. Edmonds
Suffolk IP32 6BN England
0284-63277
RESTRICTIONS: Awards for undergraduate and graduate students to study hydraulic mechanisms, particularly hydrostatic transmissions and servo mechanisms. Tenable to the institution.
AMOUNT GIVEN: 1,000 British pounds.
DEADLINE: U.K.—January 31; overseas—February 28.

Pulp and Paper Research Institute
McGill University
Harold Hibbert Fellowship
Attn: Chairman, Education Committee
Montreal, Quebec
Canada
RESTRICTIONS: Fellowship in chemistry, chemical engineering, mechanical engineering in relation to the pulp and paper industry. Open to students of all nationalities who have a Ph.D. or equivalent in chemistry or physics from an approved university. Full-time study and research in department of chemistry at McGill and in the Pulp and Paper Research Institute of Canada is required.
AMOUNT GIVEN: Canadian $20,000.
DEADLINE: February 1.

Pulp and Paper Research Institute
McGill University
F.L. Mitchell Fellowship
Attn: Chairman, Education Committee
Montreal, Quebec
Canada
RESTRICTIONS: Fellowship open to applicants from the U.S. or from the Commonwealth for research in chemistry, chemical engineering, and mechanical engineering in relation to the pulp and paper industry.
AMOUNT GIVEN: Canadian $11,000.
DEADLINE: February 1.

Pulp and Paper Research Institute of Canada
Fowler Fellowships; Papricorn Fellowships
570 St. John's Boulevard
Pointe Claire, Quebec H9R 3J9 Canada
514-630-4100
RESTRICTIONS: Open to graduate and postdoctorate students in mechanical engineering, chemical engineering and electrical engineering to research topics relevant to the pulp and paper industry.
AMOUNT GIVEN: Up to Canadian $20,000.
DEADLINE: February 1.

Queen's University at Kingston
R. Samuel Mclaughlin Teaching Fellowships
School of Graduate Studies and Research
Kingston, Ontario
Canada
RESTRICTIONS: Fellowships in mechanical engineering for applicants of all nationalities. Recipients must fulfill teaching or demonstrating duties.
AMOUNT GIVEN: Canadian $5,000 per year.
DEADLINE: March 1.

Society of Manufacturing Engineering Education Foundation
Alfred V. Bodine/SME Award
One SME Drive; P.O. Box 930
Dearborn, MI 48121
313-271-1500
RESTRICTIONS: Granted for best paper on machine tool justification and its relationship to manufacturing productivity submitted by a graduate student. Must be U.S. or Canadian citizen.
AMOUNT GIVEN: 1 student award of $5,000 per year; $1,500 and a medallion awarded to the winning student's major professor.
DEADLINE: February 1.

ENGLISH

Notre Dame Seishin University
President of the University
2-16-9 Ifukucho
Okayma 700 Japan
RESTRICTIONS: Awards available to foreign female students of all nationalities over the age of 18 for study in the fields of English language and literature, Japanese language and literature, home economics, child welfare, food and human nutrition. Must have completed 12 years of schooling and be proficient in Japanese.
AMOUNT GIVEN: 50,000 yen per month and or tuition.
DEADLINE: December 31.

Queen's University at Kingston
Gerald Row Foundation Scholarship
School of Graduate Studies and Research
Kingston, Ontario
Canada
RESTRICTIONS: English fellowship available to graduate students of all nationalities. Recipients must assist in teaching English composition.
AMOUNT GIVEN: Canadian $3,000 per year.
DEADLINE: March 1.

University of London—Bedford College
Attn: Registrar
Engham Hill
Engham, Surrey TW20 OEX England
RESTRICTIONS: Awards available to students of any nationality holding a higher degree in English or who have completed a minimum of 2 years of research towards a higher degree.
AMOUNT GIVEN: Equivalent to a British Academy Major Scholarship.

ENVIRONMENTAL DESIGN

University of Calgary
Environmental Design Scholarships
Design Graduate Assistantships
2500 University Dr.
Rm. 275 Arts Bldg.
Calgary Alberta T2N 1N4 Canada
220-5690
RESTRICTIONS: Open to graduate students who are or will be enrolled in the Department of Environmental Design at the university. Based on merit.
AMOUNT GIVEN: 10–12 scholarships of Canadian $1,000. 8 month duration. 25 assistantships of Canadian $3,232 renewable session by session.

ENVIRONMENTAL STUDIES

University of Dundee
Postgraduate Office
Dundee DD1 4HN Scotland
RESTRICTIONS: Awards available to foreign nationals in the fields of medicine, dentistry, science, law, engineering, arts, social sciences, environmental studies, and education. Applicants must have a minimum of an upper second-class honors degree or equivalent.
AMOUNT GIVEN: Up to 2,860 British pounds.
DEADLINE: March 31.

University of Tasmania
Post-Graduate Course Awards
GPO Box 252 C
Hobart, Tasmania 7001 Australia
RESTRICTIONS: For graduate study at the university in the fields of educational studies, environmental studies, financial studies, fine arts, humanities, music, psychology, social science, special education and welfare law. Open to postgraduate students from Australia and overseas who hold a first- or second-class honors degree or equivalent qualifications from a recognized institution or other university.
AMOUNT GIVEN: Aus. $7,000. Renewable for 2 years maximum or length of degree (whichever is lesser).
DEADLINE: October 31.

EUROPEAN STUDIES

American College in Paris
French Nationality Scholarships
Attn: Director of Financial Aid
Office of Admission
31 Avenue Bosquet
75007 Paris, France
RESTRICTIONS: Scholarships for students of all nationalities in the fields of art history, comparative literature, computer science, European cultural studies, French studies, international affairs, international business administration, and international economics who have demonstrated English proficiency and established need.
AMOUNT GIVEN: Full tuition.
DEADLINE: July 31 or December 15.

American College in Paris
Work/Study and Tuition reductions
Attn: Director of Financial Aid
Office of Admission
31 Avenue Bosquet
75007 Paris, France
RESTRICTIONS: Scholarships for students of all nationalities in the fields of art history, comparative literature, computer science, European cultural studies, French studies, international affairs, international business administration, and international economics who have demonstrated English proficiency and established need. Must be 18 years of age.
AMOUNT GIVEN: ½ of yearly tuition.
DEADLINE: July 31 or December 15.

American School of Classical Studies at Athens
Gennadeion Fellowships
41 E. 72nd Street
New York, NY 10021
212-861-0302
RESTRICTIONS: Open to graduate students in the fields of Byzantine and Greek studies to support work and study at the Gennadeion in Athens. Must be U.S. or Canadian citizen.
AMOUNT GIVEN: $4,000 + room and board.
DEADLINE: January 15.

Bologna Center of the Johns Hopkins University
School of Advanced International Studies
Via Belmeloroll
I-40126 Bologna, Italy
051-23-21-85678

RESTRICTIONS: For graduate students with adequate preparation in the social sciences who are interested in the problems confronting European nations and international relations. For study at Johns Hopkins Bologna Center.
AMOUNT GIVEN: 60 awards per year. Tuition + $500–$700 per month stipend.
DEADLINE: March 15.

British Federation of University Women
Theodora Bosanquet Bursary
Crosby Hall; Cheyne Walk
London SW3 5BA England
01-352-5354
RESTRICTIONS: Open to female undergraduate and graduate students who are carrying out research in the field of English literature or English history requiring use of reference libraries or other sources of information in London.
AMOUNT GIVEN: Residential fees and board for up to 6 weeks.
DEADLINE: November 23.

CDS International Inc.
Robert Bosch Foundation Fellowships
425 Park Ave; 27th Floor
New York, NY 10022
212-593-3004
RESTRICTIONS: 9-month fellowship in Germany involving work internships in the federal government and then in regional government or private industry, supplemented by special seminars in Berlin, Paris, and Brussels. Must be U.S. citizen with a graduate degree or equivalent professional experience in the fields of business administration, communications, economics, German studies, journalism, law, political science, or public affairs.
AMOUNT GIVEN: 3,000 Deutsche Marks per month + travel expenses.
DEADLINE: October 15.

Gladys Frieble Delmos Foundation
40 W. 57th Street; 27th Floor
New York, NY 10019
RESTRICTIONS: Grants are available for pre-doctoral and postdoctoral research in Venice. Must be U.S. citizen and have some experience in advanced research. Graduate students must have fulfilled all doctoral requirements except dissertation.
AMOUNT GIVEN: $500–$10,000
DEADLINE: December 15.

European University Institute
Via de Roccettini 5

San Domenico di Fiesole
50016 Italy
0039-055-50921
RESTRICTIONS: For graduate students in the fields of political science, social sciences, law, economics, and history. Open to qualified candidates with honors degree, and a research project with a European dimension.
AMOUNT GIVEN: $615–$1,000 per month + travel, medical, and family allowances.
DEADLINE: November 30.

European University Institute
Jean Monnet Fellowship
Via de Roccettini 5
San Domenico di Fiesole
50016 Italy
0039-055-50921
RESTRICTIONS: Postdoctoral fellowships in the fields of political science, social sciences, law, economics and history. Recipients required to make scholarly contribution to research on Europe within one of EUI's research projects or on topics falling within the general interests of the institute. Publication of research is expected.
AMOUNT GIVEN: 25 fellowships per year of $1,400–$2,100 per month + medical and family allowances.
DEADLINE: November 30.

Germanistic Society of America
Foreign Study Scholarships
809 U.N. Plaza
New York, NY 10017
212-984-5330
RESTRICTIONS: Must be a U.S. citizen with a bachelor's degree. For graduate study at a German university in the fields of history, international relations, language, literature, philosophy, political science, and public affairs. Selection based on promised project, language fluency, academic achievement, and references.
AMOUNT GIVEN: $6,000.
DEADLINE: October 31.

Institute für Europäisch Geschichte
Fellowship Program
Alte Universitatsstrasse 19
D-6500 Mainz; Germany
06131-26143 or 06131-24870
RESTRICTIONS: Open to Ph.D. candidates and postdoctoral applicants in European history, preferably for completion of dissertation. Also for research in German archives.

AMOUNT GIVEN: Approximately 30 awards. DM 960-Dm 1240.
DEADLINE: Open.

Istituto Italiano per gli Studi Storici
Federico Chabod and Adolfo Amodeo Scholarships
12 Via Benedetto
80134 Naples Italy
081-207704
RESTRICTIONS: For graduate students under 30 years of age for study in the field of European history at the institute.
AMOUNT GIVEN: 5,000,000 lire.
DEADLINE: October.

Queen's University of Belfast
Junior Research Fellowships
Secretary to Academic Council
Belfast BT7 INN Northern Ireland
245-133 ext. 3006
RESTRICTIONS: Fellowships for graduate students with honors degree and research experience. For 1 year of study at the university in the field of Irish studies.
AMOUNT GIVEN: 3,548 British pounds + fees.
DEADLINE: January 22.

United Chapters of Phi Beta Kappa
Mary Isabel Sibley Fellowship
1811 Q Street, NW
Washington, DC 20009
RESTRICTIONS: Postdoctoral fellowships for study in the fields of Greek language, literature, history, or archaeology, open to single women ages 25–30 who have proved ability to carry on original research. Must have Ph.D. or have completed all requirements except dissertation. Must research full-time during fellowship. Tenable anywhere.
AMOUNT GIVEN: $6,000. One fellowship per year.

University of Stockholm
International Graduate Scholarships
S-106 Stockholm, Sweden
08-16-34-66
RESTRICTIONS: One-year graduate diploma program with emphasis on Scandinavia. Open to foreign students of all nationalities who have completed an academic degree in a field of social science. Minimum of a "B" average and fluency in English required.
AMOUNT GIVEN: Tuition + $350.
DEADLINE: March 1.

FINE ARTS

Academy of Korean Studies
Graduate School
50 Unjung-dong, Seongnam-si
Gyenggi-do, 130-17 Korea
RESTRICTIONS: Scholarships available to students of all nationalities who have graduated from an accredited institution. For study in the fields of history, philosophy, political science, economics, sociology, anthropology, education, literature, and fine arts. Must speak English, Korean, and one other language.
AMOUNT GIVEN: Tuition, room and board, and stipend.
DEADLINE: April 30; October 30.

Archaeological Institute of America
Olivia James Travelling Fellowship
675 Commonwealth Avenue
Boston, MA 02215
617-353-9361
RESTRICTIONS: For graduate or postgraduate study in Greece, Aegean Islands, Sicily, Southern Italy, Asia Minor, or Mesopotamia. Preference for dissertation or recent Ph.D. research. Not for field excavation. Must be U.S. citizen or legal resident for study in the fields of archaeology, architecture, classics, history, or sculpture.
AMOUNT GIVEN: $10,000 stipend.
DEADLINE: November 15.

Banff Centre School of Fine Arts
Scholarships
P.O. Box 1020
Banff Alberta T0L 0C0 Canada
403-762-6180
RESTRICTIONS: Scholarships for study at the university for artists who have completed formal training and are pursuing studies at advanced levels. Young artists are given an opportunity to design postgraduate work programs.
AMOUNT GIVEN: 150 scholarships per year of approximately Canadian $6,000 each. Renewable for two years.
DEADLINE: March 15.

British School at Rome
Abbey Major Scholarships
c/o Regent's College
Inner Circle
Regent's Park

London NWI 4N5 England
01-935-9576
RESTRICTIONS: Open to postgraduate students who wish to work and study in the field of painting for 1 year at the British School at Rome. Must be a citizen of the U.S. or Great Britain.
AMOUNT GIVEN: Approximately 4,500 British pounds.
DEADLINE: January 15.

Foundation des Etats Unis
Harriet Hale Wolley Scholarships
15 Boulevard Jourdan
75690 Paris-Cedex 14 France
45-89-35-79
RESTRICTIONS: Art and music scholarships for U.S. citizens for graduate study in France. Must be between 21 and 30 years of age. Preference given to mature students who have already done graduate study. Must have good knowledge of French and live at Foundation des Etats Unis.
AMOUNT GIVEN: $6,000 stipend + living quarters.
DEADLINE: None.

John Simon Guggenheim Memorial Foundation
Guggenheim Fellowships
90 Park Avenue
New York, NY 10016
RESTRICTIONS: Fellowships for study in the U.S. and abroad available to applicants between 30 and 45 years of age who have demonstrated superior capacity for scholarship or creative ability in the fine arts.
AMOUNT GIVEN: Varies.
DEADLINE: October 1 of previous year.

Kyungpook National University
Bureau of Student Affairs
370 San Kyuk-dong, uk-gu
Daegu 635 Korea
RESTRICTIONS: Scholarships and loans available to applicants of all nationalities in the fields of humanities, social sciences, natural sciences, economics, commerce, law, engineering, agriculture, teaching, medicine, dentistry, music, and visual arts. Must have completed 12 years of schooling and 2 years of pre-medical or pre-dental courses for study in these fields.
DEADLINE: One semester prior to start of studies.

Nova Scotia College of Art and Design
5163 Duke St.
Halifax, Nova Scotia B3J 3J6 Canada
902-422-7381

RESTRICTIONS: Individual grants awarded to advanced graduate students during the fall and spring semesters for study at the college in the Master of Fine Arts program.
AMOUNT GIVEN: Canadian $300–$500.

University of Regina
Teaching Assistantships
Dean of Graduate Studies and Research
Regina, Saskatchewan S4S 0A2 Canada
RESTRICTIONS: Teaching assistantships in education, engineering, fine arts, humanities, science, and social science available to students from all nationalities.
AMOUNT GIVEN: 35 awards of up to Canadian $3,310 per semester (limit of 2 semesters).
DEADLINE: April 1.

University of Regina
Graduate Scholarships
Dean of Graduate Studies and Research
Regina, Saskatchewan S4S 0A2 Canada
RESTRICTIONS: Scholarships for graduate students accepted by the graduate faculty as fully qualified participants in the master's or Ph.D. programs in the fields of education, fine arts, humanities, interdisciplinary sciences, science, and social science available to students from all nationalities.
AMOUNT GIVEN: 11 awards of up to Canadian $3,100 per semester (limit of 3 semesters).
DEADLINE: April 1.

University of Tasmania
Post-Graduate Course Awards
GPO Box 252 C
Hobart, Tasmania 7001 Australia
RESTRICTIONS: For graduate study at the university in the fields of educational studies, environmental studies, financial studies, fine arts, humanities, music, psychology, social science, special education and welfare law. Open to postgraduate students from Australia and overseas who hold qualifications from a recognized institution or other university.
AMOUNT GIVEN: Aus. $7,000. Renewable for 2 years maximum or length of degree (whichever is lesser).
DEADLINE: October 31.

FOOD SCIENCE

Institute of Food Technologies
Graduate Fellowships

221 North La Salle Street, #300
Chicago, IL 60601
312-782-8424
RESTRICTIONS: Graduate fellowships to encourage and support research in food science and technology at an accredited institution in the U.S. or Canada.
AMOUNT GIVEN: 23 awards of $1,000–$10,000 per year.
DEADLINE: February 1.

Institute of Food Technologies
Undergraduate Scholarships
221 North La Salle St. #300
Chicago, IL 60601
312-782-8424
RESTRICTIONS: Open to high school graduates planning to enroll/enrolled in an accredited institution in the U.S. or Canada in fields related to food science and technology. Based on academics (minimum 2.5 average) and personality.
AMOUNT GIVEN: $500–$2,000. 30 freshman/sophomore + 52 junior/senior awards per year.
DEADLINE: February 1 (junior/senior); February 15 (freshman); March 1 (sophomore).

Natural Sciences and Engineering Research Council of Canada
Science and Engineering Scholarships
200 Kent Street
Ottawa, Ontario K1A 1H5 Canada
613-996-2009
RESTRICTIONS: For graduate students in the fields of agriculture, biology, chemistry, computer science, engineering, food science, forestry and geography with superior scholastic or research ability for study and research in Canada leading to Ph.D.
AMOUNT GIVEN: 60 awards per year of Canadian $17,500.
DEADLINE: December 8.

Natural Sciences and Engineering Research Council of Canada
Undergraduate Student Research Awards
200 Kent Street
Ottawa, Ontario K1A 1H5 Canada
613-996-2009
RESTRICTIONS: Open to Canadian citizens or legal residents for undergraduate research at universities or industrial labs in fields of agriculture, biology, computer science, engineering, food science, forestry, geography and geology to encourage students to undertake graduate studies. Tenable during summer or may be used during academic year.
AMOUNT GIVEN: Canadian $750 for a maximum of 4 months.
DEADLINE: Set by university.

Notre Dame Seishin University
President of the University
2-16-9 Ifukucho
Okayma 700 Japan
RESTRICTIONS: Awards available to female foreign students of all nationalities over the age of 18 for study in the fields of English language and literature, Japanese language and literature, home economics, child welfare, food and human nutrition. Must have completed 12 years of schooling and be proficient in Japanese.
AMOUNT GIVEN: 50,000 yen per month and/or tuition.
DEADLINE: December 31.

FORESTRY

Natural Sciences and Engineering Research Council of Canada
Science and Engineering Scholarships
200 Kent Street
Ottawa, Ontario K1A 1H5 Canada
613-996-2009
RESTRICTIONS: For graduate students in the fields of agriculture, biology, chemistry, computer science, engineering, food science, forestry and geography with superior scholastic or research ability for study and research in Canada leading to Ph.D.
AMOUNT GIVEN: 60 awards per year of Canadian $17,500.
DEADLINE: December 8.

Natural Sciences and Engineering Research Council of Canada
Undergraduate Student Research Awards
200 Kent Street
Ottawa, Ontario K1A 1H5 Canada
613-996-2009
RESTRICTIONS: Open to Canadian citizens or legal residents for undergraduate research at universities or industrial labs in fields of agriculture, biology, computer science, engineering, food science, forestry, geography, and geology to encourage students to undertake graduate studies. Tenable during summer or may be used during academic year.
AMOUNT GIVEN: Canadian $750 for a maximum of 4 months.
DEADLINE: Set by university.

University of Aberdeen
Regent Walk
Aberdeen AB9 1FX Scotland
RESTRICTIONS: Postgraduate studentships available to applicants of all nationalities accepted at the university in the fields of social sciences, science, engineering, agriculture, forestry, divinity, law, and medicine.

Must have a minimum of first-class honors degree and a TOEFL score of at least 500 or equivalent. Provisions for handicapped.
AMOUNT GIVEN: 10 awards per year.
DEADLINE: July 31.

University of New Brunswick
School of Graduate Studies and Research
P.O. Box 4400
Fredericton, New Brunswick E3B 5A3 Canada
RESTRICTIONS: Graduate assistantships and teaching assistantship in the fields of computer science, education, engineering, forestry, humanities, mathematics, physical education and recreation, science and social sciences. Available to students of all nationalities who fulfill requirements for admission as higher degree candidates in the School of Graduate Studies and Research.
AMOUNT GIVEN: Up to Canadian $12,000 per year.
DEADLINE: March 1.
CONTACT: Director of appropriate department.

GEOGRAPHY

AUCC
Awards Division
Emergency Planning Canada Research Fellowship
151 Slater St.; Enquiries Clerk
Ottawa, Ontario K1P 5N1 Canada
613-563-1236
RESTRICTIONS: For graduate research fellowships. Open to Canadian citizens or legal residents who have a first Canadian degree or equivalent. Particularly to encourage applicants in planning; geography; risk analysis; system science; sociology; business aministration; health administration to develop ongoing interest in emergency planning. Preference to Ph.D. candidates, but master's candidates are considered.
AMOUNT GIVEN: Tuition fees + Canadian $10,810 stipend. Awards tenable for 4 years at a Canadian institution.
DEADLINE: February 1.

Natural Sciences and Engineering Research Council of Canada
Science and Engineering Scholarships
200 Kent Street
Ottawa, Ontario K1A 1H5 Canada
613-996-2009
RESTRICTIONS: For graduate students in the fields of agriculture, biology, chemistry, computer science, engineering, food science, forestry

and geography with superior scholastic or research ability for study and research in Canada leading to Ph.D.
AMOUNT GIVEN: 60 awards per year of Canadian $17,500.
DEADLINE: December 8.

Natural Sciences and Engineering Research Council of Canada
Undergraduate Student Research Awards
200 Kent Street
Ottawa, Ontario K1A 1H5 Canada
613-996-2009
RESTRICTIONS: Open to Canadian citizens or legal residents for undergraduate research at universities or industrial labs in fields of agriculture, biology, computer science, engineering, food science, forestry, geography, and geology to encourage students to undertake graduate studies. Tenable during summer or may be used during academic year.
AMOUNT GIVEN: Canadian $750 for a maximum of 4 months.
DEADLINE: Set by university.

Trent University
Graduate Teaching/Research Assistantships
P.O. Box 4800; Graduate Studies & Research Officer
Peterborough, Ontario K9J 7B8 Canada
705-748-1245
RESTRICTIONS: Open to master's candidates in the fields of anthropology, archaeology, biology, Canadian studies, and geography. For teaching/research assistantships at the university.
AMOUNT GIVEN: 28 awards of Canadian $2,140 per year for up to 2 years of study.

GEOLOGY

British Federation of University Women
Johnstone & Florence Stoney Studentship
Crosby Hall; Cheyne Walk
London SW3 5BA England
01-352-5354
RESTRICTIONS: Open to members of the British and Irish Federations of University Women for postgraduate research in Australia, New Zealand, or South Africa.
AMOUNT GIVEN: Up to 3,000 British pounds.
DEADLINE: September 15.

Canadian Society of Exploration Geophysicists
206 7th Avenue, SW; Suite 501

Calgary, Alberta T2P OW7 Canada
403-262-0015
RESTRICTIONS: Scholarships available to students in an academic program leading to an exploration geophysics career in teaching, industry, or research. For study at Canadian universities or technical schools.
AMOUNT GIVEN: Approximately 35 awards per year. Canadian $1,250–1,500.
DEADLINE: June 30.
CONTACT: W. J. McCormack, Chairman.

Geological Society of America
Research Grants Program
P.O. Box 9140; 3300 Penrose Place
Boulder, CO 80301
303-447-2020
RESTRICTIONS: Open to master's and Ph.D. candidates at colleges and universities in U.S., Canada, Mexico, and Central America in the field of geology. To help support thesis research. GSA membership not required.
AMOUNT GIVEN: Approximately 200 awards per year. $500–$1,700.
DEADLINE: February 15.

Institution of Mining and Metallurgy
G. Vernon Hobson Bequest
44 Portland Place
London W1N 4BR England
01-580-3802
RESTRICTIONS: Awards for the advancement of teaching geology as applied to mining. Open to graduate students. Preference to institution members.
AMOUNT GIVEN: 1,500 British pounds.
DEADLINE: March 16.

La Trobe University
Registrar
Attn: Scholarships Officer
Bundoora, Victoria 3083 Australia
RESTRICTIONS: Research scholarships for master's and Ph.D. candidates. Available to students from any country holding the equivalent to a 4-year, first-class honors degree from an Australian university. Proof of significant written work required. Must be efficient in English. Renewable if progress is satisfactory.
AMOUNT GIVEN: Aus. $7,000 + possible spousal and dependents allowance. Thesis allowance up to Aus. $800 and possible general service fee and travel allowance. 2 years. (master's) 4 years. (Ph.D.).
DEADLINE: July 31.

Natural Sciences and Engineering Research Council of Canada
Undergraduate Student Research Awards
200 Kent Street
Ottawa, Ontario K1A 1H5 Canada
613-996-2009
RESTRICTIONS: Open to Canadian citizens or legal residents for undergraduate research at universities or industrial labs in fields of agriculture, biology, computer science, engineering, food science, forestry, geography, and geology to encourage students to undertake graduate studies. Tenable during summer or may be used during academic year.
AMOUNT GIVEN: Canadian $750 for a maximum of 4 months.
DEADLINE: Set by university.

HEALTH SCIENCES

University of Saskatchewan
College of Graduate Studies and Research
Saskatoon, Saskatchewan
Canada
RESTRICTIONS: Graduates of all nationalities with B.A. (honors) or equivalent from recognized university. Scholarships available in the fields of agriculture, education, engineering, health sciences, humanities, physical education, science, and social sciences.
AMOUNT GIVEN: Up to Canadian $8,800 for eight months with possible addition of Canadian $4,400 for summer months.
DEADLINE: February 1.

HISTORY

Academy of Korean Studies
Graduate School
50 Unjung-dong, Seongnam-si
Gyenggi-do, 130-17 Korea
RESTRICTIONS: Scholarships available to students of all nationalities who have graduated from an accredited institution. For study in fields of history, philosophy, political science, economics, sociology, anthropology, education, literature, and fine arts. Must speak English, Korean, and one other language.
AMOUNT GIVEN: Tuition, room and board, and stipend.
DEADLINE: April 30; October 30.

Archaeological Institute of America
Olivia James Travelling Fellowship

675 Commonwealth Ave.
Boston, MA 02215
617-353-9361
RESTRICTIONS: For graduate or post graduate study in Greece, Aegean Islands, Sicily, Southern Italy, Asia Minor, or Mesopotamia. Preference for dissertation or recent Ph.D. research. Not for field excavation. Must be U.S. citizen or legal resident for study in fields of archaeology, architecture, classics, history, or sculpture.
AMOUNT GIVEN: $10,000 stipend.
DEADLINE: November 15.

British Federation of University Women
Theodora Bosanquet Bursary
Crosby Hall; Cheyne Walk
London SW3 5BA England
01-352-5354
RESTRICTIONS: Open to female undergraduate and graduate students who are carrying out research in the field of English literature or English history requiring use of reference libraries or other sources of information in London.
AMOUNT GIVEN: Residential fees and board for up to 6 weeks.
DEADLINE: November 23.

European University Institute
Via de Roccettini 5
San Domenico di Fiesole
50016 Italy
0039-055-50921
RESTRICTIONS: For graduate students in the fields of political science, social sciences, law, economics, and history. Open to qualified candidates with honors degree and a research project with a European dimension.
AMOUNT GIVEN: $615–$1,000 per month + travel, medical, and family allowances.
DEADLINE: November 30.

European University Institute
Jean Monnet Fellowship
Via de Roccettini 5
San Domenico di Fiesole
50016 Italy
0039-055-50921
RESTRICTIONS: Postdoctoral fellowships in the fields of political science, social sciences, law, economics and history. Recipients required to make scholarly contribution to research on Europe within one of EUI's research projects or on topics falling within the general interests of the Institute. Publication of research is expected.

AMOUNT GIVEN: 25 fellowships per year of $1,400–$2,100 per month + medical and family allowances.
DEADLINE: November 30.

Germanistic Society of America
Foreign Study of Scholarships
809 U.N. Plaza
New York, NY 10017
212-984-5330
RESTRICTIONS: Must be a U.S. citizen with a bachelor's degree. For graduate study at a German university in the fields of history, international relations, language, literature, philosophy, political science, and public affairs. Selection based on promised project, language fluency, academic achievement, and references.
AMOUNT GIVEN: $6,000
DEADLINE: October 31.

Human Sciences Research Council Merit Bursary
Private Bag X41
Pretoria, South Africa 0001
012-28-3944
RESTRICTIONS: Open to graduate students in the fields of sociology and history. Must obtain at least 65% in the graduate exam for sociology or history. Award must be used in South Africa. Enrollment in a full-time program required.
AMOUNT GIVEN: 3,600 rand per year. 6–10 awards per year.
DEADLINE: January 15.

Institute für Europäisch Geschichte
Fellowship Program
Alte Universitätsstrasse 19
D-6500 Mainz; West Germany
06131-26143 or 06131-24870
RESTRICTIONS: Open to Ph.D. candidates and postdoctoral applicants in European history preferable for completion of dissertation. Also for research in German archives.
AMOUNT GIVEN: Approximately 30 awards. 960–1,240 Deutsche Marks.
DEADLINE: Open.

Istituto Italiano per gli Studi Storici
Federico Chabod and Adolfo Amodeo Scholarships
12 Via Benedetto
80134 Naples Italy
081-207704
RESTRICTIONS: For graduate students under 30 years of age for study in the field of European history at the institute.
AMOUNT GIVEN: 5,000,000 lire.
DEADLINE: October.

La Trobe University
Registrar
Attn: Scholarships Officer
Bundoora, Victoria 3083 Australia
RESTRICTIONS: Research scholarships for master's and Ph.D. candidates. Available to students from any country holding the equivalent to a 4-year, first-class honors degree from an Australian university. Proof of significant written work required. Must be efficient in English. Renewable if progress is satisfactory.
AMOUNT GIVEN: Aus. $7,000 + possible spousal and dependents allowance. Thesis allowance up to Aus. $800 and possible general service fee and travel allowance. 2 years. (master's); 4 years. (Ph.D.).
DEADLINE: July 31.

Ministry of Culture and Education
Huerfisenta 6
150 Reykjavik, Iceland
RESTRICTIONS: Scholarships available for study in Icelandic language, literature, and history. Open to students from countries chosen yearly or applicants of Icelandic origin from the U.S. or Canada.
AMOUNT GIVEN: Tuition, room and board.
CONTACT: Institute of International Education
              809 United Nations Plaza
              New York, NY 10017
or concurring department of applicant's country.

Rhodes University
Hugh Le May Fellowship
P.O. Box 94
Grahamstown 6140 South Africa
RESTRICTIONS: Graduate fellowships available for students qualified to pursue advanced study in philosophy, theology, classics, history, languages, politics, and law.
AMOUNT GIVEN: 2,800 rand + room and board.
DEADLINE: July 31.

Scuola Normale Superiore
Post-Graduate Scholarships for Non-Italians
Piazza dei Cavaliere 7
The Director
I-56100 Pisa, Italy
RESTRICTIONS: Scholarships for postgraduate study in the fields of humanities, history, mathematics, physics, biology and chemistry.
AMOUNT GIVEN: Tuition + 54,300 lire stipend per month.
DEADLINE: November 30.

Tokyo's Women's Christian University
Registrar's Office

Tokyo Joshi Daigaku
2-6-1, Zempukuji
Suginami-ku
Tokyo 167
RESTRICTIONS: Graduate scholarships in the fields of philosophy, Japanese language and literature, English and American literature, history, and math. Undergraduate scholarships available in these fields as well as sociology, economics, and psychology. Open to students in financial need of all nationalities. Must be proficient in Japanese.
AMOUNT GIVEN: Tuition + fees.

United Chapters of Phi Beta Kappa
Mary Isabel Sibley Fellowship
1811 Q St., NW
Washington, DC 20009
RESTRICTIONS: Postdoctoral fellowships for study in the fields of Greek language, literature, history, or archaeology open to single women ages 25–30 who have proved ability to carry on original research. Must have Ph.D. or have completed all requirements except dissertation. Must research full-time during fellowship. Tenable anywhere.
AMOUNT GIVEN: $6,000. One fellowship per year.

University of Jordan
Attn: President
Amman, Jordan
RESTRICTIONS: Awards available to female foreign students of all nationalities in the fields of Arabic language and literature, Arab and Islamic history, Middle Eastern studies for graduate and undergraduate study. Must be enrolled in a known university and have a knowledge of Arabic.
AMOUNT GIVEN: Tuition + board.
DEADLINE: August.

University of London
Warburg Institute
Frances A Yates Fellowships
Weburn Square; Head Tutor
London WC1H OAB England
01-580 9663
RESTRICTIONS: Postgraduate fellowships to study any aspect of cultural and intellectual history. Preference is given to those with special interest in the study of medieval and renaissance history, to which Dame Frances Yates contributed.
AMOUNT GIVEN: Short-term—500–1,200 British pounds. Long-term—5,000–8,500 British pounds.
DEADLINE: Early December.

HORTICULTURE

Landscape Architecture Foundation
Harriet Barnhart Wimmer Scholarship
c/o Wimmer Yamada & Associates
516 Fifth Ave.
San Diego, CA 92101
619-232-4004
RESTRICTIONS: Awarded to a female undergraduate student in her
final year of studies in landscape architecture at a university in the U.S.
or Canada who has demonstrated excellence in her design ability and
sensitivity to the environment and quality of life.
AMOUNT GIVEN: $500.
DEADLINE: April 15–May 15.

Landscape Architecture Foundation
Grace & Robert Fraser Landscape Award
4401 Connecticut Ave NW; Suite 500
Washington, DC 20008
202-628-0068
RESTRICTIONS: Awarded to graduate or postgraduate students to rec-
ognize innovative horticulture research or design as it relates to the
profession of landscape architecture.
AMOUNT GIVEN: $500.
DEADLINE: November 1.

Lincoln College
MacMillian Brown Agricultural Scholarships
Registrar
Christchurch 252 811 New Zealand
RESTRICTIONS: For graduate students studying to become Ph.D.s who
wish to research some problem bearing on agriculture or horticulture.
AMOUNT GIVEN: NZ $1,000.
DEADLINE: February 1.

Professional Plant Growers Scholarship Foundation
Carl Dietz Memorial Scholarships
P.O. Box 27517
Lansing, MI 48909
517-694-7700
RESTRICTIONS: Open to undergraduate and graduate students in hor-
ticulture with a specific interest in bedding plants. Tenable at ac-
credited universities in the U.S. and Canada.
AMOUNT GIVEN: $1,000 (undergraduate)–1,500 (graduate).
DEADLINE: May 1.

Professional Plant Growers Scholarship Foundation
Harold Bettinger Memorial Scholarship
P.O. Box 27517
Lansing, MI 48909
517-694-7700
RESTRICTIONS: Open to graduate and undergraduate horticulture majors with business and/or marketing emphasis or business and/or marketing majors with horticulture emphasis. Tenable at accredited 4 year universities or colleges in the U.S. or Canada.
AMOUNT GIVEN: $1,000.
DEADLINE: May 1.

Royal Society
Executive Secretary
Pinkering Research Fellowship
6 Carlton House Terrace
London SW1Y 5AG England
RESTRICTIONS: Fellowships in chemistry, horticulture, or botany available to students of all nationalities who have proven ability to do independent scientific research. Preference for applicants under the age of 26.
AMOUNT GIVEN: 10,670 pounds per year.

HUMANITIES

American Numismatic Society
Broadway and 156th Street
New York, NY 10032
RESTRICTIONS: Graduate fellowships for study in the U.S. and abroad in humanities or social science. Must have completed all requirements for the doctoral degree except dissertation. For dissertation research on a topic involving the use of numismatics. Applicant must have previously attended an A.N.S. summer seminar.
AMOUNT GIVEN: $3,500.
DEADLINE: March 1.

American Research Institute in Turkey
c/o University Museum 33rd and Spruce St.
Philadelphia, PA 19104
215-898-3474
RESTRICTIONS: Open to Ph.D. candidates at U.S. and Canadian institutes who have completed all coursework except dissertation. For doctoral dissertation research in Turkey in the fields of humanities and social sciences.

AMOUNT GIVEN: $1,000–$4,000.
DEADLINE: November 15.

Australian National University
Master's Degree Scholarships
Registrar
G.P.O. Box 4
Canberra ACT 2601 Australia
49-5111
RESTRICTIONS: Open to students holding a first degree with a minimum level of second-class honors (upper division) or equivalent for study in arts, Asian studies, economics, law, and science.
AMOUNT GIVEN: Aus. $7,375 per year + possible dependent's allowance. One-year duration, possibly renewable.
DEADLINE: October 31.

De La Salle University
Admissions Director
2401 Taft Avenue
Manila, Philippines
RESTRICTIONS: Scholarships available to students of all nationalities with a secondary school diploma. English required. Must be 18–22 years of age. For study in fields of liberal arts, commerce, engineering, natural sciences, and computer science.
DEADLINE: October.

Fundaco Calouste Gulbenkian
International Department
Avenida de Berna 45
Lisbon 1, Portugal
RESTRICTIONS: Postgraduate research awards in sciences and arts. Tenable in Portugal. Research project must be approved by the institution where applicant intends to study.
AMOUNT GIVEN: Maintenance awards + dependents' fees.
DEADLINE: May 31 and October 31.

Girton College Fellowships
Secretary to the Council
Cambridge CB3 OJG England
338-999
RESTRICTIONS: Research fellowships in the areas of humanities and science open to graduate students of any university. Tenable at Girton College.
AMOUNT GIVEN: Up to 9,200 British pounds per year.
DEADLINE: October 14.

Japan Society for the Promotion of Science
Yamato Bldg. 5-3-1 Kojimachi
Chiyoda-ku
Tokyo 102 Japan
03-263-1721
RESTRICTIONS: Pre-doctoral and postdoctoral fellowships awarded for study and research in the fields of humanities, math, physics, chemistry and Biology. Tenure for both is 2 years.
AMOUNT GIVEN: 12,300–21,400 yen per month.
DEADLINE: May and October.

Kyungpook National University
Bureau of Student Affairs
370 San Kyuk-dong, uk-gu
Daegu 635 Korea
RESTRICTIONS: Scholarships and loans available to applicants of all nationalities in the fields of humanities, social sciences, natural sciences, economics, commerce, law, engineering, agriculture, teaching, medicine, dentistry, music, and visual arts. Must have completed 12 years of schooling and 2 years of pre-medical or pre-dental courses for study in these fields.
DEADLINE: One semester prior to start of studies.

National Academy of Sciences
Graduate Program—Grants for Study in the PRC
2101 Constitution Ave. NW
Washington, DC 20418
202-334-2718
RESTRICTIONS: Grant support for graduate students enrolled in the social sciences or humanities to do coursework in an academic discipline at a Chinese university. Also support for dissertation and coursework. Must be U.S. citizen with proficiency in the Chinese language.
AMOUNT GIVEN: Amount varies.
DEADLINE: October 10.

National Academy of Sciences
Post-Doctoral Visiting Scholar Exchange Program
2101 Constitution Ave. NW
Washington, DC 20418
202-334-2718
RESTRICTIONS: Postdoctoral grants to support research in the People's Republic of China by U.S. scholars and research in the U.S. by Chinese scholars. Open to U.S. or PRC citizens in fields of engineering, humanities, natural sciences, and social sciences. For 1–3 month research visits only; does not support study leading to academic degree.
AMOUNT GIVEN: Amount varies.
DEADLINE: October 10.

Newberry Library
Newberry-British Academy Fellowship
  for Study in Great Britain
60 West Walton St.
Chicago, IL 60610
312-943-9090
RESTRICTIONS: Exchange fellowships open to established postdoctoral scholars, readers, and staff members of the Newberry Library for research in the humanities.
AMOUNT GIVEN: $6,000.
DEADLINE: March 1.

Queen's University at Kingston
D. W. Stewart Graduate Fellowship
School of Graduate Studies and Research
Kingston, Ontario
Canada
RESTRICTIONS: Fellowships for master's and doctoral degrees in humanities open to applicants of all nationalities who hold degrees from recognized universities.
AMOUNT GIVEN: 1-year fellowship of Canadian $6,500. Not renewable.
DEADLINE: March 1.

Royal Academy of Dramatic Art
Scholarships and Grants
62–64 Gower Street
London WC1E 6ED England
01-636-7076
RESTRICTIONS: Open to U.K. and overseas candidates. Audition and fluency in English required. Auditions held in New York and England.
AMOUNT GIVEN: Partial to full tuition.
DEADLINE: February 1.

Scuola Normale Superiore
Post-Graduate Scholarships for Non-Italians
Piazza dei Cavaliere 7
The Director
I-56100 Pisa, Italy
RESTRICTIONS: Scholarships for postgraduate study in the fields of humanities, history, mathematics, physics, biology, and chemistry.
AMOUNT GIVEN: Tuition + 54,300 lire stipend per month.
DEADLINE: November 30.

Social Science Research Council
Fellowships Coordinator
605 Third Ave.

New York, NY 10158
212-661-0280
RESTRICTIONS: Doctoral dissertation research fellowships for Ph.D. candidates of all nationalities at U.S. institutions or U.S. citizens or legal residents enrolled at any accredited institution in the U.S. or abroad. For research in the fields of social sciences, humanities, demography, urban planning, education.
AMOUNT GIVEN: 50–100 fellowships per year.
DEADLINE: November 1.

Swann Foundation
Fellowship for the Study of Caricature and Cartoon
655 Madison Avenue
New York, NY 10021
212-838-2424
RESTRICTIONS: Doctoral dissertation fellowship in caricature/cartoon open to students enrolled in a doctoral program at a university in the U.S. or Canada. Award must be used in the school year following its receipt.
AMOUNT GIVEN: $10,000.
DEADLINE: February 15.

University of Dundee
Postgraduate Office
Dundee DD1 4HN Scotland
RESTRICTIONS: Awards available to foreign nationals in the fields of medicine, dentistry, science, law, engineering, arts, social sciences, environmental studies, and education. Applicants must have a minimum of an upper second-class honors degree or equivalent.
AMOUNT GIVEN: Up to British 2,860 pounds.
DEADLINE: March 31.

University of Durham
Old Shire Hall
Durham DH1 3HP England
RESTRICTIONS: Fellowships available to senior researchers with Ph.D. standing from any country. For research in arts and social sciences.
AMOUNT GIVEN: 6,070–10,575 pounds.
DEADLINE: Announced annually.

University of Guelph
Dean of Graduate Studies
Guelph, Ontario N1G 2W1 Canada
RESTRICTIONS: Awards for postgraduate study in fields of agriculture, arts, biological sciences, physical sciences, social sciences, veterinary sciences. Open to students of all nationalities having graduated from recognized universities.

AMOUNT GIVEN: Canadian $2,400–$3,000 per year.
CONTACT: Department to which you are applying.

University of New Brunswick
School of Graduate Studies and Research
P.O. Box 4400
Fredericton, New Brunswick E3B 5A3 Canada
RESTRICTIONS: Graduate assistantships and teaching assistantships in the fields of computer science, education, engineering, forestry, humanities, mathematics, physical education and recreation, science, and social sciences. Available to students of all nationalities who fulfill requirements for admission as higher degree candidates in the School of Graduate Studies and Research.
AMOUNT GIVEN: Up to Canadian $12,000 per year.
DEADLINE: March 1.
CONTACT: Director of appropriate department.

University of Ottawa
Merit Graduate Research Scholarships
School of Graduate Studies
115 Wilbrod
Ottawa, Ontario K1N 6N5 Canada
RESTRICTIONS: Scholarships for study at the University of Ottawa in fields of humanities and social sciences available to qualified applicants of all nationalities. Fluency in English or French required.
AMOUNT GIVEN: Canadian $4,600 (masters); Canadian $6,000 (Ph.D.).
DEADLINE: Fall session by July 1. Winter session by December 1. Summer session by April 1.

University of Ottawa
Excellence Supplementary Scholarships
School of Graduate Studies
115 Wilbrod
Ottawa, Ontario K1N 6N5 Canada
RESTRICTIONS: Scholarships for study at the University of Ottawa in fields of humanities and social sciences available to qualified applicants of all nationalities. Fluency in English or French required.
AMOUNT GIVEN: Maximum of Canadian $4,500.
DEADLINE: Fall session by July 1. Winter session by December 1. Summer session by April 1st.

University of Regina
Teaching Assistantships
Dean of Graduate Studies and Research
Regina, Saskatchewan S4S 0A2 Canada

RESTRICTIONS: Teaching assistantships in education, engineering, fine arts, humanities, science, and social sciences available to students from all nationalities.
AMOUNT GIVEN: 35 awards of up to Canadian $3,310 per semester (limit of 2 semesters).
DEADLINE: April 1.

University of Regina
Graduate Scholarships
Dean of Graduate Studies and Research
Regina, Saskatchewan S4S 0A2 Canada
RESTRICTIONS: Scholarships for graduate students accepted by the graduate faculty as fully qualified participants in the master's or Ph.D. programs in the fields of education, fine arts, humanities, interdisciplinary sciences, science, and social sciences available to students of all nationalities.
AMOUNT GIVEN: 11 awards of up to Canadian $3,100 per semester (limit of 3 semesters).
DEADLINE: April 1.

University of Saskatchewan
College of Graduate Studies and Research
Saskatoon, Saskatchewan
Canada
RESTRICTIONS: Graduates of all nationalities with B.A. (honors) or equivalent from recognized university. Scholarships available in fields of agriculture, education, engineering, health sciences, humanities, physical education, science and social sciences.
AMOUNT GIVEN: Up to Canadian $8,800 for eight months with possible addition of Canadian $4,400 for summer semester.
DEADLINE: February 1.

University of Sheffield
Registrar
Sheffield S10 2TN England
RESTRICTIONS: Awards available in the areas of arts, economics, social studies, law, and architecture. Open to graduate students of all nationalities.
AMOUNT GIVEN: 2 studentships and 1 fellowship per year.
DEADLINE: June 1.

University of Tasmania
Post-Graduate Course Awards
GPO Box 252 C
Hobart, Tasmania 7001 Australia
RESTRICTIONS: For graduate study at the university in the fields of educational studies, environmental studies, financial studies, fine arts,

humanities, music, psychology, social sciences, special education, and welfare law. Open to postgraduate students from Australia and overseas who hold a first- or second-class honors degree or equivalent qualifications from a recognized institution or other university.
AMOUNT GIVEN: Aus. $7,000. Renewable for 2 years maximum or length of degree (whichever is lesser).
DEADLINE: October 31.

INDUSTRIAL DESIGN

Victoria College
Prahen Faculty of Art and Design
142 High Street
Prahen, Victoria 381 Australia
Attn: Lecturer in Charge, Industrial Design
RESTRICTIONS: For undergraduate students of all nationalities for study leading to a diploma of art and design in industrial design or a B.A. in industrial design or graphic design, with minors in exhibition, furniture, and work environments. Interview, folio, and possible entry tests required. Arrangements available for handicapped students.
AMOUNT GIVEN: 16 awards per year for 3 years for diploma of art and design and 4 years for B.A.
DEADLINE: November 30.
APPLICATIONS: Written inquiry for interview.

INTERNATIONAL RELATIONS

American College in Paris
French Nationality Scholarships
Attn: Director of Financial Aid
Office of Admission
31 Avenue Bosquet
75007 Paris, France
RESTRICTIONS: Scholarships for students of all nationalities in the fields of art history, comparative literature, computer science, European cultural studies, French studies, international affairs, international business administration, international economics who have demonstrated English proficiency and established need.
AMOUNT GIVEN: Full tuition.
DEADLINE: July 31 or December 15.

American College in Paris
Work/Study and Tuition Reductions

Attn: Director of Financial Aid
Office of Admission
31 Avenue Bosquet
75007 Paris, France
RESTRICTIONS: Scholarships for students of all nationalities in the fields of art history, comparative literature, computer science, European cultural studies, French studies, international affairs, international business administration, international economics who have demonstrated English proficiency and established need. Must be 18 years of age.
AMOUNT GIVEN: ½ of yearly tuition.
DEADLINE: July 31 or December 15.

Bologna Center of the Johns Hopkins University
School of Advanced International Studies
Via Belmeloroll
I-40126 Bologna, Italy
051-23-21-85678
RESTRICTIONS: For graduate students with adequate preparation in the social sciences who are interested in the problems confronting European nations and international relations. For study at Johns Hopkins Bologna Center.
AMOUNT GIVEN: 60 awards per year. Tuition + $500–$700 per month stipend.
DEADLINE: March 15.

Germanistic Society of America
Foreign Study Scholarships
809 U.N. Plaza
New York, NY 10017
212-984-5330
RESTRICTIONS: Must be a U.S. citizen with a bachelor's degree. For graduate study at a German university in the fields of history, international relations, language, literature, philosophy, political science, and public affairs. Selection based on promised project, language fluency, academic achievement, and references.
AMOUNT GIVEN: $6,000.
DEADLINE: October 31.

Graduate Institute of International Studies
132 Rue de Lausanne
P.O. Box 36 1211 Geneva 21 Switzerland
31-17-30
RESTRICTIONS: Open to graduate students in the field of international relations. Must have solid background in discipline of specialization and sufficient knowledge of French and English.
AMOUNT GIVEN: 350 Swiss francs per month.
DEADLINE: June 1.

International Peace Research Institute, Oslo
Fuglehaugsgt 11
0260 Oslo 2 Norway
RESTRICTIONS: Awards available to postgraduate researchers of all nationalities in the field of peace research. Must be proficient in English.
AMOUNT GIVEN: 8,000 Norwegian kroner per month.
CONTACT: Tor Andreas Gitlesen, Adm. Director.

International University of Japan
I.U.J. Scholarships
Yamato-machi, Minamiuonuma-gun
Niigata-ken 949-72 Japan
RESTRICTIONS: All nationalities. Graduate students in the field of International Relations. Master's candidates must show proof of completion of at least 16 years of schooling. Must be proficient in English (TOEFL score of 550 acceptable). Preference for unmarried students.
AMOUNT GIVEN: Scholarship for 1 academic year. Renewable.

University of Manitoba
J. W. Dafoe Graduate Fellowship
Financial Aid and Awards
Winnipeg, Manitoba R3T 2N2 Canada
204-474-9836
RESTRICTIONS: For graduate students of all nationalities planning to earn a higher degree in international studies. Must have B.A. honors degree or equivalent and fluent English.
DEADLINE: February 15.

JAPANESE STUDIES

Japan Foundation
Japan Foundation Fellowships
Park Building 3–6 Kioi-cho, Chiyodo-ku
Tokyo 102 Japan
RESTRICTIONS: Awards available to students from nations having diplomatic relations with Japan. For studies in all fields relating to Japanese studies (except natural science). Knowledge of Japanese required.
AMOUNT GIVEN: Approximately 190 fellowships.
CONTACT: Japan Foundation, New York office.

Notre Dame Seishin University
President of the University
2-16-9 Ifukucho
Okayma 700 Japan

RESTRICTIONS: Awards available to foreign female students of all nationalities over the age of 18 for study in the fields of English language and literature, Japanese language and literature, home economics, child welfare, food and human nutrition. Must have completed 12 years of schooling and be proficient in Japanese.
AMOUNT GIVEN: 50,000 yen per month and/or tuition.
DEADLINE: December 31.

Tokyo Women's Christian University
Registrar's Office
Tokyo Joshi Daigaku
2-6-1, Zempukuju
Suginami-ku
Tokyo 167 Japan
RESTRICTIONS: Graduate scholarships in the fields of philosophy, Japanese language and literature, English and American literature, history, and math. Undergraduate scholarships available in these fields as well as sociology, economics, and psychology. Open to students in financial need of all nationalities. Must be proficient in Japanese.
AMOUNT GIVEN: Tuition + fees.

JOURNALISM

CDS International Inc.
Robert Bosch Foundation Fellowships
425 Park Ave; 27th Floor
New York, NY 10022
212-593-3004
RESTRICTIONS: 9-month fellowship in Germany involving work internships in the federal government and then in regional government or private industry, supplemented by special seminars in Berlin, Paris, and Brussels. Must be U.S. citizen with a graduate degree or equivalent professional experience in the fields of business administration, communications, economics, German studies, journalism, law, political science and public affairs.
AMOUNT GIVEN: 3,000 Deutsche Marks per month + travel expenses.
DEADLINE: October 15.

Inter American Press Association
Scholarships for Study in Latin America and the West Indies
2911 NW 39th St.
Miami, FL 33142
305-634-2465

RESTRICTIONS: For young journalists and graduate students (ages 21–35). Must be U.S./Canadian citizen.
AMOUNT GIVEN: 1 academic year of study/research in a Latin American or West Indian country. Fluency in the country's language is required.
DEADLINE: August 1.

National Federation of Press Women Inc.
Helen Malloch Scholarship
P.O. Box 99
1105 Main St.
Blue Springs, MO 64015
816-229-1666
RESTRICTIONS: For undergraduate juniors and seniors or graduate students majoring in journalism at an accredited university in the U.S. or Canada.
AMOUNT GIVEN: $1,000.
DEADLINE: April 15.

LANGUAGES

American Institute of Indian Studies
AIIS Language Program.
c/o University of Chicago
1130 East 59th St.
Foster Hall #212
Chicago, IL 60637
312-702-8638
RESTRICTIONS: Undergraduate fellowships for research in languages of India open to students who have a minimum of 2 years or 240 hours of classroom instruction in a language of India. Must be U.S. citizen.
AMOUNT GIVEN: 12 awards per year. $3,000 + travel.
DEADLINE: January.

Chung-Ang University
Dean
International Education Department
221 Hukusk-dong, Dongjak-ku
Seoul 151 Korea
RESTRICTIONS: Teaching assistantships in the fields of English, Chinese, Japanese, French and German languages and Korean studies. Must be 22–30 years of age, hold a B.A., and have a minimum GPA of 3.0 and two letters of reference. Must be proficient in Korean.
AMOUNT GIVEN: 5–7 awards per year.
DEADLINE: September 30.

Germanistic Society of America
Foreign Study Scholarships
809 U.N. Plaza
New York, NY 10017
212-984-5330
RESTRICTIONS: Must be a U.S. citizen with a bachelor's degree. For graduate study at a German university in the fields of history, international relations, language, literature, philosophy, political science, and public affairs. Selection based on promised project, language fluency, academic achievement, and references.
AMOUNT GIVEN: $6,000
DEADLINE: October 31.

La Trobe University
Registrar
ATTN: Scholarship officer
Bundoora, Victoria 3083 Australia
RESTRICTIONS: (French, Italian, Spanish) research scholarships for master's and Ph.D. candidates. Available to students from any country holding the equivalent of a 4-year, first-class honors degree from an Australian university. Proof of significant written work required. Must be efficient in English. Renewable if progress is satisfactory.
AMOUNT GIVEN: Aus. $7,000 + possible spousal and dependents allowance. Thesis allowance up to Aus. $800 and possible general service fee and travel allowance. 2 years (master's) 4 years (Ph.D.).
DEADLINE: July 31.

Ministry of Culture and Education
Huerfisenta 6
150 Reykjavik, Iceland
RESTRICTIONS: Scholarships available for study in Icelandic language, literature, and history. Open to students from countries chosen yearly or applicants of Icelandic origin from the U.S. or Canada.
AMOUNT GIVEN: Tuition, room and board.
CONTACT: Institute of International Education
            809 United Nations Plaza
            New York, NY 10017
or concurring department of applicant's country.

Ministry of Education
Scholarship Centre
Pohoisvant 4 A 4
00170 Helsinki 17 Finland
RESTRICTIONS: Scholarships open to undergraduate and postgraduate students of all nationalities for studies in the Finnish language and related subjects at Finnish Universities.

AMOUNT GIVEN: 2,200 Finnish Markka per-month (4–9 months).
DEADLINE: March 1.

Norwich Jubilee Esperanto Foundation
37 Granville Court
Oxford OX3 OHS England
0865-245509
RESTRICTIONS: Scholarships for anyone to travel to the U.K. to improve their use of Esperanto. Candidates should be competent in the use of the language.
AMOUNT GIVEN: Maximum of 25 awards per year. Up to 1,000 British pounds.
DEADLINE: None.

Notre Dame Seishin University
President of the University
2-16-9 Ifukucho
Okayma 700 Japan
RESTRICTIONS: Awards available to female foreign students of all nationalities over the age of 18 for study in the fields of English language and literature, Japanese language and literature, home economics, child welfare, food and human nutrition. Must have completed 12 years of schooling and be proficient in Japanese.
AMOUNT GIVEN: 50,000 yen per month and or tuition.
DEADLINE: December 31.

Reitaku University
Dean of Students
2-1-1, Hikarigaoka
Kashiwa City
Chiba-pref 277 Japan
RESTRICTIONS: Scholarships available to foreign students of any nationality applying to the university for study of Japanese. Must be over 18 years of age.
AMOUNT GIVEN: 400,000–700,000 yen per year + tuition, room and board.
DEADLINE: November.

Rhodes University
Hugh Le May Fellowship
P.O. Box 94
Grahamstown 6140 South Africa
RESTRICTIONS: Graduate fellowships available for students qualified to pursue advanced study in philosophy, theology, classics history, languages, politics, and law.
AMOUNT GIVEN: 2,800 rand + room and board.
DEADLINE: July 31.

Tokyo Women's Christian University
Registrar's Office
Tokyo Joshi Daigaku
2-6-1, Zempukuji
Suginami-ku
Tokyo 167
RESTRICTIONS: Graduate scholarships in the fields of philosophy, Japanese language and literature, English and American literature, history, and math. Undergraduate scholarships available in these fields as well as sociology, economics, and psychology. Open to students in financial need of all nationalities. Must be proficient in Japanese.
AMOUNT GIVEN: Tuition + fees.

United Chapters of Phi Beta Kappa
Mary Isabel Sibley Fellowship
1811 Q St., NW
Washington, DC 20009
RESTRICTIONS: Postdoctoral fellowships for study in the fields of Greek language, literature, history, or archaeology open to single women ages 25–30 who have proved ability to carry on original research. Must have Ph.D. or have completed all requirements except dissertation. Must research full-time during fellowship. Tenable anywhere.
AMOUNT GIVEN: $6,000. One fellowship per year.

University of Aberdeen
Clerk to the Faculty of Divinity
University Office
Regent Walk
Aberdeen AB9 1FX Scotland
RESTRICTIONS: Scholarships open to applicants of all nationalities with an honors degree in Hebrew or a Semitic language for study at the University.
AMOUNT GIVEN: Standard research council rates.

University of Jordan
Attn: President
Amman, Jordan
RESTRICTIONS: Awards available to foreign female students of all nationalities in the fields of Arabic language and literature, Arab and Islamic history and Middle Eastern studies for graduate and undergraduate study. Must be enrolled in a known university and have a knowledge of Arabic.
AMOUNT GIVEN: Tuition + board.
DEADLINE: August.

LAW

Australian National University
Master's Degree Scholarships
Registrar
G.P.O. Box 4
Canberra ACT 2601 Australia
49-5111
RESTRICTIONS: Open to students holding a first degree with a minimum level of second-class honors (upper division) or equivalent for study in arts, Asian studies, economics, law and science.
AMOUNT GIVEN: Aus. $7375 per year + possible dependents' allowance. 1-year duration, possibly renewable.
DEADLINE: October 31.

CDS International Inc.
Robert Bosch Foundation Fellowships
425 Park Ave; 27th Floor
New York, NY 10022
212-593-3004
RESTRICTIONS: 9-month fellowship in Germany involving work internships in the federal government and then in regional government or private industry, supplemented by special seminars in Berlin, Paris, and Brussels. Must be U.S. citizen with a graduate degree or equivalent professional experience in the fields of business administration, communications, economics, German studies, journalism, law, political science, and public affairs.
AMOUNT GIVEN: 3,000 Deutsche Marks per month + travel expenses.
DEADLINE: October 15.

European University Institute
Via de Roccettini 5
San Domenico di Fiesole
50016 Italy
0039-055-50921
RESTRICTIONS: For graduate students in the fields of political science, social sciences, law, economics, and history. Open to qualified candidates with honors degree and a research project with a European dimension.
AMOUNT GIVEN: $615–$1,000 per month + travel, medical, and family allowances.
DEADLINE: November 30.

European University Institute
Jean Monnet Fellowship

Via de Roccettini 5
San Domenico di Fiesole
50016 Italy
0039-055-50921
RESTRICTIONS: Postdoctoral fellowships in the fields of political science, social sciences, law, economics, and history. Recipients required to make scholarly contribution to research on Europe within one of EUI's research projects or on topics falling within the general interests of the Institute. Publication of research is expected.
AMOUNT GIVEN: 25 fellowships per year of $1400–$2100 per month + medical and family allowances.
DEADLINE: November 30.

Institute of Chartered Secretaries and Administrators
16 Park Crescent
London W1N 4AH England
01-580-4741
RESTRICTIONS: Applications accepted for final year undergraduate students, graduate students, members of the institute, and others who are eligible for admission to postgraduate work at a university or polytechnic or its equivalent in the United Kingdom in the fields of law, business administration, economics, and public administration.
AMOUNT GIVEN: 2,000 British pounds.
DEADLINE: April 30.

Kyungpook National University
Bureau of Student Affairs
370 San Kyuk-gong, uk-gu
Daegu 635 Korea
RESTRICTIONS: Scholarships and loans available to applicants of all nationalities in the fields of humanities, social sciences, natural sciences, economics, commerce, law, engineering, agriculture, teaching, medicine, dentistry, music, and visual arts. Must have completed 12 years of schooling and 2 years of pre-medical or pre-dental courses for study in these fields.
DEADLINE: One semester prior to start of studies.

La Trobe University
Registrar
Attn:. Scholarships Officer
Bundoora, Victoria 3083 Australia
RESTRICTIONS: Research scholarships for master's and Ph.D. candidates. Available to students from any country holding the equivalent to a 4-year, first-class honors degree from an Australian university. Proof of significant written work required. Must be efficient in English. Renewable if progress is satisfactory.

AMOUNT GIVEN: Aus $7,000 + possible spousal and dependents allowance. Thesis allowance up to Aus. $800 and possible general service fee and travel allowance. 2 years (master's); 4 years (Ph.D.).
DEADLINE: July 31.

London School of Economics and Political Science
Houghton St. Scholarships Office
London WC2A England
01-955-7163
RESTRICTIONS: Open to graduate students who wish to undertake either contemporary or historical research at the school in a socio-legal area of law.
AMOUNT GIVEN: Varies.
DEADLINE: September 1.

Rhodes University
Hugh Le May Fellowship
P.O. Box 94
Grahamstown 6140 South Africa
RESTRICTIONS: Graduate fellowships available for students qualified to pursue advanced study in philosophy, theology, classics, history, languages, politics, and law.
AMOUNT GIVEN: 2,800 rand + room and board.
DEADLINE: July 31.

University of Aberdeen
C. B. Davidson Scholarships
Clerk to the Faculty of Law
University Office
Regent Walk
Aberdeen AB 9 1FX Scotland
RESTRICTIONS: Scholarships in comparative law available to applicants of all nationalities with an honors degree in law.
AMOUNT GIVEN: Standard research council rates.

University of Aberdeen
Regent Walk
Aberdeen AB9 1FX Scotland
RESTRICTIONS: Postgraduate studentships available to applicants of all nationalities accepted at the university in the fields of social sciences, science, engineering, agriculture, forestry, divinity, law, and medicine. Must have a minimum of first-class honors degree and a TOEFL score of at least 500 or equivalent. Provision for handicapped.
AMOUNT GIVEN: 10 awards per year.
DEADLINE: July 31.

University of Birmingham
Hugh Morton Scholarships
The Registry; P.O. Box 363
Birmingham B15 2TT England
RESTRICTIONS: For a student enrolled in the faculty of law pursuing an approved course of study for the higher degree of Ph.D. or LL.D. Must be nominated by the faculty of law and have taken or qualified for the LL.B. degree with honors. Recipients will remain, in regards to study and discipline, under the control of the dean of the faculty.
AMOUNT GIVEN: Tuition and fees.
DEADLINE: None.

University of Cambridge
Hughes Hall Studentship
Senior Tutor; Hughes Hall
Cambridge CB1 2EW England
02223-334893
RESTRICTIONS: Studentships are open to students who are accepted for graduate studies in the areas of medicine, law, and education at Cambridge University.
AMOUNT GIVEN: 15–20 studentships per year. 750 British pounds.
DEADLINE: July.

University of Dundee
Postgraduate Office
Dundee DD1 4HN Scotland
RESTRICTIONS: Awards available to foreign nationals in the fields of medicine, dentistry, science, law, engineering, arts, social sciences, environmental studies, and education. Applicants must have a minimum of an upper 2nd class honors degree or equivalent.
AMOUNT GIVEN: Up to 2,860 British pounds.
DEADLINE: March 31.

University of Glasgow
Post-Graduate Awards in Law and Financial Studies
Glasgow 912 8QQ Scotland
041-339-8855
RESTRICTIONS: For graduate students for research in topic specified by applicant and approved by the school of law. Must have good honors degree. Tenable at the university.
AMOUNT GIVEN: 2 awards per year.
DEADLINE: February 28.
CONTACT: Mrs. A. E. Wilson, Clerk of the Faculty, for more information.

University of Sheffield
Registrar
Sheffield S10 2TN England

RESTRICTIONS: Awards available in the areas of arts, economics, social studies, law, and architecture. Open to graduate students of all nationalities.
AMOUNT GIVEN: 2 studentships and 1 fellowship per year.
DEADLINE: June 1.

University of Sydney
Scholarships Office
Sydney NSW 2006 Australia
02-692-2222
RESTRICTIONS: Graduate research scholarships tenable at the university's selection based on academic merit. Open to law students from Australia or overseas. Accepted at the University of Sydney.
AMOUNT GIVEN: Aus. $10,500 plus travel allowances.
DEADLINE: November 30.

University of Tasmania
Post-Graduate Course Awards
GPO Box 252 C
Hobart, Tasmania 7001 Australia
RESTRICTIONS: For graduate study at the university in the fields of educational studies, environmental studies, financial studies, fine arts, humanities, music, psychology, social science, special education, and welfare law. Open to postgraduate students from Australia and overseas who hold a first- or second-class honors degree or equivalent qualifications from a recognized institution or other university.
AMOUNT GIVEN: Aus. $7,000. Renewable for 2 years maximum or length of degree (whichever is the lesser).
DEADLINE: October 31.

LINGUISTICS

Macquarie University
Attn: Registrar
North Ryde, New South Wales
Australia 2113
RESTRICTIONS: For students of all nationalities to obtain an M.A. in linguistics and its applications. Must have completed a first degree in linguistics or a related subject such as language, literature, psychology, or speech pathology.
AMOUNT GIVEN: Tuition + student activities fee.
DEADLINE: November 1.

LITERATURE

Academy of Korean Studies
Graduate School
50 Unjung-dong, Seongnam-si
Gyenggi-do, 130-17 Korea
RESTRICTIONS: Scholarships available to students of all nationalities who have graduated from an accredited institution. For study in the fields of history, philosophy, political science, economics, sociology, anthropology, education, literature, and fine arts. Must speak English, Korean, and one other language.
AMOUNT GIVEN: Tuition, room and board, and stipend.
DEADLINE: April 30–October 30.

British Federation of University Women
Theodora Bosanquet Bursary
Crosby Hall; Cheyne Walk
London SW3 5BA England
01-352-5354
RESTRICTIONS: Open to female undergraduate and graduate students who are carrying out research in the field of English Literature or English history requiring use of reference libraries or other sources of information in London.
AMOUNT GIVEN: Residential fees and board for up to 6 weeks.
DEADLINE: November 23.

Germanistic Society of America
Foreign Study Scholarships
809 U.N. Plaza
New York, NY 10017
212-984-5330
RESTRICTIONS: Must be a U.S. citizen with a bachelor's degree. For graduate study at a German university in the fields of history, international relations, language, literature, philosophy, political science, and public affairs. Selection based on promised project, language fluency, academic achievement, and references.
AMOUNT GIVEN: $6,000.
DEADLINE: October 31.

Ministry of Culture and Education
Huerfisenta 6
150 Reykjavik, Iceland
RESTRICTIONS: Scholarships available for study in Icelandic language, literature, and history. Open to students from countries chosen yearly or applicants of Icelandic origin from the U.S. or Canada.

AMOUNT GIVEN: Tuition, room and board.
CONTACT: Institute of International Education
            809 United Nations Plaza
            New York, NY 10017
or concurring department of applicant's country.

Notre Dame Seishin University
President of the University
2-16-9 Ifukucho
Okayma 700 Japan
RESTRICTIONS: Awards available to foreign female students of all nationalities over the age of 18 for study in the fields of English language and literature, Japanese language and literature, home economics, child welfare, food and human nutrition. Must have completed 12 years of schooling and be proficient in Japanese.
AMOUNT GIVEN: 50,000 yen per month and or tuition.
DEADLINE: December 31.

Showa Women's University
Dept. of Educational Affairs
1–7 Taishido, Setagaya
Tokyo 154 Japan
RESTRICTIONS: Scholarships in Japanese literature available to overseas female candidates of all nationalities. Must be over 18 years of age and must prove financial need.
AMOUNT GIVEN: Tuition + lodging.
DEADLINE: May.

University of Cambridge
St. John's College
Harper-Wood Studentship
Cambridge CB2 1TP England
RESTRICTIONS: Studentship available in field of creative writing in English poetry and literature. Open to graduate students in country of choice sponsored by St. John's. Must be a graduate of any university of the U.K., the Commonwealth, or the U.S. Must be under 30 years of age.
AMOUNT GIVEN: Up to 2,815 British pounds.
DEADLINE: June 30.

Tokyo Women's Christian University
Registrar's Office
Tokyo Joshi Daigaku
2-6-1, Zempukuji
Suginami-ku
Tokyo 167
RESTRICTIONS: Graduate scholarships in the fields of philosophy, Japanese language and literature, English and American literature, history,

and math. Undergraduate scholarships available in these fields as well as sociology, economics and psychology. Open to students in financial need of all nationalities. Must be proficient in Japanese.
AMOUNT GIVEN: Tuition + fees.

United Chapters of Phi Beta Kappa
Mary Isabel Sibley Fellowship
1811 Q St., NW
Washington, DC 20009
RESTRICTIONS: Postdoctoral fellowships for study in the fields of Greek language, literature, history, or archaeology open to single women ages 25–30 who have proved ability to carry on original research. Must have Ph.D. or have completed all requirements except dissertation. Must research full-time during fellowship. Tenable anywhere.
AMOUNT GIVEN: $6,000. One fellowship per year.

University of Jordan
Attn: President
Amman, Jordan
RESTRICTIONS: Awards available to female foreign students of all nationalities in the fields of Arabic language and literature, Arab and Islamic history, Middle Eastern studies for graduate and undergraduate study. Must be enrolled in a known university and have a knowledge of Arabic.
AMOUNT GIVEN: Tuition + board.
DEADLINE: August.

Vergilian Society Scholarships
c/o University of Maryland; Classics Dept.
College Park MD 20742
301-454-2510
RESTRICTIONS: For teachers and graduate students interested in classical civilization as revealed by archaeology, art, and literature in Greece and Italy.
AMOUNT GIVEN: $100–$500.
DEADLINE: February 1.

MATHEMATICS

Japan Society for the Promotion of Science
Yamato Bldg. 5-3-1 Kojimachi
Chiyoda-ku
Tokyo 102 Japan
03-263-1721

RESTRICTIONS: Pre-doctoral and postdoctoral fellowships awarded for study and research in the fields of humanities, math, physics, chemistry, and biology. Tenure for both is 2 years.
AMOUNT GIVEN: 12,300–21,400 yen per month.
DEADLINE: May and October.

La Trobe University
Registrar
Attn: Scholarships officer
Bundoora, Victoria 3083 Australia
RESTRICTIONS: Research scholarships for master's and Ph.D. candidates. Available to students from any country holding the equivalent to a 4-year, first-class honors degree from an Australian university. Proof of significant written work required. Must be efficient in English. Renewable if progress is satisfactory.
AMOUNT GIVEN: Aus. $7,000 + possible spousal and dependents allowance. Thesis allowance up to Aus. $800 and possible general service fee and travel allowance. 2 years (master's); 4 years (Ph.D.).
DEADLINE: July 31.

Scuola Normale Superiore
Post-Graduate Scholarships for Non-Italians
Piazza dei Cavaliere 7
The Director
I-56100 Pisa, Italy
RESTRICTIONS: Scholarships for postgraduate study in the fields of humanities, history, mathematics, physics, biology, and chemistry.
AMOUNT GIVEN: Tuition + 54,300 lire stipend per month.
DEADLINE: November 30.

Tokyo Women's Christian University
Registrar's Office
Tokyo Joshi Daigaku
2-6-1, Zempukuji
Suginami-ku
Tokyo 167
RESTRICTIONS: Graduate scholarships in the fields of philosophy, Japanese language and literature, English and American literature, history, and math. Undergraduate scholarships available in these fields as well as sociology, economics, and psychology. Open to students in financial need of all nationalities. Must be proficient in Japanese.
AMOUNT GIVEN: Tuition + fees.

University of Cambridge—St. Johns College
Norman Laski Senior Studentship
Master; St. Johns College
Cambridge CB2 1TP England

RESTRICTIONS: Awards available to graduate students from any country for study in the fields of economics, engineering, and applied mathematics. Preference for study or research related to business or management. Must not be working for postgraduate qualification at the beginning of tenure. Must be over 23 years of age.
AMOUNT GIVEN: Up to 7,530 British pounds.
DEADLINE: March 31.

University of New Brunswick
School of Graduate Studies and Research
P.O. Box 4400
Fredericton, New Brunswick E3B 5A3 Canada
RESTRICTIONS: Graduate assistantships and teaching assistantships in the fields of computer science, education, engineering, forestry, humanities, mathematics, physical education and recreation, science, and social sciences. Available to students of all nationalities who fulfill requirements for admission as higher degree candidates in the School of Graduate Studies and Research.
AMOUNT GIVEN: Up to Canadian $12,000 per year.
DEADLINE: March 1.
CONTACT: Director of appropriate department.

MEDICINE

American Academy for Dermatology
ADA Student Fellowship Program
1567 Maple Ave.
Evanston, IL 60201
312-869-3950
RESTRICTIONS: Graduate fellowships for medical students in the field of dermatology. Work undertaken must be done at a university or college in the U.S. or Canada not for credit or degree. Must be U.S. or Canadian citizen.
AMOUNT GIVEN: Up to $1050.
DEADLINE: March 30.

American Heart Association
Division of Research Awards
British-American Research Fellowships
7320 Greenville Ave.
Dallas, TX 75231
214-706-1453
RESTRICTIONS: Postdoctoral awards open to U.S. citizens who seek research training in the United Kingdom.

AMOUNT GIVEN: $22,000 stipend.
DEADLINE: July 1.

American Lung Association
1740 Broadway
New York, NY 10019
212-245-8000
RESTRICTIONS: Open to U.S. citizens for study in U.S. or Canada or Canadian citizens to train in the U.S. Must be physicians entering at least second year of residency in lung-related specialities. Also open to M.D., Ph.D., or S.C.D. holders for further training as investigators in this field.
AMOUNT GIVEN: $25,000.
DEADLINE: October 1.

American Medical Association
Rock Cleyster Memorial Scholarship
Director of Undergraduate Medical Education
535 North Dearborn St.
Chicago, IL 60610
312-645-4691
RESTRICTIONS: Open to rising undergraduate seniors who are nominated by their medical school. Awards based on demonstration of interest and need and are tenable at accredited medical schools in the U.S. or Canada. Must be U.S. citizen of legal resident.
AMOUNT GIVEN: Approximately 20 scholarships. $2,500.
DEADLINE: May 1.

Arthritis Society
Studentships
250 Bloor St. E. #401
Toronto, Ontario M4W 3P2 Canada
416-967-1414
RESTRICTIONS: Highly competitive awards open to qualified candidates to promote research training in the general area relating to arthritis research. Research training may be part of an M.D./Ph.D. program. Preference to Canadian citizens/legal residents. 12-month awards renewable with satisfactory progress.
AMOUNT GIVEN: Canadian $12,570.
DEADLINE: February 1.

Canadian Heart Foundation
Research Traineeships
1 Nicholas Street, Suite 1200
Ottawa, Ontario K1N 7B7 Canada
613-237-4361
RESTRICTIONS: Research fellowships for qualified research workers of all nationalities in cardiovascular research at approved Canadian in-

stitutions. Applicants must make their own arrangement with the university or institution and submit a statement of acceptance from the head of the department with their application.
AMOUNT GIVEN: Canadian $11,550–$46,500
DEADLINE: December 1.
APPLICATIONS: Send written inquiry for prescribed forms.

Canadian Lung Association
Canadian Nurses Respiratory Society
Fellowships & Research Grants
72 Albert Suite 908
Ottawa, Ontario K1P 5E7 Canada
613-237-1208
RESTRICTIONS: For those studying at master's level or above. To increase the number of nurses with expertise in the clinical practice of respiratory nursing resulting in improved quality of patient care.
AMOUNT GIVEN: Varies.
DEADLINE: November 1.

Dermatology Foundation
Post-Doctoral Fellowship Award Program
1567 Maple Ave.
Evanston, IL 60201
312-869-3950
RESTRICTIONS: Competitive awards to support training in research skills and methods or research projects. Must be U.S. or Canadian citizen.
AMOUNT GIVEN: 18 awards. $15,000–$25,000 per year.
DEADLINE: September 15; February 1.
CONTACT: Sandra Rahn Goldman, Executive Director.

Dermatology Foundation
Post-Doctoral Grant Program
1567 Maple Ave.
Evanston, IL 60201
312-869-3950
RESTRICTIONS: Postdoctoral grants for M.D.s for "seed support" of research projects. Competitive awards. Must be Canadian or U.S. citizen.
AMOUNT GIVEN: $5,000–$10,000.
DEADLINE: September 15.
CONTACT: Sandra Rahn Goldman, Executive Director.

Indian Council of Medical Research Fellowships
Post Box 4508
Ansari Nagar New Delhi–110029
India 660235

RESTRICTIONS: For young scientists to research in the field of biomedical sciences at the permanent institutes of the council. Maximum tenure for all fellowships is three years subject to annual review.
AMOUNT GIVEN: Amount varies.

Institut Pasteur de Tunis
Bourses Charles Nicolle
13 Place Pasteur
1002 Tunis Belvedere-Tunisia
283-022
RESTRICTIONS: Graduate awards for study in Tunisia in the fields of medicine and biology.
AMOUNT GIVEN: 2,000 Tunisian dinars.
CONTACT: Nearest Tunisian embassy for more information.

Sigrid Juselins Foundation
Medical Research Grants
Aleksanterinkatu 48 B
00100 Helsinki, Finland
90-634461
RESTRICTIONS: Grants for advanced postdoctoral research work in the field of medicine. For study in Finland.
AMOUNT GIVEN: 10,000–650,000 Finnish markka.
DEADLINE: November 15.

Kidney Foundation of Canada
Nephrology/Urology Scholarship Fellowship and Grant Programs
4060 Ste-Catherine St. W.; #555
Montreal, Quebec H3Z 2Z3 Canada
514-934-4806
RESTRICTIONS: To support study & research in fields of nephrology/urology. Open to graduate and postgraduate teachers/doctors/Ph.D.'s and researchers. Many programs limited to Canadian citizens.
AMOUNT GIVEN: Amount varies with program.
DEADLINE: Varies.

Kyungpook National University
Bureau of Student Affairs
370 San Kyuk-dong, uk-gu
Daegu 635 Korea
RESTRICTIONS: Scholarships and loans available to applicants of all nationalities in the fields of humanities, social sciences, natural sciences, economics, commerce, law, engineering, agriculture, teaching, medicine, dentistry, music, and visual arts. Must have completed 12 years of schooling and 2 years of pre-medical or pre-dental courses for study in these fields.
DEADLINE: One semester prior to start of studies.

Medical Research Council
Studentships
20th Floor, Jeanne Mance Bldg.
De'Lengantine St.
Tunney's Pasture, Ottawa, Ontario K1A 0W9 Canada
RESTRICTIONS: Awards for Canadian citizens and non-citizens tenable
in Canada. Applicants must have or be about to receive an honors B.S.
degree (or its equal).
AMOUNT GIVEN: Canadian $11,400.
DEADLINE: December 1; April 1.

Medical Research Council of New Zealand
Post-Doctoral Fellowships
P.O. Box 5541; Wellesley St.
Auckland, New Zealand
798-227
RESTRICTIONS: Scholarships for biomedical research open to appli-
cants with Ph.D.s or equivalent degrees based on academic standing and
research capabilities. Applicants should be under 35 years of age.
AMOUNT GIVEN: 30,500 New Zealand dollars.
DEADLINE: April 1; October 1.

Smith and Nephew Foundation
Research Fellowships
2 Temple Place
Victoria Embankment
London WC2R 3BP England
RESTRICTIONS: Postdoctoral research fellowships open to citizens of
any country between the ages of 25 and 35 who have had 2 years of
general clinical experience. Awards tenable in the U.K. in the fields of
surgery research and internal medicine. Fellows must return to their
home county after completion of studies.
AMOUNT GIVEN: 14,000 British pounds.
DEADLINE: April.

University of Aberdeen
Regent Walk
Aberdeen AB9 1FX Scotland
RESTRICTIONS: Postgraduate studentships available to applicants of all
nationalities accepted at the university in the fields of social sciences,
science, engineering, agriculture, forestry, divinity, law, and medicine.
Must have a minimum of first-class honors degree and a TOEFL score of
at least 500 or equivalent. Provision for handicapped.
AMOUNT GIVEN: 10 awards per year.
DEADLINE: July 31.

University of Cambridge
Hughes Hall Studentship

Senior Tutor; Hughes Hall
Cambridge CB1 2EW England
02223-334893
RESTRICTIONS: Studentships are open to students who are accepted for graduate studies in the areas of medicine, law, and education at Cambridge University.
AMOUNT GIVEN: 15–20 studentship per year. 750 British pounds.
DEADLINE: July.

University of Dundee
Postgraduate Office
Dundee DD1 4HN Scotland
RESTRICTIONS: Awards available to foreign nationals in the fields of medicine, dentistry, science, law, engineering, arts, social sciences, environmental studies, and education. Applicants must have a minimum of an upper second-class honors degree or equivalent.
AMOUNT GIVEN: Up to 2,860 British pounds.
DEADLINE: March 31.

University of London
JFH Knight Fellowship
Senate House; Room 21A
Malet Street
London, WC1E 7HU England
RESTRICTIONS: For postgraduate research into the social epidemiological or preventive aspects of diseases of adult life with special reference to the problems of venereal disease, alcohol, drugs of addiction, and similar matters. Open to university graduates who are registered medical practitioners or who hold equivalent qualifications. Tenable at the London School of Hygiene & Tropical Medicine.
AMOUNT GIVEN: 2,995 British pounds.
DEADLINE: March 1.

University of Sheffield
Medical Research Fellowships
Attn: Registrar
Sheffield S10 2TN England
RESTRICTIONS: Awards in all branches of medicine approved by the faculty open to graduate students of all nationalities.
AMOUNT GIVEN: Varies.

University of Western Australia
James & Sith Annie Chester Scholarships
Mounts Bay Rd.
Crawley Perth 6009 Western Australia
09-380-3838 or 09-380-3030

RESTRICTIONS: Open to medical graduates from U.W.A. or other recognized universities. For study at the University of Western Australia.
AMOUNT GIVEN: Variable stipend plus travel allowances.
DEADLINE: July 31.

METALLURGY

American Society for Metals
ASM Scholarship Selection Committee
Metals Park, OH 44073
216-338-5151
RESTRICTIONS: Open to undergraduate students in the fields of metallurgy or materials science who have completed at least 1 year of study. For citizens of the U.S., Canada, or Mexico who are enrolled in a recognized college or university.
AMOUNT GIVEN: $500– $2,000
DEADLINE: June 15.

Institution of Mining and Metallurgy
Stanley Moore Fellowships
44 Portland Place
London W1N 4BR England
01-580-3802
RESTRICTIONS: For graduate research into all branches of extractive metallurgy and mineral processing. Tenable at U.K. universities. Preference given to members of the institution.
AMOUNT GIVEN: 1,500–1,600 British pounds.
DEADLINE: March 16.

Institution of Mining and Metallurgy
G. Vernon Hobson Bequest
44 Portland Place
London W1N 4BR England
01-580-3802
RESTRICTIONS: Awards for the advancement of teaching geology as applied to mining. Open to graduate students. Preference to institution members.
AMOUNT GIVEN: 1,500 British pounds.
DEADLINE: March 16.

Institution of Mining and Metallurgy
Bosworth Smith Trust Fund
44 Portland Place
London W1N 4BR England
01-580-3802

RESTRICTIONS: Grants available for postgraduate research in metal mining, nonferrous extraction, metallurgy, or mineral dressing. For use towards working expenses and costs of visits to mines. Preference given to members of the institution.
AMOUNT GIVEN: 3500 British pounds.
DEADLINE: March 16.
CONTACT: The secretary of the institution.

University of Manchester
Institute of Science and Technology
Mohn Research Fellowships
P.O. Box 88
Manchester M60 1QD England
061-236-3311
RESTRICTIONS: Postgraduate fellowships for persons who wish to pursue research in the faculty of technology. Preference given to studies in the areas of metallurgy, materials science, and chemical engineering.
AMOUNT GIVEN: Approximately 4,000 British pounds.
DEADLINE: None.

MIDDLE EASTERN STUDIES

American Jewish League for Israel
University Scholarship Fund
30 E. 60th Street
New York, NY 10022
212-371-1452
RESTRICTIONS: All fields. Must be Jewish. For Americans who have been accepted for a year of undergraduate or graduate study in Israel at Bar Ilan University, Ben Gurion Technion University, Tel Aviv University, or Weismann Institute of Science.
AMOUNT GIVEN: 5–6 awards per year of $1,000.
DEADLINE: June 1.

Archaeological Institute of America
Harriet Pomerance Fellowship
675 Commonwealth Avenue
Boston, MA 02215
617-353-9361
RESTRICTIONS: Graduate fellowships to enable work on a scholarly project relating to the Aegean Bronze Age in archaeology. Preference given to persons whose project requires travel to the Mediterranean. Must be U.S. or Canadian citizen.

AMOUNT GIVEN: $3,000.
DEADLINE: November 15.

Archaeological Institute of America
Olivia James Travelling Fellowship
675 Commonwealth Avenue
Boston, MA 02215
617-353-9361
RESTRICTIONS: For graduate or postgraduate study in Greece, Aegean Islands, Sicily, Southern Italy, Asia Minor, or Mesopotamia. Preference for dissertation or recent Ph.D. research. Not for field excavation. Must be U.S. citizen or legal resident for study in fields of archaeology, architecture, classics, history, or sculpture.
AMOUNT GIVEN: $10,000 stipend.

Hebrew University
Attn: Secretary
Moritz and Charlotte Warburg Prize
Jerusalem, Israel
RESTRICTIONS: Graduate and postgraduate awards available to students of all nationalities in the field of Jewish studies.
AMOUNT GIVEN: $6,500–$7,000 per year.
DEADLINE: November.

University of Jordan
Attn: President
Amman, Jordan
RESTRICTIONS: Awards available to foreign female students of all nationalities in the fields of Arabic language and literature, Arab and Islamic history, Middle Eastern studies. For graduate and undergraduate study. Must be enrolled in a known university and have a knowledge of Arabic.
AMOUNT GIVEN: Tuition + board.
DEADLINE: August.

MUSIC

Academy of Korean Studies
Graduate School
50 Unjung-dong, Seongnam-si
Gyenggi-do, 130-17 Korea
RESTRICTIONS: Scholarships available to students of all nationalities who have graduated from accredited institutions. For study in fields of history, philosophy, political science, economics, sociology, anthropol-

ogy, education, literature, fine arts, and music. Must speak English, Korean, and one other language.
AMOUNT GIVEN: Tuition, room and board, and stipend.
DEADLINE: April 30–October 30.

Federal Ministry of Science and Research
Minoritenplatz 5
1014 Wien 1 Austria
RESTRICTIONS: Scholarships for music students of any nationality with very high musical ability.
AMOUNT GIVEN: 5,700–7,200 schillings per month for 1 year.
DEADLINE: March 1.
CONTACT: Austrian embassy.

Foundation des Estats Unis
Harriet Hale Wolley Scholarships
15 Boulevard Jourdan
75690 Paris-Cedex 14 France
45-89-35-79
RESTRICTIONS: Art and music scholarships for U.S. citizens for graduate study in France. Must be between 21 and 30 years of age. Preference given to mature students who have already done graduate study. Must have good knowledge of French and live at Foundation des Estats Unis.
AMOUNT GIVEN: $6,000 stipend + living quarters.
DEADLINE: None.

La Trobe University
Registrar
Attn: Scholarships officer
Bundoora, Victoria 3083 Australia
RESTRICTIONS: Research scholarships for master's and Ph.D. candidates. Available to students from any country holding the equivalent of a 4-year, first-class honors degree from an Australian university. Proof of significant written work required. Must be efficient in English. Renewable if progress is satisfactory.
AMOUNT GIVEN: Aus. $7,000 + possible spousal and dependents' allowance. Thesis allowance up to Aus. $800 and possible general service fee and travel allowance. 2 years (master's), 4 years (Ph.D.).
DEADLINE: July 31.

University of Music and Performing Arts
Lothrinerstrasse 18
Postfach 146
1037 Wien III Austria
RESTRICTIONS: Postgraduate students of all nationalities for studies in performance using all musical instruments, composition, and voice. Must

have outstanding musical ability and good knowledge of German. Must be between 17 and 30 years of age.
AMOUNT GIVEN: 6,500 schillings per month for 1 year. Renewable.
DEADLINE: February.
CONTACT: Austrian embassy.

Kyungpook National University
Bureau of Student Affairs
370 San Kyuk-dong, uk-gu
Daegu 635 Korea
RESTRICTIONS: Scholarships and loans available to applicants of all nationalities in the fields of humanities, social sciences, natural sciences, economics, commerce, law, engineering, agriculture, teaching, medicine, dentistry, music, and visual arts. Must have completed 12 years of schooling and 2 years of pre-medical or pre-dental courses for study in these fields.
DEADLINE: One semester prior to start of studies.

University of Tasmania
Post-Graduate Course Awards
GPO Box 252 C
Hobart, Tasmania 7001 Australia
RESTRICTIONS: For graduate study at the university in the fields of educational studies, environmental studies, financial studies, fine arts, humanities, music, psychology, social science, special education, and welfare law. Open to postgraduate students from Australia and overseas who hold a first- or second-class honors degree or equivalent qualifications from a recognized institution or other university.
AMOUNT GIVEN: Aus. $7,000. Renewable for 2 years maximum or length of degree (whichever is the lesser).
DEADLINE: October 31.

PHILOSOPHY

Academy of Korean Studies
Graduate School
50 Unjung-dong, Seongnam-si
Gyenggi-do, 130–17 Korea
RESTRICTIONS: Scholarships available to students of all nationalities who have graduated from accredited institutions. For study in the fields of history, philosophy, political science, economics, sociology, anthropology, education, literature, and fine arts. Must speak English, Korean, and one other language.
AMOUNT GIVEN: Tuition, room and board, and stipend.
DEADLINE: April 30–October 30.

Australian National University
Ph.D. Scholarships
G.P.O. Box 4; Graduate Students Section
Canberra ACT 2601 Australia
49-5111
RESTRICTIONS: Full-time study for doctorate of philosophy. High academic record with capacity for research.
AMOUNT GIVEN: Aus. $7,375 per year. Scholarship for 3 years.
DEADLINE: September 30.

Germanistic Society of America
Foreign Study Scholarships
809 U.N. Plaza
New York, NY 10017
212-984-5330
RESTRICTIONS: Must be a U.S. citizen with a bachelor's degree. For graduate study at German university in the fields of history, international relations, language, literature, philosophy, political science, and public affairs. Selection based on promised project, language fluency, academic achievement, and references.
AMOUNT GIVEN: $6,000.
DEADLINE: October 31.

La Trobe University
Registrar
Attn: Scholarships officer
Bundoora, Victoria 3083 Australia
RESTRICTIONS: Research scholarships for Masters and Ph.D. candidates. Available to students from any country holding the equivalent to a 4-year, first-class honors degree from an Australian university. Proof of significant written work required. Must be efficient in English. Renewable if progress is satisfactory.
AMOUNT GIVEN: Aus. $7,000 + possible spousal and dependents' allowance. Thesis allowance up to Aus. $800 and possible general service fee and travel allowance. 2 years (master's); 4 years (Ph.D.).
DEADLINE: July 31.

Rhodes University
Hugh Le May Fellowship
P.O. Box 94 Grahamstown 6140
South Africa
RESTRICTIONS: Graduate fellowships available for students qualified to pursue advanced study in philosophy, theology, classics history, languages, politics, and law.
AMOUNT GIVEN: 2,800 rand + room and board.
DEADLINE: July 31.

Tokyo Women's Christian University
Registrar's Office
Tokyo Joshi Daigaku
2-6-1, Zempukuji
Suginami-ku
Tokyo 167
RESTRICTIONS: Graduate scholarships in the fields of philosophy, Japanese language and literature, English and American literature, history, and math. Undergraduate scholarships available in these fields as well as sociology, economics, and psychology. Open to students in financial need of all nationalities. Must be proficient in Japanese.
AMOUNT GIVEN: Tuition + fees.

PHYSICAL EDUCATION

Jewish Welfare Board
JWB Scholarship Program
Grants Coordinator
15 E. 26th Street
New York, NY 10010
212-532-4949
RESTRICTIONS: Open to U.S. and Canadian citizens of the Jewish faith. For master's degree programs only in the fields of adult education, early childhood education, physical education, and social work. Should have a strong desire to enter and work in the Jewish community center field.
AMOUNT GIVEN: $7,500. 18 awards per year.
DEADLINE: February 1.

University of New Brunswick
School of Graduate Studies and Research
P.O. Box 4400
Fredericton, New Brunswick E3B 5A3 Canada
RESTRICTIONS: Graduate assistantships and teaching assistantships in the fields of computer science, education, engineering, forestry, humanities, mathematics, physical education and recreation, science, and social sciences. Available to students of all nationalities who fulfill requirements for admission as higher degree candidates in the School of Graduate Studies and Research.
AMOUNT GIVEN: Up to Canadian $12,000 per year.
DEADLINE: March 1.
CONTACT: Director of appropriate department.

University of Saskatchewan
College of Graduate Studies and Research
Saskatoon, Saskatchewan Canada

RESTRICTIONS: Graduates of all nationalities with B.A. (honors) or equivalent from recognized university. Scholarships available in the fields of agriculture, education, engineering, health sciences, humanities, physical education, science, and social sciences.
AMOUNT GIVEN: Up to $8,800 for eight months with possible addition of Canadian $4,400 for summer semester.
DEADLINE: February 1.

PHYSICS

Canadian Society of Exploration Geophysicists
206 7th Ave SW; suite 501
Calgary Alberta T2P 0W7 Canada
403-262-0015
RESTRICTIONS: Scholarships available to students in an academic program leading to an exploration geophysics career in teaching, industry, or research. For study at Canadian universities or technical schools.
AMOUNT GIVEN: Approximately 35 awards per year. Canadian $1250–$1500.
DEADLINE: June 30.
CONTACT: W. J. McCormack, Chairman.

Dublin Institute for Advanced Studies
Research Scholarships
10 Burlington Road
Dublin 4 Ireland
(DUBLIN) 680748
RESTRICTIONS: Must hold Ph.D. or equivalent in an appropriate subject. Also may be available to candidates holding an honors degree or its equivalent. For research in astronomy, Celtic studies, cosmic physics, and theoretical physics at the Dublin Institute. The Dublin Institute is not a university.
AMOUNT GIVEN: $8,600–$12,500. 18 awards per year.
DEADLINE: March 31.

Inter-American Foundation
Doctoral Dissertation Fellowship
1515 Wilson Boulevard
Rosslyn, VA 22209
703-841-3800
RESTRICTIONS: Open to Ph.D. candidates in social sciences and physical sciences enrolled in a U.S. university who have fulfilled all degree requirements other than the dissertation before they travel to their country of intended study. Research themes must deal directly with

developing activities among the poor. Candidates must speak the language of the country of intended study.
AMOUNT GIVEN: Approximately $550 per month stipend. Approximately 15 awards per year.
DEADLINE: December 5.

Japan Society for the Promotion of Science
Yamato Bldg. 5-3-1 Kojimachi
Chiyoda-ku
Tokyo 102 Japan
03-263-1721
RESTRICTIONS: Pre-doctoral and postdoctoral fellowships awarded for study and research in the fields of humanities, math, physics, chemistry, and biology. Tenure for both is 2 years.
AMOUNT GIVEN: 12,300–21,400 yen per month.
DEADLINE: May and October.

La Trobe University
Registrar
Attn: Scholarships officer
Bundoora, Victoria 3083 Australia
RESTRICTIONS: Research scholarships for master's and Ph.D. candidates. Available to students from any country holding the equivalent to a 4-year, first-class honors degree from an Australian university. Proof of significant written work required. Must be efficient in English. Renewable if progress is satisfactory.
AMOUNT GIVEN: Aus $7,000 + possible spousal and dependents' allowance. Thesis allowance up to Aus. $800 and possible general service fee and travel allowance. 2 years (master's); 4 years (Ph.D.).
DEADLINE: July 31.

Scuola Normale Superiore
Post-Graduate Scholarships for Non-Italians
Piazza dei Cavaliere 7
The Director
I-56100 Pisa, Italy
RESTRICTIONS: Scholarships for postgraduate study in the fields of humanities, history, mathematics, physics, biology, and chemistry.
AMOUNT GIVEN: Tuition + 54,300 lire stipend per month.
DEADLINE: November 30.

University of Guelph
Dean of Graduate Studies
Guelph, Ontario N1G 2WI Canada
RESTRICTIONS: Awards for postgraduate study in fields of agriculture, arts, biological sciences, physical sciences, social sciences, and veteri-

nary sciences. Open to students of all nationalities having graduated from a recognized university.
AMOUNT GIVEN: Canadian $2,400–$3,000 per year.
CONTACT: The department to which you are applying.

POLITICAL SCIENCE

Academy of Korean Studies
Graduate School
50 Unjung-dong, Seongnam-si
Gyenggi-do, 130-17 Korea
RESTRICTIONS: Scholarships available to students of all nationalities who have graduated from an accredited institution. For study in fields of history, philosophy, political science, economics, sociology, anthropology, education, literature, and fine arts. Must speak English, Korean, and one other language.
AMOUNT GIVEN: Tuition, room and board, and stipend.
DEADLINE: April 30–October 30.

American Friends of the London School of Economics
AFLSE Scholarship Program
1025 Thomas Jefferson Street, NW
#400 East Lobby
Washington, DC 20007
202-944-3640
RESTRICTIONS: All fields. Graduate awards open to U.S. citizens or legal residents for one year of study at the London School of Economics. Preference to students who have not previously studied in Great Britain. For newly enrolled students only.
AMOUNT GIVEN: 8 scholarships per year. $2,500.
DEADLINE: March 1.

CDS International Inc.
Robert Bosch Foundation Fellowships
425 Park Ave; 27th floor
New York, NY 10022
212-593-3004
RESTRICTIONS: 9-month fellowship in Germany involving work internships in the federal government and then in regional government or private industry, supplemented by special seminars in Berlin, Paris, and Brussels. Must be U.S. citizen with a graduate degree or equivalent professional experience in the fields of business administration, communications, economics, German studies, journalism, law, political science, and public affairs.

AMOUNT GIVEN: 3,000 Deutsche Marks per month + travel expenses.
DEADLINE: October 15.

European University Institute
Via de Roccettini 5
San Domenico di Fiesole
50016 Italy
0039-055-50921
RESTRICTIONS: For graduate students in the fields of political science, social sciences, law, economics, and history. Open to qualified candidates with honors degree and a research project with a European dimension.
AMOUNT GIVEN: $615–$1,000 per month + travel, medical, and family allowances.
DEADLINE: November 30.

European University Institute
Jean Monnet Fellowship
Via de Roccettini 5
San Domenico di Fiesole
50016 Italy
0039-055-50921
RESTRICTIONS: Postdoctoral fellowships in the fields of political science, social sciences, law, economics, and history. Recipients required to make scholarly contribution to research on Europe within one of EUI's research projects or on topics falling within the general interests of the institute. Publication of research is expected.
AMOUNT GIVEN: 25 fellowships per year of $1,400–$2,100 per month + medical and family allowances.
DEADLINE: November 30.

Germanistic Society of America
Foreign Study Scholarships
809 U.N. Plaza
New York, NY 10017
212-984-5330
RESTRICTIONS: Must be a U.S. citizen with a bachelor's degree. For graduate study at a German university in the fields of history, international relations, language, literature, philosophy, political science, and public affairs. Selection based on promised project, language fluency, academic achievement, and references.
AMOUNT GIVEN: $6,000.
DEADLINE: October 31.

London School of Economics and Political Science
Houghton St. Scholarships Office

London WC2A 2AE England
01-955-7163
RESTRICTIONS: Awards and prizes available to students wishing to attend the university as graduate or undergraduate students in the fields of accounting, economics, finance, and political science.
AMOUNT GIVEN: Varies.

Rhodes University
Hugh Le May Fellowship
P.O. Box 94
Grahamstown 6140 South Africa
RESTRICTIONS: Graduate fellowships available for students qualified to pursue advanced study in philosophy, theology, classics, history, languages, politics, and law.
AMOUNT GIVEN: 2,800 rand + room and board.
DEADLINE: July 31.

POPULATION AND DEVELOPMENT

Macquarie University
Attn: Registrar
North Ryde, New South Wales
Australia 2113
RESTRICTIONS: For students of all nationalities to obtain an M.A. in population and development (in English). Must have a sound background in economics or demography and a knowledge of first year statistics and computing.
AMOUNT GIVEN: Tuition + student activities fees.
DEADLINE: November 1.

Social Science Research Council
Fellowships Coordinator
605 Third Avenue
New York, NY 10158
212-661-0280
RESTRICTIONS: Doctoral dissertation research fellowships for Ph.D. candidates of all nationalities at U.S. institutions, or U.S. citizens or legal residents enrolled at any accredited institution in the U.S. or abroad. For research in the fields of social sciences, humanities, demography, urban planning, and education.
AMOUNT GIVEN: 50–100 fellowships per year.
DEADLINE: November 1.

PSYCHOLOGY

Murdoch University
Attn: Secretary, Board of Research and Post-Graduate Studies
Murdoch, Western Australia 6150 Australia
RESTRICTIONS: Postgraduate students of all nationalities not already holding a Ph.D. For study leading to a master's degree in fields of applied psychology, education, or public policy.
AMOUNT GIVEN: 4 scholarships per year. Aus. $7,000 + dependents' incidentals, thesis, and fares allowances.
DEADLINE: September 30.

Radio Free Europe/Radio Liberty
Summer Student Research Internship Program
1201 Connecticut Ave. NW
Washington, DC 20036
RESTRICTIONS: Open to graduate students in the fields of international communications, mass communications, collective behavior, or social psychology. For full-time research producing a publishable paper.
AMOUNT GIVEN: Daily stipend of 45 Deutsche marks + living accommodations.
DEADLINE: February 14.
CONTACT: Mr. Alan Dodds.

Tokyo Women's Christian University
Registrar's Office
Tokyo Joshi Daigaku
2-6-1, Zempukuji
Suginami-ku
Tokyo 167 Japan
RESTRICTIONS: Graduate scholarships in the fields of philosophy, Japanese language, and literature, English and American literature, history, and math. Undergraduate scholarships available in these fields as well as sociology, economics, and psychology. Open to students in financial need of all nationalities. Must be proficient in Japanese.
AMOUNT GIVEN: Tuition + fees.

University of Tasmania
Post-Graduate Course Awards
GPO Box 252 C
Hobart, Tasmania 7001 Australia
RESTRICTIONS: For graduate study at the university in the fields of educational studies, environmental studies, financial studies, fine arts, humanities, music, psychology, social science, special education, and welfare law. Open to post-graduate students from Australia and overseas

who held a first- or second-class honors degree or equivalent qualifications from a recognized institution or other university.
AMOUNT GIVEN: Aus. $7,000. Renewable for 2 years maximum or length of degree (whichever is lesser).
DEADLINE: October 31.

REHABILITATION

Kappa Kappa Gamma
Rehabilitation Scholarships
c/o Mrs. La Williams
4720 Pickett Rd.
Fairfax, VA 22032
RESTRICTIONS: Open to U.S. or Canadian citizens. For women who are undergraduate students in their last two years or graduate students having completed at least 2 years of study on a campus with a KKG chapter. Limited to study in rehabilitation or related fields (e.g., mental health rehabilitation and speech/hearing therapy). Membership not required.
AMOUNT GIVEN: $750 (undergraduate); $1,000 (graduate).
DEADLINE: February 15.

RELIGIOUS STUDIES

Hebrew University
Attn: Secretary
Moritz and Charlotte Warburg Prize
Jerusalem, Israel
RESTRICTIONS: Graduate and postgraduate awards available to students of all nationalities in the field of Jewish studies.
AMOUNT GIVEN: $6,500–$7,000 per year.
DEADLINE: November.

International Order of the Kings Daughters and Sons
Student Ministry Scholarship Fund
Headquarters; P.O. Box 1017
34 Vincent Ave.
Chataqua, NY 14722
716-357-6200
RESTRICTIONS: Available to graduate students accepted or enrolled in an accredited U.S. or Canadian school or seminary or those preparing for a full-time religious career. Must have minimum of "B" average. Must be U.S. or Canadian citizens.

AMOUNT GIVEN: 18–25 awards of $1,000 per year.
DEADLINE: April 30.
APPLICATIONS: Send a self-addressed, stamped, legal sized envelope to the director:
Mrs. Thad Welch Jr.
1318 Walthour Rd.
Savannah, GA. 31410

Kings College London
Cleave Cocherill Post-Grad Studentship
Office of the Dean
Strand, London WC2R 2LS England
RESTRICTIONS: Awarded to a candidate for holy orders in the Church of England who wishes to proceed to a higher degree in theology. Preference given to graduates of Kings College.
AMOUNT GIVEN: 500 British pounds.
DEADLINE: None.

Rhodes University
Hugh Le May Fellowship
P.O. Box 94
Grahamstown 6140 South Africa
RESTRICTIONS: Graduate fellowships available for students qualified to pursue advanced study in philosophy, theology, classics, history, languages, politics, and law.
AMOUNT GIVEN: 2,800 rand + room and board.
DEADLINE: July 31.

University of Aberdeen
Regent Walk
Aberdeen AB9 1FX Scotland
RESTRICTIONS: Postgraduate studentships available to applicants of all nationalities accepted at the university in the fields of social sciences, science, engineering, agriculture, forestry, divinity, law, and medicine. Must have a minimum of first-class honors degree and a TOEFL score of at least 500 or equivalent. Provision for handicapped.
AMOUNT GIVEN: 10 awards per year.
DEADLINE: July 31.

University of Oxford
Squire and Marriott Bursaries
University Office; Wellington Square
Oxford OX1 2JD England
0865-270001
RESTRICTIONS: Undergraduate and graduate scholarships. Applicants must intend to offer themselves for ordination in the Church of England or any church in communion therewith. Must show financial need.

AMOUNT GIVEN: 6 awards per year.
DEADLINE: March or September

University of Oxford
Hall-Houghton Studentship
University Office; Wellington Square
Oxford OX1 2JD England
0865-270001
RESTRICTIONS: For postgraduate study at the University of Oxford in the field of theology, with emphasis on the Greek New Testament or Septuagint version of the Hebrew scriptures in its relation to the Bible and the Greek testament or the Syriac versions of the Holy Scriptures.
AMOUNT GIVEN: 500 British pounds
DEADLINE: Early February.

University of Oxford
Denyer and Johnson Studentships
University Office; Wellington Square
Oxford OX1 2JD England
0865-270001
RESTRICTIONS: For postgraduate study at the University of Oxford. Applicants for higher degrees under the Board of the Faculty at the university.
AMOUNT GIVEN: Up to 1,300 British pounds.
DEADLINE: February 1.

SCIENCES, GENERAL

American Society for Enology and Viticulture
P.O. Box 1855
Davis, CA 95617
916-753-3142
RESTRICTIONS: Candidate must be enrolled/accepted in an accredited college in North America in curriculum stressing a science basic to the wine and grape industry. Must be North American resident.
AMOUNT GIVEN: $1,000–$3,000.
DEADLINE: March 1.

American Society for Metals
ASM Scholarship Selection Committee
Metals Park, OH 44073
216-338-5151
RESTRICTIONS: Open to undergraduate students in the fields of metallurgy or materials science who have completed at least 1 year of

study. For citizens of the U.S., Canada, or Mexico who are enrolled in a recognized college or university.
AMOUNT GIVEN: $500–$2,000.
DEADLINE: June 15.

American Vacuum Society
Russell and Sigurd Varian Fellow Award
335 E. 45th Street
New York, NY 10017
212-661-9404
RESTRICTIONS: Award to recognize and encourage excellence in graduate studies in vacuum science. Recipients selected on academic merit. Finalists must interview with trustees. Candidates must be full-time graduate students in a regular institution in North America.

AUCC
Awards Division
Petro Canada Inc. Graduate Research Program
151 Slater St.; Enquiries Clerk
Ottawa, Ontario K1P 5N1 Canada
613-563-1236
RESTRICTIONS: For full-time graduate study at an accredited Canadian institution. Granted primarily on the basis of academic standing and demonstrated potential for advanced study/research. Must be Canadian citizen or legal resident.
AMOUNT GIVEN: Canadian $10,000. Possibly renewable pending satisfactory progress.
DEADLINE: February 1.

Australian National University
Master's Degree Scholarships
Registrar
G.P.O. Box 4
Canberra ACT 2601 Australia
49-5111
RESTRICTIONS: Open to students holding a first degree with a minimum level of second-class honors (upper division) or equivalent for study in arts, Asian studies, economics, law, and science.
AMOUNT GIVEN: Aus. $7,375 per year + possible dependents allowance. 1 year duration, possibly renewable.
DEADLINE: October 31.

British Federation of University Women
Johnstone & Florence Stoney Studentship
Crosby Hall; Cheyne Walk
London SW3 5BA England
01-352-5354

RESTRICTIONS: Open to members of the British and Irish Federations of University Women for postgraduate research in Australia, New Zealand, or South Africa.
AMOUNT GIVEN: Up to 3,000 British pounds.
DEADLINE: September 15.

De La Salle University
Admissions Director
2401 Taft Avenue
Manila, Philippines
RESTRICTIONS: Scholarships available to students of all nationalities with a secondary school diploma. English required. Must be 18–22 years of age. For study in fields of liberal arts, commerce, engineering, natural sciences, and computer science.
DEADLINE: October.

Department of Education
Headquarters Section 3
Marlborough Street
Dublin 1 Ireland
RESTRICTIONS: Postdoctoral fellowships for approved research in the fields of science, engineering, and architecture at Irish universities or colleges. Must be under 30 years of age.
AMOUNT GIVEN: 8,375–10,946 Irish pounds.
DEADLINE: March 31.

Entomology Society of America
4603 Calvert Road
College Park, MD 20740
301-864-1334
RESTRICTIONS: Must be enrolled at a recognized college or university in the U.S. or Canada or Mexico and have accumulated at least 30 semester hours at the time award is presented. For study in fields of entomology, biology, or related science.
AMOUNT GIVEN: $500–$1,000.
DEADLINE: July 1.

European Science Foundation
European Brain Research Fellowships
1 Quay Lezay-Marnesia
67000 Strasbourg, France
88-35-30-63
RESTRICTIONS: For graduate students in the field of science who have some research experience but need further training to broaden their research scopes. Tenable in Europe and Israel. Preference for candidates under 30 years of age.

AMOUNT GIVEN: 7,300 francs per month.
DEADLINE: March 1; September 15.

Fundaco Calouste Gulbenkian
International Department
Avenida De Berna 45
Lisbon 1, Portugal
RESTRICTIONS: Postgraduate research awards in sciences and arts. Tenable in Portugal. Research project must be approved by the institution where applicant intends to study.
AMOUNT GIVEN: Maintenance awards + dependents' fees.
DEADLINE: May 31 and October 31.

Girton College Fellowships
Secretary to the Council
Cambridge CB3 OJG England
338-999
RESTRICTIONS: Research fellowships in the areas of humanities and science open to graduate students of any university. Tenable at Girton College.
AMOUNT GIVEN: Up to 9,200 British pounds per year.
DEADLINE: October 14.

Hungarian Academy of Sciences
Roosevelt ter 9
1059 Budapest V Hungary
RESTRICTIONS: Tertiary scholarships available under bilateral agreements for scientific cooperation. Open to qualified citizens of the U.S., Canada, and other countries for fundamental scientific research and study visits.
AMOUNT GIVEN: 180–450 forints per day (for up to 12 months) + lodging, medical care, and transportation within Hungary.
CONTACT: Corresponding national institution.

Konrad-Adenauer Stiftung
Post-Graduate Awards
Postfach 1260
5205 Sankt Augustin 1 Bei Bonn, Germany
02241 2 46-0
RESTRICTIONS: KAS promotes scientific training of foreign graduate students in Germany at German universities. Should have adequate command of German language.
AMOUNT GIVEN: Monthly grant of 940 Deutsche marks.
DEADLINE: None.

Kyungpook National University
Bureau of Student Affairs

370 San Kyuk-dong, uk-gu
Daegu 635 Korea
RESTRICTIONS: Scholarships and loans available to applicants of all nationalities in the fields of humanities, social sciences, natural sciences, economics, commerce, law, engineering, agriculture, teaching, medicine, dentistry, music, and visual arts. Must have completed 12 years of schooling and 2 years of pre-medical or pre-dental courses for study in these fields.
DEADLINE: One semester prior to start of studies.

National Academy of Sciences
Post-Doctoral Visiting Scholar Exchange Program
2101 Constitution Ave NW
Washington, DC 20418
202-334-2718
RESTRICTIONS: Postdoctoral grants to support research in the People's Republic of China by U.S. scholars and research in the U.S. by Chinese scholars. Open to U.S. or PRC citizens in fields of engineering, humanities, natural sciences, and social sciences. For 1–3 month research visits only; does not support study leading to academic degree.
AMOUNT GIVEN: Varies.
DEADLINE: October 10.

National Research Council of Canada
Research Associateships
Research Associates Office
Ottawa, Ontario K1A 1H5 Canada
RESTRICTIONS: Open to recent Ph.D.s in natural sciences or recent master's or Ph.D.'s in engineering. Tenable at NRCC laboratories throughout Canada. 2–5 years' duration. Preference to Canadian citizens or legal residents.
AMOUNT GIVEN: Up to Canadian $31,423 stipend.
DEADLINE: November 30.

Natural Sciences and Engineering Research Council of Canada
200 Kent Street
Visiting Fellowships in Canadian Government Laboratories
Ottawa, Ontario K1A 1H5 Canada
RESTRICTIONS: Fellowships for research in science and engineering available to applicants of all nationalities who meet all Canadian immigration requirements. Must possess a Ph.D. from an accepted university or a master's degree with a minimum of two years of post-master's experience. Must have proven ability to successfully conduct independent research. No more than five years may have passed since applicant received their doctorate.
AMOUNT GIVEN: Canadian $28,992 per year + travel allowances.
DEADLINE: December 15.

North Atlantic Treaty Organization
NATO Science Fellowships for U.S.A. Citizens
B-1110; Science Affairs Division
Brussels, Belgium
2-241-00-40
RESTRICTIONS: Graduate and postdoctoral fellowships for almost all scientific areas, including interdisciplinary areas. Open to U.S. citizens who wish to study/conduct research in another NATO member country. Administered in each country by a national administration. Write for address of your country's administration.
AMOUNT GIVEN: Amount varies with country.
DEADLINE: January 1; March 1.

Queen's Fellowships Committee
Marine Science Grants
Department of Science and Technology
P.O. Box 65
Belconnen, ACT 2616 Australia
RESTRICTIONS: For fellowships in marine science. Applicants of all nationalities holding a Ph.D. or equivalent in research and work experience in marine science. Must be under 30.
AMOUNT GIVEN: 2-year fellowships.
APPLICATIONS: Send written inquiry to the National Research Fellowships Scheme at the above address.

Royal Norwegian Council for Scientific and Industrial Research
P.O. Box 70 Tasen
N-0801 Oslo 8 Norway
47-2-23-76-85
RESTRICTIONS: Postdoctoral fellowships in the fields of applied sciences and engineering open to foreign scientists under the age of 36 who wish to do research work in Norway. Qualifications must be equivalent to at least a British or American Ph.D. in applied science or engineering.
AMOUNT GIVEN: 20 awards per year. 9,000 Norwegian kroner if single, 11,000 Norwegian kroner if married + expenses.
DEADLINE: March 1; September 1.

University of Aberdeen
Regent Walk
Aberdeen AB9 1FX Scotland
RESTRICTIONS: Postgraduate studentships available to applicants of all nationalities accepted at the university in the fields of social sciences, science, engineering, agriculture, forestry, divinity, law, and medicine. Must have a minimum of first-class honors degree and a TOEFL score of at least 500 or equivalent. Provision for handicapped.

AMOUNT GIVEN: 10 awards per year.
DEADLINE: July 31.

University of Dundee
Postgraduate Office
Dundee DD1 4HN Scotland
RESTRICTIONS: Awards available to foreign nationals in the fields of medicine, dentistry, science, law, engineering, arts, social sciences, environmental studies, and education. Applicants must have a minimum of an upper second-class honors degree or equivalent.
AMOUNT GIVEN: Up to 2,860 British pounds.
DEADLINE: March 31.

University of Guelph
Dean of Graduate Studies
Guelph, Ontario N1G 2WI Canada
RESTRICTIONS: Awards for postgraduate study in fields of agriculture, arts, biological science, physical sciences, social sciences, veterinary sciences. Open to students of all nationalities having graduated from a recognized university.
AMOUNT GIVEN: Canadian $2,400–$3,000 per year.
CONTACT: Desired department.

University of Manchester
Institute of Science and Technology
Mohn Research Fellowships
P.O. Box 88
Manchester M60 1QD England
061-236-3311
RESTRICTIONS: Postgraduate fellowships for persons who wish to pursue research in the faculty of technology. Preference given to studies in the areas of metallurgy; materials science and chemical engineering.
AMOUNT GIVEN: Approximately 4,000 British pounds.
DEADLINE: None.

University of New Brunswick
School of Graduate Studies and Research
P.O. Box 4400
Fredericton, New Brunswick E3B 5A3 Canada
RESTRICTIONS: Graduate assistantships and teaching assistantships in the fields of computer science, education, engineering, forestry, humanities, mathematics, physical education and recreation, science, and social sciences. Available to students of all nationalities who fulfill requirements for admission as higher degree candidates in the School of Graduate Studies and Research.
AMOUNT GIVEN: Up to Canadian $12,000 per year.

DEADLINE: March 1.
CONTACT: Director of appropriate department.

University of Ottawa
Merit Graduate Research Scholarships in Sciences and Engineering
Graduate Studies Scholarships
School of Graduate Studies
115 Wilbrod
Ottawa, Ontario K1N 6N5 Canada
RESTRICTIONS: Scholarships for study at the University of Ottawa in fields of sciences and engineering available to qualified applicants of all nationalities. Fluency in English or French required.
AMOUNT GIVEN: Canadian $1,000– $2,000.
DEADLINE: Fall session by July 1. Winter session by December 1. Summer session by April 1.

University of Ottawa
Research Excellence Scholarships in Sciences and Engineering
School of Graduate Studies
115 Wilbrod
Ottawa, Ontario K1N 6N5 Canada
RESTRICTIONS: Scholarships for study at the University of Ottawa in fields of sciences and engineering available to qualified applicants of all nationalities. Fluency in English or French required.
AMOUNT GIVEN: Canadian $3,500 per year. Renewable for one year at $2,500.
DEADLINE: Fall session by July 1. Winter session by December 1. Summer session by April 1.

University of Ottawa
Entrance Scholarships in Sciences and Engineering
Graduate Studies Scholarships
School of Graduate Studies
115 Wilbrod
Ottawa, Ontario K1N 6N5 Canada
RESTRICTIONS: Scholarships for study at the University of Ottawa in fields of sciences and engineering available to qualified applicants of all nationalities. Fluency in English or French required.
AMOUNT GIVEN: Canadian $1,500.
DEADLINE: Fall session by July 1. Winter session by December 1. Summer session by April 1.

University of Regina
Teaching Assistantships
Dean of Graduate Studies and Research
Regina, Saskatchewan S4S 0A2 Canada

RESTRICTIONS: Teaching assistantships in education, engineering, fine arts, humanities, science, and social sciences available to students from all nationalities.
AMOUNT GIVEN: 35 awards of up to Canadian $3,310 per semester (limit of 2 semesters).
DEADLINE: April 1.

University of Regina
Graduate Scholarships
Dean of Graduate Studies and Research
Regina, Saskatchewan S4S 0A2 Canada
RESTRICTIONS: Scholarships for graduate students accepted by the graduate faculty as fully qualified participants in the master's or Ph.D. programs in the fields of education, fine arts, humanities, interdisciplinary sciences, science, and social sciences available to students of all nationalities.
AMOUNT GIVEN: 11 awards of up to Canadian $3,100 per semester (limit of 3 semesters).
DEADLINE: April 1.

University of Saskatchewan
College of Graduate Studies and Research
Saskatoon, Saskatchewan
Canada
RESTRICTIONS: Graduates of all nationalities with B.A. (honors) or equivalent from recognized university. Scholarships available in fields of agriculture, education, engineering, health sciences, humanities, physical education, science, and social sciences.
AMOUNT GIVEN: Up to Canadian $8,800 for eight months with possible addition of Canadian $4,400 for summer semester.
DEADLINE: February 1.

SOCIAL SCIENCES

American Numismatic Society
Broadway and 156th Street
New York, NY 10032
RESTRICTIONS: Graduate fellowships for study in the U.S. and abroad in humanities or social sciences. Must have completed all requirements for the doctoral degree except dissertation. For dissertation research on a topic involving the use of numismatics. Applicant must have previously attended an A.N.S. summer seminar.
AMOUNT GIVEN: $3,500.
DEADLINE: March 1.

American Research Institute in Turkey
c/o University Museum 33rd and Spruce St.
Philadelphia, PA 19104
215-898-3474
RESTRICTIONS: Open to Ph.D. candidates at U.S. and Canadian institutes who have completed all coursework except dissertation. For doctoral dissertation research in Turkey in the fields of humanities and social sciences.
AMOUNT GIVEN: $1,000– $4,000.
DEADLINE: November 15.

AUCC
Awards Division
Petro Canada Inc. Graduate Research Program
151 Slater St.; Enquiries Clerk
Ottawa, Ontario K1P 5N1 Canada
613-563-1236
RESTRICTIONS: For full-time graduate study at an accredited Canadian institution. Granted primarily on the basis of academic standing
and demonstrated potential for advanced study/research. Must be Canadian citizen or legal resident.
AMOUNT GIVEN: Canadian $10,000. Possibly renewable pending sat-
isfactory progress.
DEADLINE: February 1.

Ecole des Hautes Etudes en Sciences Sociales
54 Boulevard Raspail
75270 Paris, France
RESTRICTIONS: Graduate studies in Social Sciences. Must have good
knowledge of French.
AMOUNT GIVEN: 1,000 francs.
DEADLINE: October 30.

European University Institute
Via de Roccettini 5
San Domenico di Fiesole
50016 Italy
0039-055-50921
RESTRICTIONS: For graduate students in the fields of political science,
social sciences, law, economics, and history. Open to qualified candidates with honors degree and a research project with a European dimension.
AMOUNT GIVEN: $615– $1,000 per month + travel, medical, and family
allowances.
DEADLINE: November 30.

European University Institute
Jean Monnet Fellowship

Via de Roccettini 5
San Domenico di Fiesole
50016 Italy
0039-055-50921
RESTRICTIONS: Postdoctoral fellowships in the fields of political science, social sciences, law, economics, and history. Recipients required to make scholarly contribution to research on Europe within one of EUI's research projects or on topics falling within the general interests of the institute. Publication of research is expected.
AMOUNT GIVEN: 25 fellowships per year of $1400–$2100 per month + medical and family allowances.
DEADLINE: November 30.

Inter-American Foundation
Doctoral Dissertation Fellowship
1515 Wilson Blvd.
Rosslyn, VA 22209
703-841-3800
RESTRICTIONS: Open to Ph.D. candidates in social sciences and physical sciences enrolled in a U.S. university who have fulfilled all degree requirements other than the dissertation before they travel to their country of intended study. Research themes must deal directly with developing activities among the poor. Candidates must speak the language of the country of intended study.
AMOUNT GIVEN: Approximately $550 per month stipend. Approximately 15 awards per year.
DEADLINE: December 5.

Kyungpook National University
Bureau of Student Affairs
370 San Kyuk-dong, uk-gu
Daegu 635 Korea
RESTRICTIONS: Scholarships and loans available to applicants of all nationalities in the fields of humanities, social sciences, natural sciences, economics, commerce, law, engineering, agriculture, teaching, medicine, dentistry, music, and visual arts. Must have completed 12 years of schooling and 2 years of pre-medical or pre-dental courses for study in these fields.
DEADLINE: One semester prior to start of studies.

London School of Economics and Political Science
Houghton St. Scholarships Office
London WC2A England
01-955-7163
RESTRICTIONS: Open to applicants who register as full-time students of the school and pursue graduate work in the social sciences.
AMOUNT GIVEN: 600 British pounds.

DEADLINE: September 1.

London School of Economics and Political Science
Roseberry Studentships
Houghton St. Scholarships Office
London WC2A England
01-955-7163
RESTRICTIONS: For graduate work at the school in the social sciences. Preference to students studying some aspect of transport.
AMOUNT GIVEN: 300 British pounds minimum.
DEADLINE: September 1.

National Academy of Sciences
Graduate Program–Grants for Study in the PRC
2101 Constitution Ave. NW
Washington, DC 20418
202-334-2718
RESTRICTIONS: Grant support for graduate students enrolled in the social sciences or humanities to do coursework in an academic discipline at a Chinese university. Also, support for dissertation and coursework. Must be U.S. citizen with proficiency in the Chinese language.
AMOUNT GIVEN: Varies.
DEADLINE: October 10.

National Academy of Sciences
Post-Doctoral Visiting Scholar Exchange Program
2101 Constitution Ave. NW
Washington, DC 20418
202-334-2718
RESTRICTIONS: Postdoctoral grants to support research in the People's Republic of China by U.S. scholars and research in the U.S. by Chinese scholars. Open to U.S. or PRC citizens in fields of engineering, humanities, natural sciences, and social sciences. For 1–3 month research visits only; does not support study leading to academic degree.
AMOUNT GIVEN: Varies.
DEADLINE: October 10.

Social Science Research Council
Fellowships Coordinator
605 Third Ave.
New York, NY 10158
212-661-0280
RESTRICTIONS: Doctoral dissertation research fellowships for Ph.D. candidates of all nationalities at U.S. institutions or U.S. citizens or legal residents enrolled at any accredited institution in the U.S. or abroad. For research in the fields of social sciences, humanities, demography, urban planning, and education.

AMOUNT GIVEN: 50–100 fellowships per year.
DEADLINE: November 1.

Svenska Handelsbanken Foundations for Social Science Research
Secretary of the Board
10328 Stockholm, Sweden.
RESTRICTIONS: Graduate research grants in the fields of economics
and social sciences. Area of interest must concern international payments and capital movement, domestic payments, markets, and economic planning. Tenable in Sweden for up to 1 year at Swedish research
institute.
AMOUNT GIVEN: Stipend + expenses.
DEADLINE: March 10.

University of Aberdeen
Regent Walk
Aberdeen AB9 1FX Scotland
RESTRICTIONS: Postgraduate studentships available to applicants of all
nationalities accepted at the university in the fields of social sciences,
science, engineering, agriculture, forestry, divinity, law, and medicine.
Must have a minimum of first-class honors degree and a TOEFL score of
at least 500 or equivalent. Provision for handicapped.
AMOUNT GIVEN: 10 awards per year.
DEADLINE: July 31.

University of Dundee
Postgraduate Office
Dundee DD1 4HN Scotland
RESTRICTIONS: Awards available to foreign nationals in the fields of
medicine, dentistry, science, law, engineering, arts, social sciences, en-
vironmental studies, and education. Applicants must have a minimum
of an upper second-class honors degree or equivalent.
AMOUNT GIVEN: Up to 2,860 British pounds.
DEADLINE: March 31.

University of Durham
Old Shire Hall
Durham DH1 3HP England
RESTRICTIONS: Fellowships available to senior researchers with Ph.D.
standing from any country. For research in arts and social sciences.
AMOUNT GIVEN: 6,070–10,575 British pounds.
DEADLINE: Announced annually.

University of Guelph
Dean of Graduate Studies
Guelph, Ontario N1G 2WI Canada

RESTRICTIONS: Awards for postgraduate study in fields of agriculture, arts, biological science, physical sciences, social sciences, veterinary sciences. Open to students of all nationalities having graduated from a recognized university
AMOUNT GIVEN: Canadian $2,400–$3,000 per year.
CONTACT: Desired department.

University of New Brunswick
School of Graduate Studies and Research
P.O. Box 4400
Fredericton, New Brunswick E3B 5A3 Canada
RESTRICTIONS: Graduate assistantships and teaching assistantships in the fields of computer science, education, engineering, forestry, humanities, mathematics, physical education and recreation, science, and social sciences. Available to students of all nationalities who fulfill requirements for admission as higher degree candidates in the School of Graduate Studies and Research.
AMOUNT GIVEN: Up to Canadian $12,000 per year.
DEADLINE: March 1.
CONTACT: Director of appropriate department.

University of Ottawa
Merit Graduate Research Scholarships
School of Graduate Studies
115 Wilbrod
Ottawa, Ontario K1N 6N5 Canada
RESTRICTIONS: Scholarships for study at the University of Ottawa in fields of humanities and social sciences available to qualified applicants of all nationalities. Fluency in English or French required.
AMOUNT GIVEN: Canadian $4,600 (masters); Canadian $6,000 (Ph.D.).
DEADLINE: Fall session by July 1. Winter session by December 1. Summer session by April 1.

University of Ottawa
Excellence Supplementary Scholarships
School of Graduate Studies
115 Wilbrod
Ottawa, Ontario K1N 6N5 Canada
RESTRICTIONS: Scholarships for study at the University of Ottawa in fields of humanities and social sciences available to qualified applicants of all nationalities. Fluency in English or French required.
AMOUNT GIVEN: Maximum of Canadian $4,500.
DEADLINE: Fall session by July 1. Winter session by December 1. Summer session by April 1.

University of Regina
Teaching Assistantships

Dean of Graduate Studies and Research
Regina, Saskatchewan S4S 0A2 Canada
RESTRICTIONS: Teaching assistantships in education, engineering, fine arts, humanities, science, and social sciences available to students from all nationalities.
AMOUNT GIVEN: 35 awards of up to Canadian $3,310 per semester (limit of 2 semesters).
DEADLINE: April 1.

University of Regina
Graduate Scholarships
Dean of Graduate Studies and Research
Regina, Saskatchewan S4S 0A2 Canada
RESTRICTIONS: Scholarships for graduate students accepted by the graduate faculty as fully qualified participants in the master's or Ph.D. programs in the fields of education, fine arts, humanities, interdisciplinary sciences, science, and social sciences available to students from all nationalities.
AMOUNT GIVEN: 11 awards of up to Canadian $3,100 per semester (limit of 3 semesters).
DEADLINE: April 1.

University of Saskatchewan
College of Graduate Studies and Research
Saskatoon, Saskatchewan
Canada
RESTRICTIONS: Graduates of all nationalities with B.A. (honors) or equivalent from recognized university. Scholarships available in fields of agriculture, education, engineering, health sciences, humanities, physical education, science, and social sciences.
AMOUNT GIVEN: Up to Canadian $8,800 for eight months with possible addition of Canadian $4,400 for summer semester.
DEADLINE: February 1.

University of Sheffield
Registrar
Sheffield S10 2TN England
RESTRICTIONS: Awards available in the areas of arts, economics, social studies, law, and architecture. Open to graduate students of all nationalities.
AMOUNT GIVEN: 2 studentships and 1 fellowship per year.
DEADLINE: June 1.

University of Stockholm
International Graduate Scholarships
S-106 Stockholm, Sweden
08-16-34-66

RESTRICTIONS: One-year graduate diploma program with emphasis on Scandinavia. Open to foreign students of all nationalities who have completed an academic degree in a field of social science. Minimum of a "B" average and fluency in English required.
AMOUNT GIVEN: Tuition + $350.
DEADLINE: March 1.

University of Tasmania
Post-Graduate Course Awards
GPO Box 252 C
Hobart, Tasmania 7001 Australia
RESTRICTIONS: For graduate study at the university in the fields of educational studies, environmental studies, financial studies, fine arts, humanities, music, psychology, social sciences, special education, and welfare law. Open to postgraduate students from Australia and overseas who hold a first- or second-class honors degree or equivalent qualifications from a recognized institution or other university.
AMOUNT GIVEN: Aus. $7,000. Renewable for 2 years maximum or length of degree (whichever is the lesser).
DEADLINE: October 31.

SOCIAL WORK

Council of International Programs
Youth Worker and Social Worker Exchange Programs
1030 Euclid Ave. #410
Cleveland, OH 44115
216-861-5478
RESTRICTIONS: Summer exchange program in Germany or France. Open to graduate students with 1 or more years of professional experience or to professional social workers and youth workers. Must be under 40 years of age.
AMOUNT GIVEN: Varies.
DEADLINE: None.

Jewish Welfare Board
JWB Scholarship Program
Grants Coordinator
15 E. 26th St.
New York, NY 10010
212-532-4949
RESTRICTIONS: Open to U.S. and Canadian citizens of the Jewish faith. For master's degree programs only in fields of adult education, early childhood education, physical education, and social work. Should have a strong desire to enter and work in the Jewish community center field.

AMOUNT GIVEN: $7,500. 18 awards per year.
DEADLINE: February 1.

SOCIOLOGY

Academy of Korean Studies
Graduate School
50 Unjung-dong, Seongnam-si
Gyenggi-do, 130-17 Korea
RESTRICTIONS: Scholarships available to students of all nationalities
who have graduated from an accredited institution. For study in fields
of history, philosophy, political science, economics, sociology, anthropology, education, literature, and fine arts. Must speak English, Korean,
and one other language.
AMOUNT GIVEN: Tuition, room and board, and stipend.
DEADLINE: April 30; October 30.

AUCC
Awards Division
Emergency Planning Canada Research Fellowship
151 Slater St.; Enquiries Clerk
Ottawa, Ontario K1P 5N1 Canada
613-563-1236
RESTRICTIONS: For graduate research fellowships. Open to Canadian
citizens or legal residents who have a first Canadian degree or equivalent. Particularly to encourage applicants in planning, geography, risk
analysis, system science, sociology, business administration, health administration to develop ongoing interest in emergency planning. Preference to Ph.D. candidates, but master's candidates are considered.
AMOUNT GIVEN: Tuition fees + Canadian $10,810 stipend. Awards
tenable for 4 years at a Canadian institution.
DEADLINE: February 1.

Human Sciences Research Council Merit Bursary
Private Bag X41
Pretoria, South Africa 0001
012-28-3944
RESTRICTIONS: Open to graduate students in the fields of sociology
and history. Must obtain at least 65% in the graduate exam for sociol-
ogy or history. Award must be used in South Africa. Enrollment in a full-
time program required.
AMOUNT GIVEN: 3,600 rand per year. 6–10 awards per year.
DEADLINE: January 15.

Radio Free Europe/Radio Liberty
Summer Student Research Internship Program

1201 Connecticut Avenue, NW
Washington, DC 20036
RESTRICTIONS: Open to graduate students in the fields of international communications, mass communications, collective behavior, and social psychology. For full-time research producing a publishable paper.
AMOUNT GIVEN: Daily stipend of 45 Deutsche Marks + living accommodations.
DEADLINE: February 14.
CONTACT: Mr. Alan Dodds.

Tokyo Women's Christian University
Registrar's Office
Tokyo Joshi Daigaku
2-6-1, Zempukuji
Suginami-ku
Tokyo 167
RESTRICTIONS: Graduate scholarships in the fields of philosophy, Japanese language and literature, English and American literature, history, and math. Undergraduate scholarships available in these fields as well as sociology, economics, and psychology. Open to students in financial need of all nationalities. Must be proficient in Japanese.
AMOUNT GIVEN: Tuition + fees.

University of London—Bedford College
Lady Huggins Scholarship
Attn: Registrar
Engham Hill
Engham, Surrey TW20 OEX England
RESTRICTIONS: Scholarship in the field of sociology available to women graduate students of all nationalities. Preference to applicants with honors degrees in philosophy, psychology, economics or sociology.
AMOUNT GIVEN: As funds permit.
DEADLINE: May 1.

TROPICAL PROBLEMS

International Institute of Tropical Agriculture
Training Programs
Oyo Road PMB 5320
Ibadan, Nigeria
413244-413315-413440
RESTRICTIONS: The main objective of the various training programs is to build up the agricultural capacity of the professional personnel of

developing countries. Participants for training range from secondary school levels to holders of advanced degrees.
AMOUNT GIVEN: Varies.

McGill University
Faculty of Graduate Studies and Research
Associate Dean, Faculty of Graduate Studies and Research
Fellowship Office, Dawson Hall
853 Sherbrooke Street West
Montreal, Quebec H3A 2T6 Canada
RESTRICTIONS: Fellowships open to postdoctoral students of all nationalities for study of tropical problems at Bellairs Research Institute, Barbados. Applicants must collaborate with a McGill staff member.
AMOUNT GIVEN: Canadian $20,000 year + essential travel expenses.
DEADLINE: March 16.

URBAN PLANNING

AUCC
Awards Division
Emergency Planning Canada Research Fellowship
151 Slater Street; Enquiries Clerk
Ottawa, Ontario K1P 5N1 Canada
613-563-1236
RESTRICTIONS: For graduate research fellowships. Open to Canadian citizens or legal residents who have a first Canadian degree or equivalent. Particularly to encourage applicants in planning, geography, risk analysis, system science, sociology, business administration, and health administration to develop an ongoing interest in emergency planning. Preference to Ph.D. candidates, but master's candidates are considered.
AMOUNT GIVEN: Tuition fees + Canadian $10,810 stipend. Awards tenable for 4 years at a Canadian institution.
DEADLINE: February 1.

Social Science Research Council
Fellowships Coordinator
605 Third Ave.
New York, NY 10158
212-661-0280
RESTRICTIONS: Doctoral dissertation research fellowships for Ph.D. candidates of all nationalities at U.S. institutions or U.S. citizens or legal residents enrolled at any accredited institution in the U.S. or abroad. For research in the fields of social sciences, humanities, demography, urban planning, education.

AMOUNT GIVEN: 50–100 fellowships per year.
DEADLINE: November 1.

University of Adelaide
Clive E. Boyce Fellowship
Registrar
G.P.O. Box 498
Adelaide, South Australia 5001 Australia
RESTRICTIONS: Fellowships in architecture or urban and regional planning open to students of all nationalities with proper degree from a recognized university. Tenable at the University of Adelaide.
AMOUNT GIVEN: Minimum of Aus. $5,000. Awarded as available.

VETERINARY SCIENCE

Animal Health Trust
Blount Memorial Fund Scholarship
Lanwades Hall; General Secretary
Kennett Newmarket, Suffolk CB8 7PN England
RESTRICTIONS: Scholarships to study all aspects of animal health. For graduate study at agreed centers in the U.K.
AMOUNT GIVEN: 2,000 British pounds.
DEADLINE: March 1.

Royal College of Veterinary Surgeons
Sir Fredrick Smith and Miss Aleen Cust Research Fellowships
32 Belgrave Square
London SW1X 8QP England
01-235-4971
RESTRICTIONS: Postgraduate fellowships available for research at an approved institution in the field of veterinary science.
AMOUNT GIVEN: $1,000 per annum + 200 British pounds.

University of Guelph
Dean of Graduate Studies
Guelph, Ontario N1G 2WI Canada
RESTRICTIONS: Awards for postgraduate study in fields of agriculture, arts, biological sciences, physical sciences, social sciences, and veterinary sciences. Open to students of all nationalities having graduated from a recognized university.
AMOUNT GIVEN: Canadian $2,400–$3,000 per year.
CONTACT: Department to which you are applying.

Further Reading

Fellowships, Scholarships and Related Opportunities in International Education. Knoxville, TN: The Center for International Education (201 Alumni Hall, University of Tennessee, Knoxville 615-974-3177), 1989.

Financial Resources for International Study: A Definitive Guide to Organizations Offering Awards for Overseas Study. Princeton, N.J.: Peterson's Guides, 1989.

Study Abroad. Paris: United Nations Educational, Scientific and Cultural Organization, 1989.

INDEX